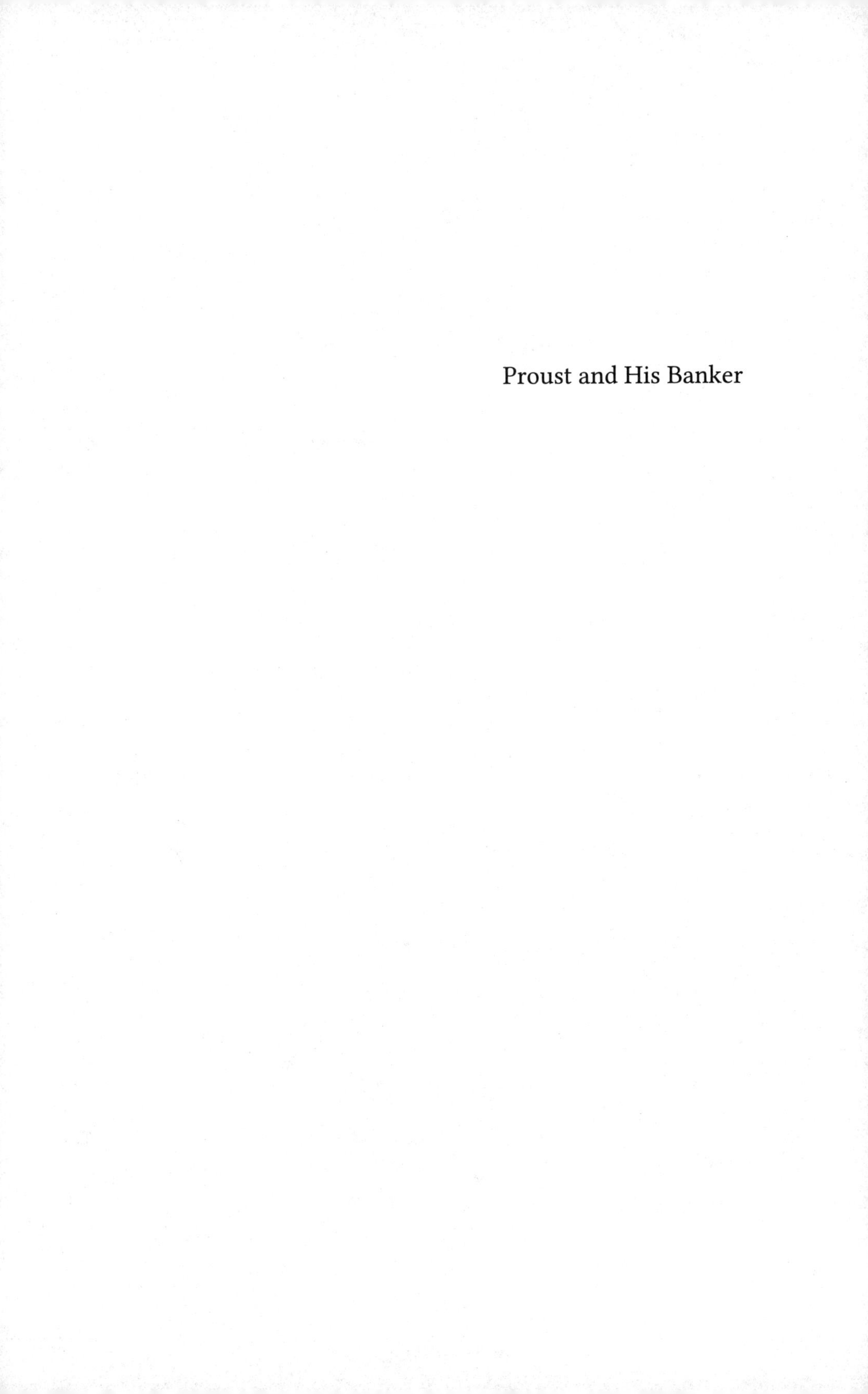

Proust and His Banker

IN SEARCH OF TIME SQUANDERED

Gian
BALSAMO

THE UNIVERSITY OF SOUTH CAROLINA PRESS

Published by the University of South Carolina Press
Columbia, South Carolina 29208

www.sc.edu/uscpress

Manufactured in the United States of America

26 25 24 23 22 21 20 19 18 17
10 9 8 7 6 5 4 3 2 1

Library of Congress Cataloging-in-Publication Data
can be found at http://catalog.loc.gov/

ISBN: 978-1-61117-736-7 (hardcover)
ISBN: 978-1-61117-737-4 (ebook)

This book was printed on a recycled paper with 30 percent postconsumer waste content.

To my *maestro di economia* in Torino, Bruno Contini.
To my mathematical nemesis in Minneapolis, Tom Sargent.
And to *you* as always and everywhere, A. B.

CONTENTS

ILLUSTRATIONS AND FIGURES

ILLUSTRATIONS

FIGURES

PREMISE

Four years before his death, Marcel Proust was still a self-published novelist. Over the course of their fifteen-year-long collaboration, his financial advisor Lionel Hauser had seen him squander three-fifths of his wealth on reckless speculations and magnificent gifts to the men and women who struck his fancy. During World War I it fell upon Hauser to stem the damage. To Hauser, time was money: Proust wasted a great deal of both time and money, gambling on the stock exchange, whiling away his days in bed as he wrote about time's ephemeral flow, or buying British cars, fabulous clothing—even an airplane!—for Alfred Agostinelli, Henri Rochat, and other such heartthrobs. For the occasional jewel to the occasional girlfriend, he sought inspiration at Cartier's.

The banker could not know what you will learn from this book, namely, that time and money (and good health as well) were mere assets to Proust to be sacrificed to the success of his artwork. Hauser saw in the writer a foolish squanderer, a virtuoso in resource mismanagement. But Proust's worldview was different. Lost Time was not only, to him, a subject worthy writing about for a whole lifetime, but also the sextant of human existence, the measure of our adjustment to its transiency. He was willing to gamble everything on this idea, from the substantial wealth he inherited from his family to the scarce amount of time his poor health allowed him to devote to his artwork.

And in the long run, Lost Time showed him the right course of action. Meanwhile (if you don't mind my sticking with the figure of the sextant), Lost Money provided him with the orientation of a magnetic pole. Here is how.

Many of Proust's losses on the stock exchange inspired him to write vital episodes of his novel, *In Search of Lost Time,* or to fashion its most important characters. The futility of his conspicuous expenses on

Agostinelli and Rochat, for instance, gave birth to his best female character, the pink-tongued and fat-cheeked Albertine Simonet, whose cagey behavior filled him, her creator, with *real* jealousy, and whose premature death filled him with *true* grief. Another source of inspiration for Albertine Simonet sprouted from Proust's assiduous courtship of the stunning yet untalented actress Louisa de Mornand, met in a brothel, who figured, on at least one occasion, as his sexual partner in—how shall I put it?—a narcoleptic sort of intercourse. The inspiration Proust drew from Louisa de Mornand more than rewarded him for the large amounts of time, money, and personal influence (and personal embarrassment as well, on occasion) which he devoted to the success of her acting career. In addition, the most irresponsible of Proust's financial speculations became the risky investments made by his novel's protagonist to cover the costs for turning Albertine, the acerbic beach nymph, into his urban captive, a refined woman of fashion—an undertaking which eventually left him with "barely one fifth" of his original patrimony (versus the two-fifths left Proust in real life during World War I).

With Proust, in sum, waste was the renewable resource that kept on giving. I'm sure I won't be getting ahead of myself if I pitch in some more evidence.

The long years that Proust squandered as an unemployed aesthete and underachieving *homme du monde* helped him give shape to the character that made his initial fame as a best-selling author: Charles Swann, an amateur and procrastinating art critic who was also modeled on the real-life Charles Haas, a gentleman for whom lack of an occupation was a matter of principle. It is *because* of his dandified and ineffectual erudition as an art historian that Charles Swann is welcome in the same aristocratic circles, well above his family's standing, that were frequented by the idle would-be writer Marcel Proust. Even Charles Swann's marriage to the courtesan Odette de Crécy, so out-of-character and ruinous to his reputation, is redolent of asset mismanagement. Unable to endure Odette's infidelities or his own undignified, nagging jealousy of her, Swann weds her. And, promptly, their domestic ménage portrays, in Proust's novel, the pecuniary arrangement worthy of people who, like the banker Lionel Hauser, deal with passion and devotion in the spirit of accountants. Based on the way Proust rated Hauser's tolerance of his erotic drives in the summer of 1918, one could say that Swann, the former ladies' man, joins eventually the ranks of *love's bookkeepers*—a sort of blunder for which his creator refused to be a model.

The character of Odette de Crécy, who makes a career out of her Botticellian beauty, and is second in importance, among the female characters of Proust's novel, only to Albertine Simonet, was modeled on Proust's association with exclusive *demi-mondaines,* or kept-women, a costly milieu which Hauser warned him against. Since the time he was a boy, Proust was on intimate terms with Laure Hayman, who enjoyed the keen insights of her languid young friend—her "little psychologist in porcelain," as she called him—and is by turns, on the more prosaic business side, the lover of his maternal great-uncle Louis Weil and almost certainly of his father Adrien. Marcel Proust paid her frequent visits at her address in Rue La Pérouse, near the Arc de Triomphe. She was not too pleased when she read in Proust's novel that, before her marriage, the courtesan Odette de Crécy used to live in Rue Laperouse.

Not even the financial disaster of World War I, which took away a good chunk of Proust's fortune, was detrimental to his art: the nocturnal air raids of the infamous German zeppelins turned the pitch-black passageways of the Parisian metro into a dark city, a Sodom of sorts, where his impenitent Baron de Charlus hunts for African soldiers in red skirts and Hindu soldiers in white turbans; and in the masculine solidarity of trench war, his protagonist's devoted friend Robert de Saint-Loup, a junior cavalry officer, discovers a curious blend of lower-class eroticism and heroic patriotism.

In 1919 an astute publisher, Gaston Gallimard, seized the opportunity to convert hundreds of pages of chaotic scribbling into Proust's best-seller—and in the process Gallimard became the unchallenged doyen of literary publishing in France. On top of it all, one of Proust's longest-term and sneakiest investments produced unhoped-for results after the war. Although Hauser had grown used to Proust's comparison of certain securities in his portfolio with "old mistresses," prone either to unreasonable claims or unexpected handouts, he is kept mostly in the dark regarding his friend's substantial packet of shares of Royal Dutch, the progenitor of Shell; from 1919 to the year of the writer's death, 1922, these securities counted among the writer's steadiest and most generous mistresses on the stock exchange.

So much so that when Proust died, he left behind a substantial patrimony, a novel destined not only to fill the pockets of his heirs and publishers, but also to enrich the lives of thousands of readers like you and me, and a banker friend dazed by his unorthodox yet resourceful usage of time and money.

ACKNOWLEDGMENTS

Even though I wrote this book to patch up the same gap in each of my five favorite biographies of Marcel Proust, I owe a debt of gratitude to the immense and authoritative work of documentation of their authors: Jean-Yves Tadié, William Carter, Edmund White, Roger Duchêne, and George Painter. This debt pales, however, vis-à-vis my appreciation of Philip Kolb's editorial excellence, and, on top of it, of his hugely informative annotations and comments to Proust's correspondence, published from 1970 to 1993. A relevant portion of this book's information was derived from Kolb's edited and annotated pages; hidden in full sight, their potential revelations went unnoticed for too many years, and it is my good fortune to make them available to Proust's fans at long last.

Were it not for the late Roger Duchêne, author of a decisive article on Proust's inherited wealth, I could have never started the project that led to this book. As a biographer, Duchêne had a distinctive flair for the retrieval of neglected financial information; I knew my research was on the right path the day I found evident traces of his perusal of a dusty and most unlikely dossier at a branch of the Rothschild Archives in Roubaix, France. But Duchêne was monumentally unfair to Proust's sexual tastes, and since Proust's dealings with the world of finance cannot be explained without a firm grasp of his amorous and sexual proclivities, under Duchêne's influence I could have walked into a blind alley. This is why he does not figure first in my list of favorite biographies.

In the process of composition, Gerald Gillespie was a steady and generous source of ideas, insights, German translations, survival strategies, and reflections on good and bad, useful and useless criticism; he also gave me a piece of my title. Freshly back from a long stay in Italy, Zakiya Hanafi gave me another welcome piece of it; and long before I started drafting the present version of my book, she did precious copyediting work for me. My son Tito Balsamo, who at some moment in recent years became the second of my ideal targeted readers, gave me the concept of opportunity costs, an indispensable ingredient. Pyra Wise provided me with formidable scholarship. The editor Richard Ratzlaff gave me excellent advice. In 1975 my professor of econometrics in Turin, Bruno Contini, launched me into the long journey that led to this book, of which he is one of the three dedicatees; in the process he initiated me into the beauty of numbers. In 1978 my professor of macroeconomics in Minneapolis, Tom Sargent, this book's second dedicatee, initiated me into the benefits of mathematics, as well as to some of its hidden costs (such as the motivational breakdown, subsequent to his teaching, that changed the course of my life, making of me a man of letters).

I started work on *Proust and his Banker* in 2008, at the peak of the Great Recession. I conceived my book as a humanistic response to the innumerable personal tragedies caused by it. Proust's manic conduct on the stock exchange and his survival through several crashes at the Bourse de Paris show that there may be an inherent inventiveness to our economic experiences, even the most wretched ones. This is something I meant to argue with this book. Closer to us, such inventiveness is mirrored in the increasingly rare pleasure one feels in meeting an editor still capable, in these years of growing scarcity for humanists and proportionately cumbersome obligations for academic presses, of being driven by genuine intellectual curiosity. Jim Denton of the University of South Carolina Press is such an editor, and I admire him for it.

The present one being my second book with Mr. Denton's press, I had the renewed pleasure of perfecting the publishing agreement with Linda Fogle, whose solicitude and know-how are the best guarantee that *Proust and His Banker* got an in-house treatment commensurate to its merits.

I am grateful to the Trustees of Rothschild Archive Trust Limited in London (with special thanks to the formidable researcher Claire-Amandine Soulié and the archivist Justin Cavernelis-Frost) for the permission to consult and reproduce documents in their Proust-related dossiers; to Dorothea Hauser for her consultation regarding the Warburg Bank Archives in Hamburg, the materials she kindly retrieved on my behalf, and the interest she showed in my project; to the Éditions Robert Flammarion in Paris (with special thanks to the resourceful iconographer Pascaline Bressan) for the permission to reproduce Sartony's picture of the young Céleste Albaret; to Art Resource Inc. (with special thanks to the associate Robbie Siegel) for the permission to reproduce Giovani Boldini's portrait of Robert de Montesquiou, James Tissot's "*Le Cercle de la rue Royale,*" and El Greco's *Burial of Count d'Orgaz*; to the Department of Reproductions (with special thanks to Pascale Kahn) and the SINDBAD service of the Bibliothèque nationale de France, as well as to the Service of Research and Documentation of the Musée d'Orsay in Paris (with special thanks to the efficient Denise Faïfe), for their prompt replies to my queries.

And I owe a special debt of gratitude to the Éditions Plon in Paris (with special thanks to the exquisite Florence Surmany) for permission to translate and reproduce in this book several key passages from Proust's correspondence.

From 2008 to 2014, many resourceful members of Stanford University's Philosophy Reading Group (PRG), including its chairs, Sepp Gumbrecht and Robert Harrison, and its two existential souls, Niklas Damiris and Helga Wild, helped me sift all matters aesthetic through a fine grid of alternative forms, till I found the one I was bound to pick.

Last, I'm appreciative of the support and many suggestions I received from the readers of *Alla ricerca del tempo sprecato,* published by Claudio Maria Messina, my trusty publisher of thirty years in Italy, which laid the foundations—an early draft of sorts—for this *Proust and His Banker.* The present book is not a simple revision or English version of *Alla ricerca del tempo sprecato* but the substantial completion of an interrupted project. The Italian book was squeezed out of me prematurely by sinister circumstances I have described elsewhere, which explains why I signed it Luigi Ferdinando Dagnese, the penname I had used as a novelist but never as a critic before then.

In turn, my frequently disguised identity as L. F. Dagnese explains the curious coincidence that all of this author's books and most of mine, including the present one, are dedicated to the same person, A. B, my third dedicatee today. Proust's indiscreet loves figure prominently throughout this book; it would be churlish of me thereby to stick with my customary discretion instead of taking this occasion to acknowledge once and for all that A. B. is Armanda Balsamo, my *Wonder Woman,* ideal reader, and wife of many years; she was barely a kid (striking and long, long-legged) when we first met, at the peak of the Sexual Revolution, and I was a confident young man, unaware of how long it would take me to write the right book. From the very start, she knew I would manage it eventually.

NOTE ON TRANSLATIONS, ADOPTED EDITIONS, CURRENCY EXCHANGE RATES, AND CONVENTIONS

For the French version of Proust's *À la recherche du temps perdu* I adopted the four volumes of the Gallimard edition edited by Jean-Yves Tadié et al., published from 1987 to 1989. Endnote references to the French version indicate the full title followed by the page number. For the English translations of Proust's novel, I quoted from the recent, excellent English translations of the novel's several volumes, namely, from the renderings of *Swann's Way* by Lydia Davis; of *In the Shadow of Young Girls in Flower* by James Grieve; of *The Guermantes Way* by Mark Treharne; of *Sodom and Gomorrah* by John Sturrock; of *The Prisoner* by Carol Clark; of *The Fugitive* by Peter Collier; and of *Finding Time Again* by Ian Patterson. Parenthetical and endnote references to the English translations indicate the pertinent title followed by the page number. In the rare cases of disagreement with these translators, I inserted my own rendering, followed by the original French text in square brackets, followed, in turn, by a justification—tolerably persuasive, I hope, to the cited translators—of my own word choices. All translations from *Contre Sainte-Beuve,* one of Proust's two aborted novels, and from his *Pastiches et mélanges* are mine, from the Gallimard edition of 1971. For the passages cited from *Jean Santeuil,* the second of Proust's unfinished novels, my own translations, from the Gallimard edition of 1971, have been used after consultation of the corresponding translation by Gerard Hopkins, when available, in the 1956 partial edition of *Jean Santeuil* published by Simon and Schuster.

The present study cites or refers to almost all of the 357 letters, exchanged by Marcel Proust and Lionel Hauser from 1908 to 1922, that are contained in the pertinent volumes of the French edition of Proust's *Correspondance,* edited by Philip Kolb for the Librairie Plon from 1970 to 1993. The second, third, and fourth volume of Proust's *Selected Letters,* edited by Philip Kolb and translated respectively by Philip Kilmartin (volumes 2 and 3) and Joanna Kilmartin (volume 4), include but a tiny fraction, precisely 25, of these 357 letters. I took this setback as an opportunity, opting to avail myself of my own English translations of Proust's epistolary correspondence with Lionel Hauser as well as with his other friends, bankers, and stockbrokers from 1908 to 1922. With regard to my two protagonists, Proust and Hauser, this decision had the obvious advantage of allowing me to reproduce their distinctive epistolary voices in English with a consistency of tone and word choice that could not be expected from different translators working on different letters. With few exceptions, the letters cited in the present study were translated, with the generous permission of Éditions Plon, from the 21 volumes of Proust's *Correspondance*. The individual volumes from *Correspondance* are referred to as COR both in parenthetical and endnote references, followed by the Roman number of the volume and the Arabic number of the pertinent letter; when needed, references to Kolb's annotations are included in square brackets, and references to the page numbers of Kolb's *Avant-Propos* to the pertinent volume are included in lower-case Roman numerals.

Most other English translations are mine. When this is not the case, it is specified by the reference in the pertinent endnote.

Most of my book's financial information was derived from the twenty-one volumes of Proust's *Correspondance*, by means of the ad-hoc quantitative methods briefly described in "Proust and His Banker: Numerical Documentation," Item 6. This file is posted online at http://www.academia.edu/24415226/Documentation. The data sets thus obtained provided the quantitative information shown in figs. 1 and 3 and are included, together with more detailed descriptions of my quantitative methodology, in the annotated numerical tables from the same document. The data set about France's inflation rate from 1907 to 1921, shown in fig. 2, is also included in an annotated numerical table from this file. And the financial information shown in illus. 6 comes from the dossier of Marcel Proust's inheritance papers held at the Fond Rothschild, Archives Nationales du Monde du Travail in Roubaix, France.

Last, a most relevant detail on currencies: in this book, the relative worth of the French franc versus the U.S. dollar is always measured in terms of the American currency's 2008 purchasing power.

INTRODUCTION

In 1907 Lionel Hauser entered the life of Marcel Proust through the back door. The writer's dearest friends were blue bloods: Louis d'Albufera, the Rumanian prince Antoine Bibesco, Bertrand de Fénelon, Robert de Billy, Gabriel de La Rochefoucauld, Armand de Guiche, Georges de Lauris, and Robert de Montesquiou, to name the ones we shall meet in this book. Those of Proust's friends who were not the offspring of some aristocratic family were for the most part former students of the prestigious Lycée Condorcet, attended by Proust in his teenage years. Under the supervision of Proust, who at sixteen was the eldest of the group, his former schoolmates Jacques Bizet (son of Georges, the author of *Carmen*), Daniel Halévy (son of Léon, the librettist of *Carmen*), Robert Dreyfus, and others published essays dealing with aesthetic matters in a self-financed and short-lived journal, *Le Lundi.* They also attended the contagious lectures of a young philosopher and student of personal identity, Alphonse Darlu.[1]

A competent banker, Lionel Hauser was poorly acquainted with aesthetic and philosophic matters; however, by the time of his arrival on the populous stage of Proust's life, he had been tutoring himself in the subtleties of theosophical doctrine. In the next few decades he would collect a private library of theosophical and alchemical books of great renown, frequently consulted by high-caliber esotericists such as Alfred Poisson and Eugène Léon Canseliet. But not even in finance, the professional field in which he excelled, could Hauser claim a patent advantage with respect to Proust. On his mother's side, the writer descended from the Jewish *haute bourgeoisie,* no less associated than Hauser himself with things financial; the writer's personal patrimony was managed by the Rothschild Bank.

At first blush, Hauser might have seemed more in need of Proust than vice versa. After an impressive career across Europe, the young banker had recently established himself in Paris and was looking for clients. In principle, a friendship with Proust would entail a regal introduction to the Parisian world of art and culture. What's more, several of the writer's closest friends, most of them patrons of the art world, were "burdened with a discreet number of millions" and might well avail themselves of Hauser's financial services (COR XV, 122, 127).[2] Yet Hauser's connection to Proust never bore fruit in artistic circles, and, for reasons independent of Proust's own wishes and sincere efforts, Hauser never secured a single client from Proust's entourage. Indeed, it was Proust who was truly in need of Hauser, although he was unaware of it yet.

Their financial alliance was engineered by Léon Neuberger, who managed Proust's Rothschild account and portfolio (COR VIII, 115 [note 17]). As was customary for this bank's executives, Neuberger handled personal and corporate accounts in the shrewd and wary manner that consolidated some of Europe's greatest fortunes in the nineteenth and twentieth centuries. He had no time to waste with the verbose and heedless client that the thirty-six-year-old Proust gave signs of becoming; led astray by the example of friends much too rich even for him, the young and wealthy writer had taken to handling financial investments with the same bold gusto that fueled his compulsive gambling on the green baize (COR XI, 4). Neuberger wanted to find an expeditious way to protect his cousin's fortune from major losses. When his nephew Lionel Hauser declared his intention to open a financial-services firm in Paris, Neuberger took the opportunity to benefit two cousins at once, procuring a client for the banker and a financial advisor for the writer.

Hauser was thirty-nine, three years older than Proust, when he began to advise the writer in the management of his finances, and he soon found himself playing the role of older brother. Proust was already caught in the spiral of illnesses that would put a premature end to his life fifteen years later. He rarely went out, and when he did, it was mostly to scrutinize the mannerisms and shortcomings of the acquaintances that would soon serve as models for the characters of *In Search of Lost Time* (COR XX, 98). Hauser was free of the traits and faults satirized in this novel. Hence Proust could hardly find the time to see him in person. Day in and day out, they corresponded in writing.[3]

The thick collection of their letters stands as a striking example of the kind of surrogate existence imposed on Proust by his precarious health conditions. Moreover, it provides the details of an enduring relationship that gradually turned Proust's financial advisor into one of his truest friends. In light of the profound affection permeating every page, even the ones marked by strife, their correspondence amounts to an epistolary idyll. Proust and Hauser, the two protagonists, are flanked by several crucial characters in a tapestry woven in many hues and colors, now soft, now harsh, occasionally outrageous and at times heartrending, where episodes of ruthless conflict alternate with moving scenes of affection.

As we become more familiar with Hauser, we learn to recognize in him a genuine theosophist with a pragmatic frame of mind: the commonsense approach that he favored enabled him on more than one occasion to disentangle the complex financial arrangements of Proust's making. Hauser even went so far as to identify in "common sense" the divine spark buried within every person's soul by God himself (COR XVII, 49). With the help of elementary common sense, Hauser felt he could solve all of his friend's problems, from financial troubles to chronic ailments. This ambitious plan would be only partially successful, at best.

As a decadent artist, Proust leaned instead toward an impractical approach to life: his private world was cerebral, organized around a proliferation of metaphors. To him, the urge of a noble intention was worthier than a good deed or a concrete result. In the second volume of his novel, titled *In the Shadow of Young Girls in Flower,* Proust countered the virtue of common sense extolled by his friend the banker with his own goodness of heart. There is no doubt, he wrote, that goodness of heart, *rather than* common sense, is the most widespread virtue in the world. The polemical thrust against his trusty correspondent was evidently intentional.

Also different were their respective attitudes toward the best usage of time. Hauser had a profound dislike of the products of wasted time: he shunned all situations and predicaments threatening to keep him away from activities that might be productive or profitable to himself or to his dear ones. Time was a scarce commodity to him, and he meant to optimize its usefulness. In Hauser's eyes, Proust, who spent most of his time in bed, was the personification of wasted time; more than that, he even became the eulogist of time squandered once he began publishing volume after volume of a massive novel devoted, precisely, to the passing of time. Proust, in contrast, conceived of Lost Time as the indispensable bridge linking the impermanence of our experiences and sensations with the continuity of our individuality.

Their respective attitudes toward friendship was another area of difference. Hauser was suspicious of friendship because he considered human beings too selfish to cultivate friendship in a genuine way. In his view, only believers in the theosophical doctrine that he championed were capable of recognizing or showing true friendship. His attempts to convert Proust to theosophy, in order to make the writer into a reliable friend, may thus be deemed as self-serving: were Proust truly to become Hauser's friend, thus opening up "a credit account" in his own heart, he would then make an honest effort to keep a positive balance in their mutual dealings and avoid creating overdrafts.

Proust was equally suspicious of friendship but for the opposite reason: compulsively driven to condone the superficiality and defects of the friends he frequented in his outings, he was too generous of his own time, even when conviviality and gregariousness stifled the manifestations of his true individuality, which flourished instead in a regime of isolation and introspection. His true identity was his most valuable asset, and he regretted the time he squandered on futile friendships instead of investing it in the solitude of artistic expression. As our story unwinds, we shall see that Proust sacrificed most of what mattered to him—not only friendship, wealth, health, and time, but even love—to the cultivation of what he called his "deep self" ("moi profound") or truest identity.[4]

From the start, the ups and downs in the relationship between the banker and the writer mirrored Proust's rash decisions in financial and investment matters. Since on several occasions these decisions affected the entirety of Proust's estate, his epistolary quarrels with Hauser have enabled me to trace the evolution of the writer's personal fortune year by year. Oftentimes when reading *In Search of Lost Time,* one cannot help but wonder about the nonchalance with which Proust's protagonist and alter ego throws money out the window. The accounting evidence made available in Proust's letters thus provides a welcome degree of verisimilitude to the lifestyle of the novel's protagonist, who is a notorious and incorrigible spendthrift. This evidence confirms the analogies between reality and fiction which the reader may often feel invited to make by Proust's narrative.

Little by little, as the friendship between Proust and Hauser evolved, the human side took over, and the ups and downs in their relationship increasingly mirrored the often opposite but at times touchingly similar evolution of two personalities that, equally strong willed, diverged in too many respects. Since Hauser looked at Proust's economic affairs through the gray-tinged lenses of a banker, he could only conclude that the writer was a hopeless businessman and a reckless investor. This opinion, shared for almost a century by all of the writer's biographers, is one which my book invalidates.

This is my take: Throughout his adult life, Proust pursued tenaciously the mirage of an unconditionally requited love, whose costs in gifts and various gratuities would be financed by dramatically profitable speculations. This tenacity is the manifestation of one of the most distinctive and permanent traits of the writer's temperament. Hauser's task was to make sure these speculations would not go sour (as they often did). *In Search of Lost Time,* especially its second part, where Hauser's role stands out for its absence, is the fictionalization and, at once, the monetization of this character trait of its author.

In the course of Proust's lifetime, his literary genius made itself plain through a tight symbiosis between life and art—one of whose corollaries is the well-known symbiosis of art and illness. It is a matter of controversial debate whether the story told in Proust's *In Search of Lost Time* coincides with the author's autobiography.[5] In my opinion it does, albeit not with his verifiable and documentable biography, but rather with the pseudobiography that the French writer elected to present as his own and, by the very act of writing it, left as such to posterity. The decision to substitute the documentable facts and verifiable chronologies of a day-to-day life with the pseudobiography contained in a literary work was the stroke of genius that set the French writer alongside two giants of the confessional genre, namely, Saint Augustine and Dante Alighieri. Like these two predecessors, Proust tied an indissoluble knot between his life and his writing by making them symbiotic; he is the author of his own life, the flesh-and-blood proxy of his novel's protagonist. Analogously, the life of his novel's Narrator (who is also the novel's protagonist, a squanderer of time and money, destined to become a dedicated writer) unfolds through a similar symbiosis to the one between art and life: this is the symbiosis that links art to finance.

The opinion shared by Hauser and all of Proust's biographers, that the writer's handling of his own finances was irresponsible, neglects to take this symbiosis of art and finance into account. The relevance of this symbiosis is hinted at in the second volume of the novel, *In the Shadow of Young Girls in Flower,* where we read of the wealth that is bestowed on the young Narrator in the form of a family inheritance. When she dies, his aunt Léonie bequeaths him, together with "many more objects and furniture than I knew what to do with, almost the whole of her money," which the Narrator's father is charged to manage until his son comes of age (*Young Girls in Flower,* 26).[6] It is far from accidental that the same thing happened in Proust's own experience: his great-uncle Louis Weil, who had no heirs, left half his fortune to his niece, Jeanne, the writer's mother, who at her death left it to her two sons, Marcel and the younger Robert.[7] On the occasion of a visit from Monsieur Norpois, a former French ambassador, the Narrator's father asks the diplomat for advice on his son's portfolio. As he does so, he takes the stock certificates issued by the Compagnie des Eaux out of a drawer. It is here that the Narrator first avails himself of the opportunity to slip in the interplay between art and finance, and more generally "the millennia-long association between artwork and currency," which becomes a motif in the novel:

> All the productions of a particular time look alike; the artists who illustrate the poems of a certain period are the same ones who are employed by its banking houses. There is nothing more evocative of certain episodes of Hugo's Notre Dame de Paris, or works by Gérard de Nerval, as I used to see them displayed outside the grocery store in Combray, than the river divinities wielding the beflowered rectangle that frames a stock certificate issued by the Compagnie des Eaux. (*Young Girls in Flower,* 27)[8]

In the Narrator's perceptive eyes, the interplay between the market value of a security and its graphic representation on paper is analogous with the packaging and broad market distribution of, say, Victor Hugo's literary best-sellers. This passage reads like a faithful echo of John Ruskin's theories about the interconnections between aesthetics and economics. Scarcely acquainted with the English language, with the help of Marie Nordlinger, a young and versatile artist, as well as of his own mother, Proust had scrupulously translated two books by Ruskin: *The Bible of Amiens* and *Sesame and Lilies.*[9] The passage from *In the Shadow of Young Girls in Flower* cited above may be taken as an indication of the profound impression that the ideas of the British art critic made on Proust.[10] In *Sesame and Lilies,* Ruskin argues that books are as precious as mineral gold, and they must be excavated as patiently and tenaciously as miners excavate gold mines.[11] In *The Political Economy of Art,* in which he classifies books and works of art as the "only kind [of property] which deserves the name of *real* property," Ruskin extends the excavation metaphor to all "artistical gold."[12] The bridge drawn by Proust's Narrator between the distinct worlds of visual arts and finance may be taken as a confirmation of Marc Shell's view that Proust took seriously "the economic implications of Ruskin's aesthetics." He took them so seriously, in fact, that in a late addition to *In Search of Lost Time,* discussed below in the chapter "Turning Caresses into Gold," a significant gap between the author, aged about fifty, and the Narrator, aged about forty, consists precisely of their different apprehensions of the notion of wealth: the latter identifies wealth with art as a scarce "natural resource," while the former, in the light of the passage's thematic thrust, does not seem unwilling to identify it with revenue from royalties.[13]

In order to understand why Proust was quite the opposite of a hopeless businessman and a reckless investor, one must appreciate the economic and literary implications of the symbiosis between art and finance as it is thematically developed throughout his novel. At times against his better judgment (and *always* against Hauser's advice), Proust intermingled artwork and money matters not only in his writings but also in his day-to-day existence. The high integration in his life between financial and imaginative resources induced Proust to translate every excessive expense, every incongruous cost, every hazardous risk, every acrobatic speculation (we shall see how many he made!) into an incomparable form of creative capital, one that was immensely remunerative in the long run. This creative capital consisted in the aptitude to squeeze lucrative artwork seemingly, magically, out of thin air; it was his best financial asset.

Proust was in sum an unequalled master in turning financial excess into narrative craftsmanship. His biographers complain about his financial recklessness and the conspicuous consumptions induced by his sentimental infatuations. But these real-life episodes contributed to the composition of several decisive and memorable episodes in his masterpiece. Proust was the first to acknowledge that he had "no imagination" and needed to draw inspiration from concrete experience.[14] His financial and economic misadventures are a case in point. Who better than his heirs could bear witness to the long-term profitability of his allegedly disastrous expenses and investments? This is the paradox guessed at by Hauser when he remarked that the personal shortcomings that brought about his friend's economic downfall were identical to the virtues that made him into an extraordinary artist. Hauser's intuitive understanding of this paradox probably nourished his constant and unswerving devotion to Proust, a man so different from him.

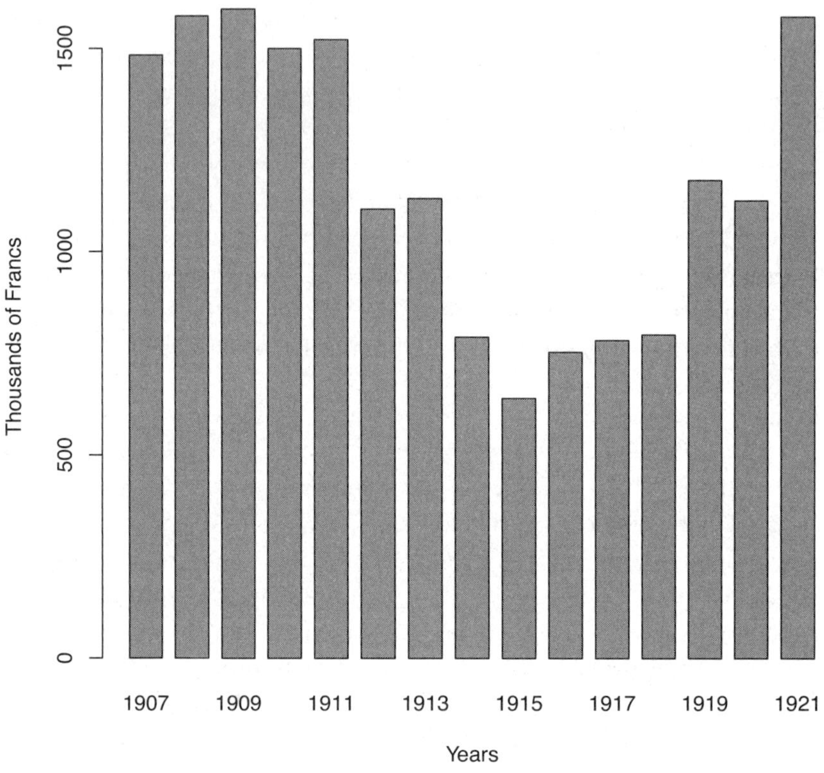

Proust's net worth (1907–1921). *Source:* Gian Balsamo, "Proust and His Banker: Numerical Documentation," Item 2.

A good index of the effects of Proust's investments and discretionary spending, negative at first but positive in the long run, can be seen in the evolution of his patrimony. His personal wealth decreased by 58 percent in real terms from 1911 to 1915, owing more to his aggressive investment strategy and conspicuous spending habits than to the devastation caused to French finances by World War I. As a matter of fact, the suspension of trading on the Bourse de Paris (the Paris stock exchange), as well as on the major European exchanges, caused by World War I, bailed Proust out of an untenable situation just a few days before he would have had to default on his collateralized debt obligations.[15] The declaration of war was initially a benefit to Proust's finances, although both he and Hauser were far from seeing it that way. But after the war, between 1918 and 1921, Proust's personal wealth grew by 98 percent in real terms.[16] He owed this to many factors, ranging from his stock-exchange strategy to the postwar economy, which benefited him no less (possibly more) than his fellow countrymen, and to the investment of time and personal health that he made through the years toward the success of his novel, which in 1920 began to pay him back generously. The above chart tells this same story in numbers.

The only period when Proust dutifully followed the guidance of Lionel Hauser was during the war years; before and after this time he steadily, if courteously, scorned the banker's advice. It was Hauser's massive intervention into the wreckage of Proust's finances after 1914 that paved the way for the miracle of Proust's financial recovery after the war—a recovery that was bound to surprise Hauser himself, who, like many other brilliant financiers, emerged in bad shape from the long conflict.

As I said, Proust was hardly able to find time for Hauser. The initial reason for this was because Hauser's bourgeois milieu was uninteresting compared to the fashionable society frequented by the writer, which he reported on from time to time in short, mordant newspaper articles. Later on, as Proust proceeded in the writing of *In Search of Lost Time* and the novel's characters became the targets of his social satire, he could not find time for Hauser because he needed to observe, methodically and from up close, the friends and acquaintances who provided him with the raw materials for the creatures of his imagination.

Albeit in an oblique manner that was never openly allusive, the characters in Proust's novel were modeled on the people he knew best and associated with most often. This made his tasks as a writer squalid and occasionally self-demeaning; these tasks often called for him to act duplicitously toward some of the friends he frequented and even fawned on, in order to satisfy his need for attitudes and mannerisms conducive to satire. One of these friends was Robert, Count of Montesquiou, who followed the strictest rules of decadence in making a languorously aesthetic artwork of his own life; in time, to his great displeasure, Montesquiou discovered that he was the main model for the increasingly objectionable character of the Baron de Charlus.

Of the many marvelous features of Proust's novel, the satirical thrust of his "corrosive gaze," as Julia Kristeva calls it, plays an indispensable role:[17] in a story that spans more than three decades, satire contributes the irreversible erosion that gradually wears away the faith that Proust's Narrator puts in his own social milieu, the aristocracy of the Faubourg Saint-Germain in Paris—which coincided, unquestioningly, with Proust's own favorite world. The writer's satirical mode hinges on the forms of social snobbery he mimicked, based on his real-life models. Several of his snobbish characters are "the most sought-after members of society," as Edmund White points out:[18] too high-ranking to be confused with ordinary snobs, with, that is, the social climbers, arrivistes and parvenus who strive to associate with people of higher social status and treat all others contemptuously. The catalogue of Proustian snobbery is more inclusive than that: it applies, as the literary critic Jean Robichez phrases so well, to all forms of "social disguise,"[19] to all forms of complacency, including, for instance, the "opposite path[s]" followed by his Narrator and the arriviste Legrandin in order to reach the same snobbish destination, namely, "to be admitted into the Guermantes circle."[20] The smugness that afflicts many of Proust's upper-class characters consists of a special kind of disguise and a deliberate act of complacency: the older they grow, the more eagerly they dismiss the temporary and perishable nature of that human condition which, whether they like it or not, they share with the most ordinary of human beings; the older they grow, the more stubbornly they wallow in a sort of plastic surgery of the soul. They work hard at forgetting their mortal condition, in sum.

Odette de Crécy is emblematic of this sort of fallacy. A woman who, as I said, made a career out of her own beauty, and that her future husband Swann liked to contemplate like a work of art, in middle age "she found in herself, or invented for herself, a personal style of face, full of a fixed character, a recognized pattern of beauty; and on her formerly undesigned features . . . she now wore this immutable model of eternal youth" (*Young Girls in Flower,* 192–93).[21] In old age this artifice leads her to a sort of mummification: "Precisely because she had not changed, she hardly seemed to be quite alive" (*Finding Time Again,* 258).[22] Of all lapses in good taste, this oblivion of mortality is certainly the gravest in a novel such as *In Search of Lost Time,* which celebrates, as the title may suggest, the process of self-transformation which memory enables us to imprint on the *times* of our lives—on the past, the present, the future, and even, through art, the postmortem.

Hauser is not vain enough. He has too much personal integrity, strength of purpose, and professional zeal to be included or to flourish in the Parisian purgatory of self-damning characters that populate *In Search of Lost Time.* Proust may even have felt, to the contrary, that if the Paris described in his novel were to be peopled with too many clones of this upright banker's human type, the poetry of snobbism that fueled his narrative would have waned like a will-o'-the-wisp (COR XV, 65; *Sodom and Gomorrah,* 149).[23] He certainly made sure that this would not happen. He explained the agenda behind his poetry of snobbism to Lucien Daudet in 1916:

> In order to accomplish the aesthetic discovery of reality . . . one must manage not to be a Parisian when one is talking of Paris. When I spoke of the Guermantes, I always made an effort not to look at them from the perspective of the homme du monde, or at least not from the perspective of someone like me who frequents or has frequented le monde, but rather from the elusively poetic perspective that can be attributed to snobbism. I didn't talk of the Guermantes in the detached tone of the homme du monde, but in the tone full of marvel proper to someone who lives far away from their world. (COR XV, 65)

In Search of Lost Time is a merciless novel, in a sense. It advances ineluctably toward the physical, social, and, in some cases, mental decay of all its characters—with the exception of the Narrator, who discovers, first of all, that Time is not a zero-sum game swaying between, if you will, Wasted Time and Saved Time, and, second of all, that the resources of memory are boundless, and who thereby contrives to defeat his own fear of the end of time that comes with death. This is the main legacy of Proust's novel, to whose wide dissemination he sacrificed all his friendships, his affections, his loves, his good health, and even, in a paradoxical, financially savvy sense, his personal fortune—savvy in this sense, that this sacrifice, or should I say, this wager of his material wealth was bound to enrich several generations of heirs and publishers.

Our need of time is inexhaustible, because it takes time, a lot of it, to transform the impermanence of our experiences and our sensations into the "enduring stability," as Paul Ricoeur calls it, of a personal identity.[24] However, Proust's novel tells us that we are not time's captives. We are not captive, that is, to the limited duration of our existence. On the contrary, we can master time and turn it into a cohesive whole made of the sum total of our active participation in life, the cohesive whole comprising all meaningful occurrences, memories, and intentions—so that time itself becomes an obliging vehicle for the personal identity that we elect as our own, just as it became an obliging vehicle, in Proust's case, for the personal identity that he told us about in his novel.

Chapter 1

THE SENTIMENTAL FINANCIER

At the age of thirty-six, Marcel Proust had a personal fortune that amounted to about 1.5 million French francs, enough to yield annual revenue of 60 thousand francs—equivalent in present-day U.S. dollars to $7 million in assets, with a yearly income of $280,000.[1] This revenue covered the ordinary expenses of his hefty domestic budget (COR XI, 8); the money he spent on medicines and various health treatments alone could have comfortably supported an entire working-class family.[2] It was in December 1907 that Proust asked Lionel Hauser—a banker of French origins but a British national, having been born thirty-nine years earlier in Gibraltar[3]—to look after his financial interests.

This convergence of mutual interests was not accidental. Marcel Proust and Lionel Hauser had met twenty-five years earlier in Auteuil, a rustic village on a hill surrounded by vineyards, near the Bois de Boulogne, where wealthy Parisians like Proust's great-uncle Louis Weil ("Uncle Louis") had their country houses. The two boys met in Uncle Louis's house.

Louis Weil would play a relevant role in Marcel Proust's future. He was an entrepreneur, part of whose wealth had come from the manufacturing of buttons and the rest from his marriage with Émilie Oppenheim, a German banker's daughter.[4] A considerable portion of Proust's patrimony would come eventually from his inheritance from Uncle Louis, who at his death in 1896 left all of his fortune to his niece, Jeanne Proust (née Weil), Marcel's mother, and to her brother Georges (Baruch Denis) Weil. The main business of Jeanne Weil's father Nathé was a limited partnership that controlled a firm of *agents de change;* it made him one of "the 166,000 French men wealthy enough to claim the right to vote."

Unfortunately, we know very little of Nathé Weil's personal worth when he died. With Jeanne's death in 1905 (two years after that of her husband Adrien), Marcel and his younger brother Robert not only inherited their parents' properties, which were quite considerable thanks to their mother's family wealth and their father's dazzling medical career; they also took possession of Uncle Louis's generous legacy.[5]

In 1882, the fifteen-year-old Lionel Hauser was brought to Auteuil by his uncle Gustave Neuberger. Gustave Neuberger, the husband of Louis Weil's sister Adèle, was an acquired cousin of Marcel Proust's mother Jeanne.[6] Hence, there was a degree of kinship, however tenuous, between the two boys. By the time Proust and Hauser met again in 1907, Gustave Neuberger had become the director of the Rothschild Bank in Paris, the sister bank of the London-based N. M. Rothschild & Sons Limited, the best-established financial institution in the world. (Just to grasp the Rothschilds' unchallenged authority over world finance, historian Niall Ferguson suggests we ought to imagine "a merger between Merrill Lynch, Morgan Stanley, J. P. Morgan, and probably Goldman Sachs too.") Gustave Neuberger's brother Léon, who was the husband of a first cousin of Proust's mother, had been appointed chief of the bank's French Correspondence (COR VIII, 115 [note 13]). Léon Neuberger went on to manage Proust's account at the Rothschild Bank until his retirement in 1918. However watered-down, the kinship between Proust and Hauser was a contributing factor in the long adventure that for fifteen years, from 1907 to 1922, tied together the lives and destinies of these two equally brilliant yet hardly compatible personalities.

As I said before, the financial alliance between Proust and Hauser was engineered by Léon Neuberger, who worried about the writer's financial speculations, which he considered equally bold and incompetent. Married to Jeanne, a Parisian woman of Catholic origins[7] who gave him two children, François and Daniel, Hauser had just settled in Paris as the agent of two financial-services firms: Warburg & Co., headquartered in Hamburg, Germany, and Kuhn & Loeb, headquartered in New York. He boasted first-class international training followed by an international career. After completing his studies in finance and accounting in Paris in 1886, crowned by the "prix d'honneur," he served a three-year apprenticeship in Hamburg and then worked as an investment banker in London for another three years. In 1893 he took a job as agent of the Crédit Lyonnais in Barcelona, and six years later followed his agency's director to Saint Petersburg. From 1900 to 1903 he was vice-director of the Crédit Lyonnais in Seville. From 1903 to 1907 he was Warburg & Co.'s proxy in Seville, which he left to move to Paris. He spent the rest of his life in the French capital, where in 1916, after nine years of work as financial agent and consultant, he established his own financial-services firm, Hauser et Cie.

In 1907 Proust had an account at the Rothschild Bank and a smaller one at the Crédit Industriel. Hauser opened an account on his behalf at Warburg & Co. At first Proust entrusted Hauser with the management of 97,000 francs, which he had earned in February 1908 from the sale of his inherited share (one-fourth) of an apartment building at 102 Boulevard Haussmann in Paris. His brother Robert owned an equivalent share, and the buyer of their half of the building was their aunt Amélie, Marcel's future landlady, who had inherited the rest of the building from her husband Georges Weil (COR VIII, 143).

Hauser immediately proved to be a scrupulous administrator. On his advice, Proust bought a block of securities from Paketfahrt, a German shipping company traded on the floor of the Berlin Stock Exchange. When they lost 6.75 percent of their market value, Hauser expressed his regret to the writer. Proust declared himself "highly amused" by his friend's zealousness, remarking, in a tone of curious naiveté, that it was not as if a financial advisor was expected to feel responsible for the floating in the price of securities bought by his clients.

> My dear Lionel,
>
> . . . If I were not so awfully ill, I would write a piece about the "Sentimental Banker" who wakes up abruptly, moaning, "My God! One of my clients just lost forty cents on the Portuguese stocks, etc. etc." In any case, if you push your kindness of heart thus far, it must be because you are pleased with yourself since the other securities you advised me to buy have all grown in value at a . . . fabulous pace. (COR VIII, 148)

At this early stage, Hauser was mainly adding securities from American railways and fixed-rate bonds to Proust's portfolio. The following month, as a token of trust and gratitude, Proust instructed the Rothschild Bank to deposit a further 52,000 francs in his Warburg account. In the letter announcing this new deposit to Hauser, not only does Proust congratulate himself on his choice of a financial advisor, but also on the savvy of their recent investments. "See how wrong my parents were, when they feared that I had no common sense and could not even read a business letter! I'm saddened at the thought that they were so anxious about me, and so needlessly" (COR VIII, 164).

If Adrien and Jeanne Proust were the first two people to be concerned about their son Marcel's financial wisdom, they would not be the last among his friends and relatives to worry about his economic prosperity. Hauser would soon join the ranks of detractors of what Proust deemed to be his own financial perspicacity. In spite of their mutual affection and growing respect, the relationship between the writer and the banker, documented in almost fifteen years of epistolary exchanges, was destined to unwind itself in the tumultuous clash between the banker's moral rectitude, unquestionable competence, and prosaic lack of imagination and the most restless, most inventive, and perhaps, in spite of Proust's best intentions, least sincere of his clients.

Proust sold securities when he was bored and bought them to have fun, writes Jean-Yves Tadié, the writer's most influential biographer. This may be true to a point. As a qualifier to this opinion, Tadié adds that Proust's investments do not so much prove his incompetence as reveal "relevant aspects of his nature."[8] Hauser was under a similar impression when he told Proust that his economic downfall was the result of his artistic talents. In writing of the relevant aspects of Proust's nature, Tadié seems to acknowledge that he is talking about the literary genius who envisioned art and finance in a sort of symbiotic coexistence. It was this special vision, peculiar to Proust's temperament, that enabled him to transform the huge expenses he incurred to support his romantic infatuations, the burdensome living costs imposed on him by his myriad maladies, and the heavy losses caused by his hasty speculations, into a matchless sort of creative capital— highly profitable in the long run. Proust turned economic costs into artistic opportunities.

We saw earlier that by 1908 Proust could claim credit for translating two books by Ruskin: *The Bible of Amiens* in 1904 and *Sesame and Lilies* in 1906. As has been documented by Cynthia J. Gamble, these two works earned him the reputation of a talented stylist but did not seem destined to signal the debut of a solid literary career.[9] The literary projects that would lead to his masterpiece, *In Search of Lost Time,* had been in the works for some time, but nobody, perhaps not even Proust himself, had the sagacity to foresee the artistic stature its author would acquire. Financial interests seemed to occupy a significant part of Proust's time and attention, easily distracting him from matters literary and artistic.

Proust associated with men and women of high social standing who were richer than he was, people who did not turn a hair at undertaking the riskiest operations on the Bourse de Paris. Louis d'Albufera figured prominently among the self-assured speculators whom Proust tried to emulate. Albufera, involved in a stormy affair with the actress Louisa de Mornand, eventually provided Proust with a model for the similarly tormented love affair of his character Robert de Saint-Loup with the actress Rachel. It was from bad influences such as Albufera's that Léon Neuberger meant to rescue Proust by promoting Hauser's entrance into his life.

In an October 1908 letter, Proust asked Albufera to give him leads concerning, respectively: safe and remunerative investments; risky, more remunerative investments; and openly speculative high-risk investments (COR VIII, 131). In a letter written a month later to the same friend, he bragged about the advice, given him, it seems, by their common friend Léon Fould, to buy securities of the Banco Español del Río de la Plata. In one year these securities had risen 6.5 percent in value. He also confided to Albufera that no speculative tip ever came to him from the Rothschild brothers (in whose bank he continued, wisely enough, to keep most of his fortune): "When anything yields more than 2.5%, the Rothschild brothers tremble with fear" (COR VIII, 131, 156). He assiduously followed the news from the Bourse de Paris in the financial columns of *Le Figaro* and the *Journal des Débats.*

What distinguished Proust from his financial advisors, both the adventurous ones like Albufera and the shrewd ones like Hauser and Neuberger, was his resourcefulness in profiting from his own profligacy; he had a flair, wholly unrelated to rational thinking, for opportunity costs. In the course of the next fifteen years, this talent would induce him to undertake expenses and investments which, although costly and unsuccessful as far as his immediate personal advantage was concerned, turned out to be unaccountably profitable to the composition of his novel. We must wonder, of course, if Proust was aware of this curious talent of his. I think he was. He was too adept at self-examination to miss this aspect of his own artistic creativity. In *The Prisoner,* he turned this very talent into a subtle metaphor of artistic inspiration, the metaphor of "Turning Caresses into Gold," discussed, as noted earlier, in the chapter of the same title.

Chapter 2

OLD MISTRESSES FROM THE STOCK EXCHANGE

As a successful author, Proust was a late bloomer. The first volume of *In Search of Lost Time* was self-published in 1913, around his forty-second birthday; but he had to wait until 1919 to receive the prestigious Prix Goncourt, at the age of forty-eight, before his royalties from the novel became remunerative. And by then he was left with only three more years to live.

In the evaluation of Proust's financial decisions from 1908 to the year of his death, 1922, we must factor in the lagging benefits that his peculiar financial moves and consistently spendthrift budget choices contributed to the market value of his novel. In other words, we must leave aside judgmental considerations of eccentricity and wastefulness and treat Proust as an investor whose financial strategies had a longer lifespan than his own existence—as it is always the case, by the way, with personal patrimony. He left behind creative equity, if you will.

One can hardly conceive of an alternative version of *In Search of Lost Time,* lacking the passages and episodes that Proust derived from his own misadventures on the Bourse de Paris and more generally in the realm of conspicuous expenditure. Would such a diminished version have enjoyed the same favorable reception, the same stratospheric sales, and the same steady circulation in the world's literary markets? It is impossible to quantify an answer to these questions, or, put differently, to gauge the long-term market value of Proust's creative equity. But it is easy to show, as in this book, that Proust transposed his liberal squandering of money into the creation of literary episodes of surprising effectiveness, both in the artistic sphere and, later on, in the commercial one. What precedents are there of such an aesthetic and economic miracle in the history of literature? The additional consideration that, eventually, he turned out to be not such a bad investor as commonly thought has its own independent relevance in this picture, of course.

Let me start by recounting two anecdotes from 1908, the first year of the collaboration between Proust and Hauser. Both stories highlight how thoroughly reality and fantasy were integrated in Proust's life experience—and, more specifically, what formidable instinct he had for combining economic and imaginative resources.

The first anecdote concerns the notorious "affaire Lemoine." Henri-Didot-Léon Lemoine was a French engineer who extorted 64,000 British pounds from Sir Julius Wernher, the president of the de Beers Company, which is still nowadays in control of a large share of the global diamond industry and was founded in 1888 with capitals from the London-based N. M. Rothschild & Sons Limited. By means of rigged experiments, Lemoine persuaded Wernher that he had discovered a procedure to make artificial diamonds. Somewhat incongruously, Lemoine's plan aimed not only at extorting blackmail money from Wernher, but also at causing a steep drop in the price of de Beers shares, so that he could buy large quantities of them at a cheap price. Eventually Wernher realized he had been duped and reported Lemoine to the authorities.

This succession of events would have likely gone wholly unnoticed by Proust, if not for the fact that he had inherited a large block of de Beers shares ("seventy or eighty"; COR VIII, 115),[1] and found himself losing at least 30,000 francs when their prices plummeted. Lemoine was first questioned by the authorities on January 9, 1909, and sentenced to six years' imprisonment on July 6, 1909. Proust published a pastiche devoted to the Lemoine affair, written in the style of Honoré de Balzac, in *Le Figaro* literary supplement of February 22, 1909, no later than seven weeks, that is, after Lemoine's first police interrogation. On March 14 he published a second pastiche devoted to the same affair, in the style of Gustave Flaubert this time, and complemented, in the same issue of *Le Figaro,* by another one in the style of Charles Augustine Sainte-Beuve. This last piece was a true virtuoso performance, consisting of a critical discussion on the apocryphal piece by Flaubert. A year later he contributed another one of his Lemoine pastiches to *Le Figaro,* this time written in the style of the symbolist poet Henri de Régnier. Ten years later, in 1919 (the year when Proust's literary endeavors finally turned remunerative), the whole collection of pastiches appeared under the title *Pastiches et mélanges,* published at the same time as the second volume of *In Search of Lost Time* and a new, revised edition of the first volume.[2]

If the purchase of de Beers shares by a relative of his, almost certainly Louis Weil (as I will show in due time), must have looked rather unfortunate to Proust during the Lemoine affair, when it became an unprofitable investment, this acquisition turned out to be the enabling factor that strengthened his literary reputation in Paris. Ten years later, when all his pastiches were collected in a volume by the prestigious publishing house directed by Gaston Gallimard, it also markedly increased the balance of his bank account.

The second anecdote concerns Proust's disloyalty toward Hauser. As we saw, Léon Neuberger referred Proust to Hauser in an attempt to wrench him free of the influence of dangerous speculators such as Albufera. But Proust soon realized that Hauser was too cautious a broker and could not satisfy all the facets of his restless personality as an investor. Without knowing it, Hauser would gradually find himself in an intermediate position between Neuberger, who was more and more unresponsive to Proust's aspiration to have a say in the management of his own huge portfolio with the Rothschild Bank, and various *agents de change* (stockbrokers) and *coulissiers* (curb brokers), all very solicitous in bringing to fruition any of Proust's speculative aspirations, no matter how audacious. (Strictly speaking, a *coulissier* was authorized to trade on securities that were not quoted on the floor of the Paris Stock Exchange.)[3]

In 1908 Proust's main stockbroker was Gustave Guastalla, who, in spite of his inefficiency, was always ready to act swiftly on Proust's instructions. In a November 1908 letter to Neuberger, Proust scoffed at the messages he received from Guastalla. When Guastalla wrote him, as he had done recently, that he had just "deposited 26,000 francs in Proust's account at the Rothschild Bank in return for 75 shares of the Banco Español del Río de la Plata, which he withdrew from his portfolio," it turned out that he had done the exact opposite, having added the 75 shares, which he bought on Proust's behalf, to his client's portfolio at the Rothschild Bank, and withdrawn the money necessary to pay for them (COR VIII, 162). By 1911, the name of Guastalla was erased from the list of Proust's stockbrokers. But for the time being, in 1908, Guastalla was Proust's source of a new and important literary inspiration.

The writer had of late been devoting some of his time to the genealogical studies that play a relevant role in his novel. From these studies he learned that Guastalla was the name of a fortified town in the central

Italian province of Reggio. The town of Guastalla had belonged to the Duke of Parma till Napoleon Bonaparte took possession of it and turned it into a small state, which he gave to his sister Pauline as a gift. The title of Duke of Guastalla was considered extinguished since 1875, after the death of its last legitimate bearer, François V, Duke of Modena and Parma. In his novel Proust pretends that this title is still used both by one of the Duke of Parma's descendants and by one of Pauline Bonaparte's descendants.

And so it is that the cue given him by the name of an unreliable stockbroker blossomed into an amusing episode in the third volume of his novel, *The Guermantes Way.* Here we read of Oriane, Duchess of Guermantes, suggesting to her friend the Princess of Parma that they should go have a look at the Empire furniture of the Iéna family. The name Iéna is Proust's invention, adopted, in memory of one of Napoleon's most celebrated victories on the battlefield, in lieu of the Bonaparte name, since the emperor's family was not yet extinct at the time of the events narrated in *The Guermantes Way.* This book defines Oriane's proposal to the Princess of Parma as "an audacious ploy," and a most brazen idea even for the very impertinent Duchess of Guermantes. There is quite a bit of malice in the duchess's proposal to the Princess of Parma, in fact, since she cannot possibly be unaware of the fact that her friend the princess deems the descendants of the Iéna lineage (that is, the Bonaparte) as impostors and parvenus, usurpers of the title of Duke of Guastalla, which belongs by right to her own son (*Guermantes Way,* 516).[4]

In another scene from the same volume, the Baron de Charlus pretends he does not even know that there are two pretenders to the title of Duke of Guastalla. In a daring mingling of fiction and real life, he confuses Pauline Bonaparte's descendant who carries this title with the Parisian stockbroker: "As for this alleged Duc de Guastalla, I thought he must be my secretary's stock broker, given that you can buy almost anything with money [even a title of nobility]" (*Guermantes Way,* 562).[5]

We now turn to the first example of Proust's speculations on the stock exchange that were guided by purely sentimental motives. This first sentimental investment was a tiny one, consisting of a single share of the Royal Dutch oil company, and it failed to move the heart of its intended beneficiary; but it set the premises for Proust's economic affluence after World War I. The reputable Proustian scholar Pierre-Louis Rey has argued that by the end of the war Proust was "almost ruined."[6] Many a brilliant financier, including Hauser himself, was not immune from the devastating effects of this long conflict. But the steady purchase of Royal Dutch shares managed by the Rothschild Bank on Proust's behalf, almost without Hauser's knowledge, expeditiously reconsolidated the writer's finances after the war, leading to Hauser's professional humiliation and a serious break between the two friends. But it is still early for us to talk of this.

The story of this first sentimental investment begins in 1908, when the writer received a stock exchange tip that was exceptional, and exceptionally reliable, in that it came from one of the Rothschild brothers—not one of the two bankers, Alphonse and Gustave, though, but the medical doctor, Henri-James Rothschild, director of the journal *Revue d'Hygiène et de Pathologie Infantile.* This tip concerned the promising prospects of Royal Dutch, one of the most aggressive and influential oil companies on the European stock markets.

In a letter to Hauser, Proust made a passing mention of the advantages of buying Royal Dutch. In any case, it must have already been clear to him by then that Hauser was disinclined to invest in industrial, mineral, or mining companies, since at this time he preferred the safer, if less profitable, venue of fixed-interest and long-term bonds and government securities. This may be the reason why Proust's letter did not insist on Doctor Rothschild's tip, although, duly impressed, the writer did act on it. Two months later Proust mentioned the Royal Dutch securities in a letter to Albufera. As he praised their 22 percent yearly increase of value, he alluded to a speculation he had made on them a little earlier, when ("I wonder if you recall," he asks his friend) he "earned quite a bit on a single share" (COR VIII, 156). Proust was referring to a speculation meant to benefit Marie Nordlinger's cousin, the musician Reynaldo Hahn, who belonged to the exclusive and rather homophile group of Proust's friends of which Hauser, owing to his stern lifestyle, could not possibly be a part.

Having bought and sold in a short interval one Royal Dutch share, Proust asked his chauffeur, Nicolas Cottin, to deliver to Hahn an envelope with 750 francs in it, a sum corresponding to the operation's entire or partial return. Hahn took one look at the banknotes and put them back into Cottin's hands. The chauffeur, who was understandably puzzled by this shuffling of money back and forth, went home and handed them over to his employer. This rejected gift was followed by a few lively and playful letters between the two friends—made even more playful than their customarily jocose correspondence by the fact that, at this time, Proust was vacationing at the sea resort of Cabourg in Normandy (whose Grand-Hôtel serves in his novel as the model for the Grand-Hôtel at the fictional sea resort of Balbec).[7]

But behind Proust's playful tone one can sense a touch of bitterness. In order to justify Hahn's refusal, he had to tell Cottin that he earned those 750 francs on behalf of Monsieur Hahn, and that the latter had returned them because of "some foolish scruple." For a while after this episode, every time Proust charged Cottin to buy some expensive item or food, the chauffeur would remark, "First we should ask Monsieur Hahn to send us some more of that money." Proust was still evidently brooding on this misunderstanding with Hahn, and the result is that, in the following two weeks, three of his letters to the musician mentioned the episode again. In the postscript to the third of these letters, he declared himself still "offended." How long would it take before his beloved "Bibibuls" (one of the many nicknames he used to address his friend) would stop objecting to Proust having acted with him in the same way as "an older cousin" would? Such a dispensation would fill him with joy (COR VIII, 86, 101, and 102). Hahn was slightly older than Marie Nordlinger; Nordlinger's collaborator and biographer P. F. Prestwich gives us reasons to believe that the young woman was fondly and hopelessly in love with Hahn, who treated her "as a younger sister."[8] Analogously, Proust was slightly older than Hahn. But I doubt that in wishing for the privilege to deal with the musician the way an older cousin would, Proust had in mind an equally unconsummated attraction as that of Nordlinger for Hahn.

The debut of Proust's trading in Royal Dutch shares was thus marked by this intense and intensely frustrated sentimental motive. Proust followed Henri-James Rothschild's advice primarily in order to earn his beloved Reynaldo Hahn's gratitude. If he failed at it, it was mainly because the affection that Hahn held for him was of a kind unconnected with mercenary considerations, as time would show. (Fourteen years later, on November 18, 1922, it would fall on Hahn to write some of the most urgent announcements of Proust's death.)[9] But from a purely financial standpoint, the speculation was successful, as it yielded a good profit which, as we saw, Proust was still boasting about two months later in his letter to Albufera. He certainly seemed inclined to repeat the same investment in Royal Dutch, but on a larger scale: this is exactly what he would soon start doing, using the services of the Rothschild Bank and not, except on one or two occasions, those of Hauser. Hauser learned of the importance and the full benefits of his friend's purchases of Royal Dutch only at the end of World War I, when, as the Hauser et Cie firm crawled tiredly out of the conflict, Hauser witnessed, dumbfounded, Proust's phoenixlike rebirth out of the ashes of his supposed financial ruin.

Certain securities grow on you like an addiction, at times of a good kind, at times bad, Proust wrote to Hauser in 1917. Intrusive "like old mistresses," there are the sweet-hearted ones that give and give and never ask for anything in return, and the cheeky ones that, long after the thrill is gone, keep demanding preposterous handouts. Proust, who showered his infatuations with gifts, was especially acquainted with the latter kind of lover. Without a doubt, among the high-maintenance addictions he developed at the Bourse de Paris, Royal Dutch securities were the most munificent ones to him.

Chapter 3

A FRIEND'S HEART

The first few years of the collaboration between Marcel Proust and Lionel Hauser were characterized by events and incidents that help us understand the fascinating human phenomenon of a writer in the making. On the one hand, Proust's reputation as an original author was growing steadily, even if it would have been premature to talk of an established personal success; on the other hand, his state of health was worsening at a remarkably brisk pace. These two aspects complemented each other and continued to do so until the writer's death. It is almost as if the sacrifice of his own health, and more specifically of the chance to live any substantial day-to-day existence or love affair, besides those narrated by the fictitious biography which Proust attributed to himself in his novel, was the steep price imposed by Proust's creative muse.

In his short life, Proust proved himself an artist endowed with titanic energy. Had he been cured of his many illnesses, he would never have profited from the interminable hours of waking and solitude necessary to the creation of his masterpiece. Of this artist's many paradoxes, this is the most absurd: illness did not function to the detriment but rather to the furthering of his career. A Marcel Proust in good health is plainly inconceivable; he would have settled for "ordinary, indolent contentment," as Walter Benjamin has argued; and we would have scanty memory of him, probably based on a sheaf of articles in the society news and a few essays in journals devoted to literary and aesthetic matters.[1]

In August 1909, Proust told Madame Émile Straus (that is, Geneviève Straus, née Halévy) that the writing of his novel was "completed, although many parts of it [were] still in need of improvement." Straus, renowned in Paris for her witticisms or *mots d'esprit,*[2] was the model for the brazen speech and conduct of Oriane de Guermantes in Proust's novel, but she was also the mother, from her previous marriage to the composer of *Carmen,* of Proust's classmate and beloved *chéri* from twenty-one years earlier, Jacques Bizet (COR XXI, 399).[3] The truth is that, at this time, Proust had only written the first and last part of *In Search of Lost Time.* He was not exactly lying, though, when he declared that his book was finished: at this early stage, he was far from guessing that his masterpiece would eventually number seven volumes (and nine books), and the first volume, *Swann's Way,* which takes its title from the character of Charles Swann, would only see the light in 1913. In November 1909, Proust wrote to Hauser that he was "kept hostage by the agonies of a work in three volumes (!), undertaken, promised, unfinished" (COR IX, 81, 110).

Two months after this letter, it was Proust's poor health that took front stage in a letter to Madame Gaston de Caillavet, the young wife Jeanne (née Pouquet) of another beloved classmate from the Lycée.[4] He wrote to Jeanne de Caillavet that the days when he felt good enough to leave his bed, get dressed, and take a stroll were rare indeed. And when he did manage to go out, it was too late in the evening for him to dare pay her a visit. Most of the time, he was prey to asthma attacks, though, and in these cases not even his personal doctor was admitted to his bedroom—only Reynaldo Hahn, who by now was used to his disease and the "fumigations" from the Legras medicinal powder that Proust inhaled to relieve his suffering. When Proust could not talk at all, he and Hahn communicated by means of handwritten notes (COR X, 9).

In the summer of this same year, 1909, Proust once again spent his holidays at the sea resort of Cabourg, from where he wrote in September to Maurice Duplay, a friend from childhood:[5]

> Three years ago I could still go out every day in a closed car, two years ago my excursions by car had become impossible, but I could still go down to the beach. Last year I could not go out at all, yet every night I would go down to the hotel (or to the gambling house, which is inside the hotel and can be reached without leaving the hotel). This year I can barely get out of bed and go downstairs for an hour or two once every two or three days. (COR X, 79)

Several generations of Proust admirers have grown well acquainted with the symbiosis of art and illness, mentioned earlier, that typifies the writer's entire adult life; they are less familiar with one of this book's topics, namely, the equally important symbiosis between Proust's creative fantasy and his financial reality. Proust's state of health kept him from meeting Hauser in person, as we know, so he and his financial advisor communicated by mail. While this created obvious obstacles to the smooth management of the writer's finances, it provides us with a valuable vantage point when it comes to reconstructing their relations. Through the evidence of the letters they exchanged, we are privy to both the financial decisions Proust and Hauser agreed upon or argued about, and the love-and-hate relationship that bound them to each other for fifteen years, and gradually got the upper hand of their common economic interests.

Hauser hid his growing concern for Proust's state of health behind his worries about the writer's household budget—concerns which were justified, if not explicitly required, by his role as financial advisor. He had recently read in the *Frankfurt Gazette* about a new asthma cure based on "a physical training of the lungs." He suggested to Proust that if he tried out this therapy with good results, he would be able to do without the costly drugs he was currently using to the detriment of his budget. Hauser reckoned that Proust would save about 6,000 francs per year (equivalent to 28,000 dollars, remembering that in this book the relative worth of the French franc versus the U.S. dollar is measured in terms of the American currency's 2008 purchasing power; COR IX, 19).

Through the years, the constant worsening of Proust's illness, the veracity of whose symptoms was questioned even by friends less pragmatic and down-to-earth than Hauser, would cause a growing conflict between the two friends. The writer was fond of treatments based on physical immobility, on long periods in bed and in sealed rooms with no air circulation, on large doses of medicines and opiates, and on constant "fumigations." For all their ineffectiveness, such measures and precautions were ideally suited to Proust's need to spend endless hours with his head bent over the pages of his writings—just as his rare and debilitating attendance at social gatherings, aimed at scrutinizing the human specimens to whom his novel devotes descriptions of astounding insight and psychological subtlety, also mainly served his needs as an author. The banker was in favor of more commonsensical measures: long hours spent outdoors, sun treatments, healthy and abundant food, and so forth. In spite of the erudition he showed in his letters, Hauser was undoubtedly not receptive to the decadent culture that Proust had cherished since he was a boy. In his early youth, the writer had been an ardent admirer of Gérard de Nerval and Charles Baudelaire; and as a young adult, he struck up a lifelong friendship with Robert de Montesquiou, his senior of seventeen years, the main model for the Baron de Charlus, and a prolific writer, for whom, as I said earlier, a decadent lifestyle was an artwork in its own right.

Montesquiou's influence on his younger friend's artwork was equally lifelong and deserves a little aside—not only because it makes evident why Hauser, the prosaic man of finance and the devoted husband and father, could not possibly be a citizen of Proust's imaginary world, but also because this influence manifests itself, paradoxically, in the least artistic and most literalistic sense of the word *decadent.* When I think of Palamède XV, nicknamed Mémé, Baron de Charlus, I envision a sort of corpulent sea lion wandering the city streets at night and making a self-demeaning spectacle of his own sexual urges—that is what my memory brings back from the closing sections of *In Search of Lost Time.* But I tend to forget that, in the earlier volumes, a younger Charlus is the sharpest mind portrayed by Proust, the sharpest dresser as well, and has the reputation, which he encourages, of being irresistible to women—the perennial protagonist of an uninterrupted performance and the secret pursuer of inadmissible transgressions. Before unwittingly posing for the characterization of Charlus, Robert de Montesquiou, who in one of his poems crowned himself "the sovereign of impermanent things," had been the model for the decadent character of Jean des Esseintes in Joris-Karl Huysmans's 1884 novel *À rebours.* Giovanni Boldini's portrait of the aristocrat, held at the Musée d'Orsay in Paris, shows a young dandy (it could very well be a young Charlus), younger than his forty-two-year-old model (Charlus was not above touching his face up with makeup to look younger), at the peak of his bodily charm—an image which reveals a great deal of the formidable narrative potential that Proust, the unrepentant satirist, must have seen in this unequalled aristocratic specimen. Even Boldini, highly praised by Montesquiou for his pictorial skills, seems to have added a touch of irony to this painting (see illus. 1).

Back to Hauser and the meticulous way he handled his duties as Proust's financial advisor. An unidentified friend of the writer who had just opened a new bank, the Comptoir des Banques, needed to sell a portion of his own shares and had invited Proust to buy them. When Proust consulted Hauser about it, the banker replied drily that Proust should never "mix business with charity." If he truly cared to help this friend of his, he would do better by simply giving him some money. And then, with a flourish not to be expected of a businessman with no time to waste, Hauser set this matter aside with a learned, scathing allusion. "Anyway, I wonder what's driving you into this galley?" he asked. He was clearly counting on the efficacy added to his words by the selfsame rhetorical question—*Que diable allait-il faire dans cette galère?*— uttered eight times by the character of Géronte in the second act of Molière's *Les Fourberies de Scapin* (COR IX, 39, 39 [note 4]).

Giovanni Boldini, *Le Comte Robert de Montesquiou* (1897; RF 1977–56), Musée d'Orsay, Paris. Photograph Hervé Lewandowski. © RMN–Grand Palais / Art Resource, N.Y.

Proust's appreciation of his advisor's industry is reflected in his decision to transfer a further 40,000 francs from the Rothschild Bank to his Warburg account in 1909. Of this sum, Hauser invested 13,000 francs in the purchase of Southern Pacific securities, an American railway company, and the same amount in the purchase of the new Argentine

National Loan with 5 percent yearly yield. Then, challenging Proust's instructions, he refused to invest the residual 14,000 francs in securities of Port de Para, a shipping company he deemed too risky, and instead deposited this sum in Proust's account at the Crédit Industriel (COR IX, 40, 41, 42). This transfer of funds from Rothschild was followed by a second one in the amount of 45,000 francs in the second trimester of 1909. Hence, by May 1909 Hauser, as the French representative of Warburg & Co., was managing 220,000 francs on Proust's behalf, the modern-day equivalent of one million dollars.

It had been almost a year since Hauser had advised Proust to buy a block of Paketfahrt securities, in the presumption that migration toward America would soon recover its strength, thus benefiting this shipping company. An upswing of this sort was late in coming, though, and Hauser had expressed his regret about his imprudent advice in a letter to Proust, as we saw. But on September 15, 1909, he was able to announce to the writer that not only had the Paketfahrt securities paid their regular 4 percent coupon, but they had also grown by 8.7 percent in value. Proust's profit was about 1,000 francs (COR IX, 39, 95). It was Proust's turn to flaunt his erudition in a learned reply to Hauser—learned as well as elaborately maritime. He thanked the banker for trying to make him rich; Hauser seemed to be working so hard at it, Proust wrote, that his moods had been going up and down, from bad to good, and back, in tandem with the floating value of the German shipping company's shares. Then Proust embarked on a commentary of "By the Ship's Moorings," a poem by Sully Prudhomme, in 1901 the first writer to be awarded the Nobel Prize for literature.

The poem describes a swaying ship at harbor, which in its ups and downs seems to drag the hearts of the wives of the soon-to-take-ship seamen, as well as the babies in the cradles being rocked by the same anxious women. Prudhomme could not have imagined, Proust remarks, the subtler swaying of a true friend's heart. Hauser's heart follows the sea crossings of the Paketfahrt steamships, whose wavelike motions reflect in turn the fluctuating trends of their value on the stock exchange; and these trends have become, at long last, "marvelous" (COR IX, 96). There is no stopping Proust's Pindaric flight: Hauser's concern for his prosperity intimates a more altruistic anxiety than the one possessing the wives and mothers described in Prudhomme's poem, he concludes in an embarrassingly overstated comparison—one that is flattering to his friend, if not to his sense of proportions.

Chapter 4

ENTER ALBERT NAHMIAS

We will return to Proust's idea of "a friend's heart." To him, a friend's heart was the emblem of generosity and altruism; he opposed it, curiously, to the selfish industriousness of bees and of artists like himself, who worked tirelessly, without worrying in the least about the people who would one day taste the fruits of their labor. We will also, later on, contrast Proust's opposite views on the generosity of the heart and the selfishness of love. In his opinion, the passion of love was nothing but the selfish and exaggerated projection, onto the contours of the beloved's body, of the affection we fantasize both giving and receiving (*Fugitive,* 462).[1] To him, love had nothing to do with altruism, just as altruism had little to do with artistic originality and prolificacy.

And we will find ourselves facing over and over, by implication, the absurdity of Marcel Proust's tortured love life: he wasted it, together with his chance to be happy, in destructive love affairs that took no account whatsoever of the true nature of the men and women he was in love with or lusting after. At the same time, he schemed to translate each one of his unrequited love affairs into new narrative threads, conceived for the benefit of his readers with the generous heart of a friend, yet carried out with the industrious indifference of a bee.

This blend of generosity, altruism, callousness, and creative prolificacy informs the moral scaffoldings that sustain the complex architecture of *In Search of Lost Time.* Just like Dante Alighieri with his *Divine Comedy* and Saint Augustine with his *Confessions,* Proust wrote an autobiography which is intentionally unverifiable—not based, that is, on the facts of his life, but rather on the account of the existential choices he made in the course of his life. In this way and by this choice, his life was to be "realized in a book" (*Finding Time Again*, 342).[2] Yet, the ultimate urge driving Proust's work was partially divergent from the vocation driving his two illustrious precursors.

The existential choices of both Dante and Augustine engage them in a love quest: as they tell of their journeys in the mysteries of their own souls, they are in search of a perfect love whose name is God. At the end of his pseudobiography, though, Proust does not find the perfect love that seals the quest of his predecessors.[3] What both Proust and his Narrator find, in the end, is the vocation to write a book about the meaningful and cohesive nature of their whole life experience, the *Book of Time and Memory*, if you will—a necessary book which they have to write because nobody else could, the real author approaching its completion while the fictional character enters its first stage of inception. As argued by many critics (and contested by almost as many), the literary output of the Narrator of *In Search of Lost Time* is destined to consist of the very novel which ends with the description of his reasons for writing it and of the way he plans to write it.[4]

A pessimist when it came to the possibility of a true, simple love, Proust let himself be oriented, both in his art and in his life, by the coexistence of amity and unconcern. His heart housed at the same time a friendly generosity toward his readers and a harsh indifference toward his friends. This is the formula, both cruel and solicitous, that enabled Proust to create a novel destined to unveil a new framework for the significance of human existence. We will pay further attention to Proust's altruism as an author and self-centeredness as a friend later on, as their effects unfold together with the evolution of Proust's fiery affection for Hauser.

In 1909, Proust's assets amounted to about 1,600,000 francs, distributed as follows: 74 percent at the Rothschild Bank, invested in fixed-income bonds and securities deemed very safe; 14 percent at Warburg & Co., managed by Hauser and invested in fixed-income bonds and securities of American railway companies; and 12 percent at the Crédit Industriel, mostly derived, I gather, from the conversion of a huge block of Vichy registered securities into shares of the Banco Español del Río de la Plata. Assuming an average 4 percent annual yield, his capital earned Proust yearly revenue of 64,000 francs.

The following year, Proust would have to spend a sum equivalent to, if not greater than, this revenue of 64,000 francs to pay off his debts, which were partly a consequence of his reckless investments and partly due to the financial crisis that hit the international stock markets, especially

American railway companies. In April 1910, Proust had instructed the Rothschild Bank to entrust a further 40,000 francs to his Warburg account, and then he had asked Hauser to invest in American railways; the values of these companies dropped in less than three months, and a large sum vanished into thin air. Proust was not exaggerating in the letter he wrote to Reynaldo Hahn at the end of July 1910, when he complained that he had lost about 50,000 francs on the securities of American railways held in his Rothschild and Warburg portfolios, and almost as much on the contracts on mineral and rubber companies negotiated on his behalf by Gustave Guastalla.

At the beginning of 1910, Proust began to follow closely the financial column in *Le Figaro* written by Armand Lévy, who went by the pseudonym of Armand Yvel. This was one of his main sources of information for devising new speculations; in the month of July, it was from Monsieur Yvel that he learned about the collapse of his finances (COR X, 10, 10 [note 11]).

The composition of Proust's portfolio changed significantly in 1910. At this time, he was the client of an investment bank (Rothschild), of a deposit bank entitled to transactions on the stock exchange (Crédit Industriel), of a German firm specializing in international transactions (Warburg), and of an *agent de change* or stockbroker (Gustave Guastalla). All too soon, other stockbrokers and several *coulissiers,* or curb brokers, would count Proust among their clients. Besides acting on Proust's behalf as intermediaries with brokerage firms entitled to operate on the floor of the Bourse de Paris, these curb brokers dealt in securities for future delivery. The curb brokers' invasion into the writer's financial interests completes the catalogue of his financial agents. Proust was now dealing with the whole range of firms and operators accredited to trade on financial markets.[5]

Proust's dealings with Guastalla did not last long, though. He parted ways with this *agent de change* at the end of 1910, but not before being initiated into forwards contracts, an instrument that allowed him to buy a certain security under the obligation to pay a predetermined price for it (the settlement price) by a given date (the settlement date). In financial jargon, investing in an instrument of this sort is equivalent to taking a "long position": the presumption of the buyer of a forwards contract is that the price of the underlying security is bound to rise in time, so that by settlement date the contract holder will be able to meet the obligation to pay the settlement price, resell the security at the current price, and make a profit out of the operation. Forwards contracts are similar to futures contracts, very common on contemporary stock markets, with the difference that the gap between the market value of a futures contract and the collateral securing the contract is evaluated daily, while the gap between a forwards contract and the collateral securing it is evaluated only at settlement date (which was the last day of each month at the Bourse de Paris in Proust's time), or at the time when the contract is closed by the holder, prior to expiration. Finally, financial-services firms, such as Gustave Guastalla's in Proust's case (and later on David Léon's, Wellhoff & Neustadtl, and Cremieux & Frankel), acted as counterparties to the forwards contract's two parties, the buyer and the seller, providing the mechanisms for settlement, based on the same principle that applies to futures contracts nowadays.

In 1910, Guastalla signed four major forwards contracts on Proust's behalf, which covered large quantities of securities in Russian and Far-Eastern mineral companies, as well as an undefined amount of Port de Para securities, the shipping company in which Hauser had refused to invest on the writer's behalf. By the end of summer 1911, the values of these securities had fallen drastically, leaving Proust with a further debt of roughly 34,000 francs in collaterals. After settling the considerable debt he had run up in the interval of just a few months, Proust stopped using Guastalla's services.

Only two years earlier, Proust had written to Hauser expressing his regret that his parents had never had the chance to witness how clever he was at wealth management (COR VIII, 164). He also sang the same tune in a letter to Léon Neuberger: "My poor parents were certain that for my entire life I would never manage to read a business letter or deal with a money-related matter with the least accuracy. I know that it was a genuine cause of anxiety for them. And I think with sadness of the satisfaction they would've had, and never did, in seeing me become such a careful bookkeeper" (COR VIII, 162). As I said, Proust did indeed prove himself to be brilliant and astute in taking advantage of the opportunity costs that enhanced both the literary and market value of his novel. But this sort of talent was the opposite of the kind his parents had wished for him: his financial maneuvers were constantly triggered by a sort of intuition that was ingenious in its longer-term results, not only artistic but also financial, but equally ruinous as far as his day-to-day balance sheet was concerned.

The woodworm of forwards contracts took root in Proust's imagination, with Hauser barely knowing about it, and it began to gnaw persistently at the writer's patrimony in the fall and winter of 1911. A catastrophic debacle was in the cards, and it coincided with the entrance of the key figure of the would-be curb broker Albert Nahmias (COR X, xxx).

The son of a financial correspondent, Nahmias went on to have a terrible influence on Proust's investment decisions, but he first entered the writer's life in the capacity of copyist and secretary. In the summer of 1911, they vacationed together in Cabourg, the sea resort where they had first met in 1908, and where Proust presently either dictated to him or had him transcribe the manuscripts for the final version of the first volume of his novel. Nahmias, who wrote by hand and also served as editor (an outstanding one at that),[6] in turn delivered sections of the manuscript to Coecilia Hayward, the young British woman who typed them up (COR X, xxx). At the end of summer, the trio moved back to Paris to finish the typescript.

Proust asked Nahmias to instruct the Crédit Industriel to buy a few forwards contracts on his behalf. He signed four new contracts through this bank in 1911, one of which covered 200 securities of Tramways de Mexico, worth at least 40,000 francs, and whose subsequent destiny, as we will see, reads like a cautionary tale about incompetent investments. At the same time, following Nahmias's advice and leaving Hauser in the dark about it, Proust instructed the *agent de change* David Léon to forwards purchase securities of mining companies on his behalf, for the alarming amount of 440,000 francs.

Through a fast alternation of buying and selling, orders and counter-orders, the end of 1911 marked Proust's fastest plunge into debt exposure in his fifteen-year-long investing career. His patrimony amounted to about 1,522,000 francs, but more than 40 percent of it, precisely 640,000 francs, was tied up in forwards contracts— a crazy level of exposure for an amateur investor. In terms of American dollars, at this time Proust owned a personal fortune of $6,864,000 and had about $2,900,000 tied up in obligations to buy.

Chapter 5

SUCKERS & BELIEVERS

Proust ended 1911 with outrageous speculations. In 1912 their consequences came home to roost, not all at once but gradually, since he had not yet reached the bottom of the hole he was digging himself into. He did so in March 1912 and liquidated his contracts at a hurtful loss—just in time to see international stock markets take off again, and especially the securities directly affected by the frictions between the Ottoman Empire and Montenegro, which positively bubbled up.

Ready to dive again into daring speculations in the hope of making good on his losses, Proust suffered a few beneficial cold showers from Hauser's glacial words to him. In contrast, Proust's new crazy speculations, instigated by some equally crazy tips from Albert Nahmias, turned into creative opportunities and greatly benefited the completion of the first volume of *In Search of Lost Time.* As he worked for Proust in his capacity as copyist and editor, the young would-be curb broker was a rich source of inspiration to the writer. Two years later, in scheming to persuade Proust's new, beloved secretary, Alfred Agostinelli, to move back in with the writer, Nahmias made an even more important contribution to Proust's novel. Soon we will go into the details.

This, then, is the rather counterintuitive scenario we have before us. If Proust's patrimony had not been eroded by the influence of Nahmias (who, incidentally, was also responsible for staking and losing lots of Proust's money on the gambling tables in Cabourg),[1] the writer's novel would have lacked the mainstay of several important episodes. However, without the chilly rebukes from Hauser, whose role as caustic censor of Proust's speculative foolishness became more and more prominent, the writer would certainly have ruined himself and, an impoverished hypochondriac, would have seen his chances to finish his seven-volume novel fade away.

From November 1911 to January 1912, Nahmias sent Proust small sums of cash earned out of various investments. Galvanized by these short-term earnings, Proust hired two new brokerage firms, namely, Wellhoff & Neustadtl and Cremieux & Frankel, and instructed them to make forwards purchases on his behalf in the amount of about 65,000 francs. Meanwhile, still a novice in forwards contracts, Proust failed to keep in mind a vital detail, namely, that the drop in value of the securities tied to his forwards contracts required him to provide David Léon with additional collaterals in the form of cash deposits, and to notify him as well, by settlement day, regarding his intention to close or renew the contracts (COR XI, 15). He did neither thing; hence, Léon extended his contracts to the following months. In March 1912, Proust's debt in additional collaterals with Léon grew to 150,000 francs, which corresponded to more than half a million francs tied up in obligations to buy. His other forwards contracts shared a similar fate. Nonetheless, in the second semester of 1912, Proust urged Nahmias not to fret over the sad state of the mining companies whose securities he had advised the writer to buy. A "friend" had just come to Proust's rescue with the offer to buy out some of his forwards contracts in the amount of 100,000 francs (COR XI, 16).

This unidentified friend was probably Robert de Billy, whom Proust had been very close to since 1890, when they both did their military service in Orléans.[2] The evening of their first encounter in Orléans, Billy sported sheepskin pants modeled on those worn by cavalry officers, a saber, and spotless white gloves—a uniform bound to make a lasting impression on Proust, who, in the words of Billy himself, wore "a baggy overcoat and floating outfit" (see illus. 2). Years later, this initial impression would contribute to the characterization of the Narrator's best friend in Proust's novel, Saint-Loup, who as a cavalry junior officer wore pants of a fabric "too fine and too pink" and vaunted a wardrobe whose "chic" was unequalled by the most elegant among the senior officers. A few years after Proust's death, Billy wrote that he could not explain why he felt instantaneous sympathy for the boy of the awkward uniform, but the sympathy was reciprocal, and, as this timely financial rescue indicates, it would eventually grow into a lifelong friendship. Their friendship had recently been strengthened by the writer's accessory role in discreetly delivering certain sums of money to Billy's intimate friend Madame Gartzen (COR X, 156; XI, 5, 5 [note 3]).[3] Since 1895, Billy had been married to Jeanne Mirabaud, daughter of the late chief executive of the Mirabaud Bank.

Marcel Proust at the garrison in Orléans.
Photograph A. Bouret. Collection G. L. Vaudoyer © BnF

Nahmias replied to the good news with the remark, knowledgeable for once, that Proust's generous friend could not simply take over Proust's contracts with the brokerage firms without also covering his additional collaterals (COR XI, 18). Proust declared that, for the time being, he would use his friend's money both to buy the securities at settlement price and to pay the additional collaterals he owed, and would refund the difference to his friend later on (COR XI, 20). Judging at least from Proust's subsequent correspondence with Billy, Proust never kept this good intention. He probably forgot about it altogether, in the chaos brought to his life by the downward spiraling of his financial endeavors, by the innumerable obstacles that kept him from completing the first volume of his novel, and by the frustrations and humiliations that he encountered in the vain task of finding himself a publisher. Moreover, the balance of Proust and Billy's account ledger was muddled up by the writer's role as middleman between his friend and Madame Gartzen: while at times Proust advanced out of pocket Billy's periodic gift to his lover, on occasion he would apologize to his friend for being short of cash and unable to deliver the agreed-upon sum before receiving it from Billy himself; at times, it seems, Billy forgot to settle his debt with the writer altogether, but at times, owing to some recent act of kindness on Billy's part, Proust begged his friend *not* to refund him any of the money he had advanced. In those days, in those Parisian circles, money could be a liquid commodity in more ways than one.

Thanks to his generous friend, by the end of March 1912, Proust's debt exposure with his three brokerage firms went down to little more than 400,000 francs (1,770,000 dollars). But he still owed 120,000 francs (530,000 dollars) in additional collaterals, and had to find a not too costly way to close his contracts altogether before being swamped by the obligation to buy worthless securities. He opened a line of credit for 218,000 francs at the Crédit Industriel, putting up as warranty his whole portfolio with this bank, compounded with transfers from the Rothschild and Warburg accounts. With the money from this loan, he paid out his debts in collaterals, closed several of his forwards contracts, and was left with about 124,000 francs in cash, which he used to buy cash-down 502 securities of Doubowaïa Balka, a Russian mining company. The 8 percent interest he was paying on the loan from the Crédit Industriel cost Proust 17,500 francs a year.

Nevertheless, by June 1912 Proust seemed to have recovered fully from the financial shocks of the last few months and was eager to return to the charge. He wrote to Hauser and admitted his financial misdemeanors, but did not go into details, wrongly assuming that Léon Neuberger, who was aware of his recent economic troubles, had informed Hauser of them. I should take the occasion to point out that Proust always suffered from the delusion of envisioning himself at the center of his friends' conversations.

In 1920, this narcissistic misperception became the cause of one of his gravest quarrels with Hauser. The letters of this quarrel followed one another, as we will see, like the pages from a sadly well-wrought epistolary novel.

Proust's letter to Hauser had not even reached the end of his financial blunders when he asked the banker's advice on a new investment in an American investment-services firm. Hauser objected that well-chosen industrial and mining companies could make for suitable, solid investments (although, as I said, he preferred bonds and Treasuries), while the worth of financial-services firms was unsubstantial and unattractive (COR XI, 73, 76). This view may appear backward to us, at a time when American banks are as big as the Gross Domestic Product in the United States, and most European countries underwrite banking systems several times larger than their GDP. But Hauser obviously did not enjoy the advantages of our hindsight—nor the disadvantages, should I add, since he could not foresee the recent global recession, the worst one in your life and mine, I surmise, which originated from various crimes and misdemeanors of the financial sector.

Proust went to Cabourg to spend his summer holidays. About August 18 or 19, although a sworn enemy of vigorous exertions, he took the exceptional initiative of arranging an outdoor excursion for Albert Nahmias and a few young people who might be of interest to his friend. On the appointed date, Nahmias did not show up. Unaware of the reason of his friend's absence (in his hurry to join the writer in Cabourg, Nahmias had run over a young girl with his car), Proust wrote one of the best and harshest love letters he ever composed.

> Dear friend,
>
> I know you cannot be improved upon. You are not even made of stone, because stone can be sculpted when good luck puts it in the hands of a sculptor (and one day you might meet sculptors more skilled than I, but I would've sculpted you with tenderness), water is what you are made of, the most trivial water, the elusive kind that is colorless, fluid, perpetually inconsistent, as quick in streaming away as it is swift in plunging into oblivion. Whoever finds it amusing can watch you pass by, unresponsive, wanting in a sense of identity. . . . But I've nourished a keen affection for you, and all of this at times makes me feel like yawning, at times like weeping, and at times like drowning myself. (COR XI, 102)

The subtlety of the closing allusion is noteworthy: in order to drown himself, Proust would need to dive into Nahmias's very watery substance, which he declares himself to be repelled by.

Nahmias's victim died two days after the car accident. Having explained the reason for his absence, Nahmias was forgiven and restored to his duties as Proust's secretary. I wonder how he must have felt, though, the day when he found himself transcribing or writing under dictation the following words, which Charles Swann tells Odette de Crécy, the courtesan destined to become his wife, after she has been rude to him. "How could anyone love you, for you're not even a person, a clearly defined entity, imperfect, but at least perfectible? You're only a formless stream of water running down whatever slope one offers it" (*Swann's Way,* 301).[4] This passage appears in *Swann's Way,* the volume which Proust was putting the last touches to with the help of Nahmias and the typist Coecilia Hayward, and whose second part, *Swann's Love,* is entirely dedicated to Charles Swann's fateful surrender to the dubious charms of Odette de Crécy. With his usual Midas-like touch, Proust turned misery into riches; he spun the pain caused him by his young secretary into a concise episode that defined Swann's far-from-flattering idea of the woman he would marry—the woman, by the way, who would give birth to Gilberte Swann, the sweetheart of the novel's protagonist in his pubescent years.

After Proust himself, as we know, the major model for Charles Swann was Charles Haas, a "man of the world" who never married but had an illegitimate daughter, Luisita, from his adulterous affair with a marquise. Like Swann before his marriage with Odette, Haas was both a notorious *homme à femmes* (Sarah Bernhard fell head over heels for him) and a member of exclusive Parisian clubs such as the Cercle de la rue Royale and the Jockey Club (like Haas, Swann was the only Jewish member of the latter). A good friend of Robert de Montesquiou, Charles Haas had a refined elegance that was immortalized by the painter James Tissot in *Le Cercle de la rue Royale,* in which Haas is standing by the French window at the right (see illus. 3).

On October 12, 1912, the first Balkan War, opposing Montenegro, Bulgaria, Serbia and Greece to the Ottoman Empire, caused panic on the Paris bourse, where Treasuries lost 12 percent of their nominal value in one day; the war made huge waves as well on all other European stock markets. With an eye on depreciated stocks, Proust wanted to take advantage of the situation. He asked his banker what he thought of the copper mines in Utah, of the Spassky Copper mines in Eastern Europe, and of the Tramways Company of Buenos Aires. This time, Proust wanted to buy his securities cash-down, though, to avoid surprises from incremental collaterals. In a laconic answer, Hauser responded that he was sorry to see that Proust's recent experiences had not taught him anything; in any event, he would wait for instructions in case Proust decided to sell securities in order to realize ready money and trade on the stock market (COR XI, 117, 118). Proust was so eager to embark on new speculations, and also so busy in his complex and inconclusive negotiations with various publishers, all of whom refused to commit themselves to his novel-in-progress, that he did not seem to notice Hauser's disappointment. A week after receiving Hauser's letter, Proust asked him to sell securities in the amount of 25,000 francs and transfer this sum to his account at the Crédit Industriel.

James Tissot, *Le Cercle de la rue Royale* (1867; RF 2011 53), Musée d'Orsay, Paris. Snark / Art Resource, N.Y.

Ten days later, Proust wrote Hauser that he had "acted like a fool." By switching from forwards contracts to buying cash-down, he had paid at least an extra twenty francs on each security he bought. It is obviously difficult for a novice of the bourse to dodge the stockbrokers' fees and commissions, as Proust was trying to do. As if this confession of ingenuousness was not enough, Proust added a postscript bound to make Hauser see red.

He had recently made the acquaintance of people who were "not too rich," friends of a Mr. Garry, president of the U. S. Steel Corporation. These new acquaintances told him that from time to time Garry gave them tips on his company's shares. What did Hauser think about it? Since these acquaintances were willing to share this confidential information with Proust, should he not profit from it? (COR XI, 124) Hauser's answer was a masterpiece of repressed fury and measured sarcasm. The shared secrets from Proust's acquaintances would impress him more, he wrote, if these people were wallowing in money and willing to acknowledge that they owed their good fortune to the American philanthropist Mr. Garry. But since Proust's postscript defined them as "not too rich," Hauser had to suppose either that the American prophet's forecasts did not always come true or that these people did not trust Garry enough to invest large sums based on his tips. In either case, why did they think they could inculcate Proust's mind with a faith that they themselves did not have? Hauser's close was lapidary: "I'm not sure that it's true, as some people think, that the number of religious believers has decreased in France . . . but I'm rather inclined to think that the number of suckers has positively grown" (COR XI, 125).

Chapter 6

BLIND EYES

We have reached 1913, the glorious year that saw the publication of the first volume of *In Search of Lost Time.* After much hesitation, Proust gave it the title *Du côté de chez Swann* (*Swann's Way*). He was never able to bring the publication of his novel to completion: it was brought to an end with three posthumous volumes from 1923 to 1927, based on the original manuscripts and edited by his brother Robert. The first full version of Proust's novel would comprise seven volumes, namely: *Du côté de chez Swann,* published in 1913; *À l'ombre des jeunes filles en fleurs* (*In the Shadow of Young Girls in Flower*), published in 1919; *Le côté de Guermantes* (*The Guermantes Way*), published in two books, the first in 1920 and the second in 1921, inclusive of the first part of *Sodome et Gomorrhe* (*Sodom and Gomorrah*); *Sodome et Gomorrhe II,* published in 1922; *La prisonnière* (*The Prisoner*), published posthumously in 1923; *Albertine disparue* (*The Fugitive*), published posthumously in 1925; and *Le temps retrouvé* (*Finding Time Again*), published posthumously in 1927.

We begin 1913 with Proust's visit to the cathedral of Notre Dame to study the statues of Porte Sainte-Anne. For several weeks, the bedridden writer had yearned in vain to make this visit, until one day in the second half of January his health conditions improved slightly, enough to allow him to throw a fur over his nightshirt and travel to the cathedral by car. Was his driver on this excursion the same Alfred Agostinelli who, six months later, would take up residence with the writer? It is certainly possible, especially given Proust's love for repeated rituals. Six years earlier, in 1907, he and the nineteen-year-old Agostinelli had paid a night visit, memorialized in one of Proust's letters, to another well-known cathedral of Notre Dame, that in the town of Lisieux, not far from Cabourg. On that occasion, Proust had to grope his way in the darkness enveloping the square in front of the cathedral. Then Agostinelli had the brilliant idea of turning on the car's headlights. As he directed the cone of light here and there, the pillars of the cathedral stood out like trees in a forest, writes Proust, the chiaroscuro effect making their stone capitals look like thick leafage. From a letter to the twenty-two-year-old Maurice Rostand, whom Proust had met in 1910 through Jean Cocteau, it seems that this time, in Paris, the writer meant to take advantage of daylight, so it is likely that his visit to Porte Sainte-Anne occurred shortly after dawn, a few hours before his customary sleeping time.

Proust's desire to visit Notre Dame de Paris was probably triggered by a book by Émile Mâle, in which the art historian complains that, in the past, people tended to identify the statues adorning Porte Sainte-Anne as the kings of France, rather than the biblical kings they were meant to represent. This visit enabled Proust to refer to these statues in the second volume of his novel, which he had started drafting in its final form. But in his book, the statues of Porte Sainte-Anne are transposed to the church of Balbec on the Normandy coast, visited by the novel's Narrator in his youth. The Narrator's older friend, the painter Elstir, explains the layout of the statues to him, echoing Mâle in defining them as "the Hebrew kings, carnal ancestors of Jesus Christ" (COR XII, 11, 11 [note 19]).

The search for a publisher spurred Proust to enervating feats. At first, he submitted his manuscript to the publishing house Fasquelle through his good friend Gaston Calmette, an influential editor at *Le Figaro* (to whom he would eventually dedicate *Swann's Way* in 1913). Jacques Normand, Fasquelle's reader, was of the opinion that the novel was a product of mental insanity. Then Proust turned to his friend Antoine Bibesco to have his manuscript submitted to Jacques Copeau, who had an editorial job with the NRF or *Nouvelle Revue Française,* and who in turn put Proust in touch with the chief editor, Gaston Gallimard. In later years, as I said, Gallimard would become the doyen of literary publishing in France, thanks mainly to the success of Proust's novel. But at this point, unwisely, Gallimard entrusted the manuscript to André Gide, whose reputation as a writer had already been established by such works as *The Immoralist* of 1902 and *Strait Is the Gate* of 1909. Gide rejected Proust's work offhandedly. And Jean Schlumberger, a member of the NRF's editorial board, complained privately that Proust's novel kept talking of the same thing over and over again, so much so that it made no difference what passages one would or would not read. Then Proust turned to the publishing house

Ollendorf, whose director Alfred Humblot found the novel needlessly wordy and convoluted.[1] Less than two years later, Gide wrote to Proust confessing that the rejection of his book was "the gravest mistake of the NRF—and (since I'm ashamed to admit I was very much responsible for it) one of my worst regrets, a scorching remorse."[2]

It is a curious coincidence that, in writing to Geneviève Straus of his night visit to Notre Dame, Proust alluded to the book of Psalms in order to complain about people who have "eyes but do not see" (COR XII, 3; Psalm 115:5). He was referring to the distraction of the passersby who failed even to notice the treasures of art displayed at Porte Sainte-Anne. But the same words could well apply to Gide, Gallimard, and all the other literary experts who forced the author of the most important French novel of their time to publish the first volume at his own expense.

Why did Gide reject *In Search of Lost Time*? "One wonders why," writes Roger Duchêne.[3] It is in fact unclear whether Gide read the manuscript at all, or just a slight part of it. According to Proust's driver Nicolas Cottin, who recognized his own knots on the thread holding together the package of the manuscript returned to Proust by the NRF, the NRF committee did not even bother to take a look at the contents. But Cottin's view, reported by Céleste Albaret, Proust's deservedly fabled housemaid, who heard of it from the writer himself, is contradicted by the fact that Gide's colleague Jean Schlumberger (the owner of one-third of the NRF's capital assets) had a clear-cut opinion about the manuscript, as mentioned above—even if Schlumberger admitted in a letter that his dislike of the manuscript was derived from "pick[ing] out, here and there, a sentence that looked discouraging." So, the original package is likely to have been opened, at least.[4] According to Gide's letter of apology to Proust, he had been provided with only one of the notebooks submitted by Proust. And his decision had been mainly influenced by his disapproval of Proust's love of society life.[5]

But really, one should rather wonder, why is a great book like Proust's novel rejected? It is not a secret, after all, that the archives of most publishing houses are filled with rejected masterpieces. Do publishers and "peer readers" ever tell the truth about their decisions? Food for thought for the economists among you: the history of literature could be entirely rewritten from the perspective of those loads of royalty money thrown to the winds. Those who are in the know claim that the realm of editorial boards is fraught with dissimulation, crowded with people whose denials of their peers' legitimate aspirations peacefully coexist with denial as an (often unconscious) alibi of self-defense. Shall we ever know Gide's true motifs for rejecting *In Search of Lost Time*? Did Gide himself know them? Edmund White has pointed out that "at the end of his life Gide was still worrying about his misjudgment [of Proust], asking himself, 'Would I have been able to recognize right away the obvious value of Baudelaire, or Rimbaud?'"[6] Such rare humility does honor to Gide. Indeed, the germ of inspiration for *In Search of Lost Time* had come to Proust at a time when he was planning to demonstrate in a book the fallacy of Charles-Augustin Sainte-Beuve's biographical approach to literary criticism. Just as Gide rejected Proust's manuscript because he knew him as a society man, "a snob" in Schlumberger's words, so did Sainte-Beuve fail to appreciate the literary talent of Stendhal and Baudelaire based on his personal acquaintance with these two writers.[7] For us, Gide's failure is one more reason to grasp the true stature of Proust among his shortsighted contemporaries. And to Proust, after he was ruthlessly rejected in 1912, Gide's apology, joined with Proust's subsequent triumph on the literary market, gave the consolation of gauging his own intellectual and artistic advantage over the best literary critics in Paris.

Proust spoke of his decision to pay the publication costs of his novel to his friend Louis de Robert, who begged him to reconsider (COR XI, 166; XII, 1). But the writer got in touch and signed a publishing contract with a small publisher, Bernard Grasset, who had the insolence, on the eve of the novel's distribution to the bookstores, to call Proust's book "unreadable."[8] On March 11, 1913 Proust gave Grasset a down payment of 1,750 francs.

Proust was worn out by his hardships with Parisian publishers and, shortly after signing the contract with Grasset, also by the barrage of galley proofs he had to correct and approve before the first volume of his novel could go to the printing press. Moreover, his financial mishaps of the previous two years had cost him at least 400,000 francs, and lowered his expectations regarding the riches to be harvested from the stock exchange. Altogether, the effect of this setback was that he no longer turned a deaf ear to Hauser's circumspect advice.

Hauser wanted him to buy the new issues of Treasury notes of San Paulo do Brasil and of Treasury notes of Japan. In the case of the former securities, which were to be sold preferably to the holders of the 1908 notes of Brazil's Treasury Department,[9] Proust replied that he would like to trade the 1908 notes in his portfolio with the new ones; but he made nothing of it, after learning from Hauser that he had already sold those 1908 notes earlier on, and did not have any left in his portfolio (COR

XII, 57, 58, 66, 66 [note 3]). As regards the Japanese Treasuries, Hauser suggested that Proust ought to buy them through the Rothschild Bank. Proust discussed the idea with Léon Neuberger, who gave his consent to the purchase, on condition that Proust give his word of honor to hold on to these bonds until the maturity date. "I had to swear on the hands of Baron Alphonse and Baron Gustave," Proust joked (COR XII, 66).

Hauser's disinterestedness should not go unremarked. Although his scatterbrained friend was not much of a client, Hauser kept suggesting transactions to Proust that were of no immediate advantage to the German investment firm he represented in Paris, and, given the small fees he charged, of little advantage to himself. We begin to see evidence that the relationship between Proust and Hauser was not limited to business matters, but rather was pervaded by mutual loyalty and intense friendship—a friendship that grew at a steady pace, but that on occasion was personally devastating and, in moments of crisis or passing estrangement, led to ferocious expressions of visceral spite.

In May 1913, the investments made on Proust's behalf at the beginning of the year by David Léon, Wellhoff & Neustadtl and Cremieux & Frankel were losing money. In a letter to Geneviève Straus, adopting a casually ironic tone, Proust blamed Austria's bad taste in declaring war on Montenegro on April 30, the settlement date when his forwards contracts were due (COR XII, 71). As a matter of fact, war had not been declared yet. But each tassel in the mosaic of international conflicts leading to World War I was falling punctually into place. At that point, Austria-Hungary had just declared its intention to take "grave measures" against Montenegro.[10]

Chapter 7

ENTER ALFRED AGOSTINELLI

In June 1913, a pivotal development intertwining love and money occurred in Proust's sentimental life and took to unfolding by stages into one of the most emblematic opportunity costs encountered by the writer—successful on the artistic side, to be sure, but at a devastating price both to his fragile inner world and to his finances. It concerned Alfred Agostinelli, the elegant young chauffeur Proust met in Cabourg in 1907 and who, in the summer of 1913, moved into Proust's apartment together with his companion, Anna Square. (Proust was deceived in thinking they were married.)[1] At this time, the writer was renting an apartment in the same building on Boulevard Haussmann that had been bought from him and his brother Robert by their aunt Amélie—the very apartment that went on to provide the interiors for his Narrator's protracted cohabitation with Albertine Simonet.

In 1907, Agostinelli had been one of the three mechanics working at Unic, a car rental company managed by one of Proust's teenage infatuations, Jacques Bizet, and based in Monaco, Agostinelli's hometown on the French Riviera. Proust was a frequent client of the Unic branch in Cabourg, using their cars and mechanics (the term *chauffeur* was not in use yet) for his outings and excursions on the Normandy coast. In the summer and fall, Unic transferred some of its drivers from the French Riviera to Cabourg, where the summer season was lucrative. In November 1907, on the occasion of their night visit to Notre Dame de Lisieux, Proust had written an admiring portrait of his favorite driver for *Le Figaro:*

> My mechanic wore a large rubber cape and a sort of hood that tightly framed his young, beardless face. As we plunged faster

> and faster into the night, it gave him the looks of a pilgrim, or rather of a nun devoted to the religion of speed. From time to time—an incarnation of Saint Cecilia playing on an even more ethereal harpsichord—he touched his keyboard and pulled one of the registers of the organ pipes hidden in the automobile. . . . But most of the time he just held his steering wheel . . . rather similar to the crosses of consecration held by the apostles who lean against the columns in the choir of the Saint Chapel in Paris.[2]

This image reminded Proust, more generally, of the medieval stylizations of the wheel of torture. Agostinelli held his steering wheel as if it were the symbol of his craft, the way the statues of saints in the porches of French cathedrals hold the instrument of the craft at which they excelled, a harp, say, or a hunting trumpet. "May the steering wheel of the young man who drove me around," he added, "always be the symbol of his talent rather than the foreshadowing of his suffering."[3] Proust could hardly foresee that, seven years later, Agostinelli would die at the wheel of a much faster vehicle than the car he drove the writer around in, namely, a single-blade propeller aircraft, after taking flying lessons near Antibes, France, under the pseudonym of Marcel Swann—a name combining the writer's first name with the surname of his most famous character at the time, Charles Swann.[4]

The patroness of musicians, Saint Cecilia, whose "incarnation" Proust saw in Agostinelli at the wheel, has been portrayed sitting at the keyboard by such artists as Artemisia Gentileschi and Peter Paul Rubens. In *The Prisoner,* Saint Cecilia is impersonated by Albertine Simonet sitting at a pianola (a kind of self-playing piano), admittedly a simpler instrument than a harpsichord or even an automobile. At this advanced stage in the novel, Albertine has become, like Agostinelli in real life, the consenting captive (for a time) of the Narrator's apartment in Paris.

Proust already had a chauffeur, Nicolas Cottin, so in 1913 Agostinelli was hired as typist for the second volume of *In Search of Lost Time.* The fact that this young man would soon adopt the pseudonym of Marcel Swann is evidence of his dedication to the task. "He was an extraordinary being endowed with the best intellectual gifts I have ever encountered in anybody," Proust later wrote about him to the husband of his dear friend Geneviève Straus (COR XIII, 130). He must have found confirmation of Agostinelli's intellectual gifts in the chauffeur's last letter to him, soon to be discussed, whose elegant phrasing is duplicated, in all likelihood, in Albertine's second-to-last letter to the novel's Narrator before her death.

It is perhaps owing to his infatuation with Agostinelli that Proust made a plan to move to Florence, Italy, together with his entire entourage, grown to four members: Nicolas Cottin and his wife Céline, Alfred Agostinelli and Anna Square. (Céleste Albaret née Gineste, the most devoted of Proust's housemaids, legendary in her multiple roles as Proust's confidant, protector, collaborator, and also source of inspiration for her wit and beauty, will soon take Céline Cottin's place; she was married with Odilon Albaret, Agostinelli's colleague in Monaco, who in Paris worked as a taxi driver and as Proust's part-time chauffeur.)[5] To pursue his plan to leave Paris, Proust rented Palazzo Caprarola, a splendid Renaissance castle in Florence (COR XIII, xxx).

This is one of the opportunity costs (far from the most burdensome) that financed the contribution Agostinelli made to one of the most devastating episodes of *In Search of Lost Time,* namely, Albertine's flight from the Narrator's apartment after sharing it with him for a long and not always pleasant interlude. It seems that the costly rent of Palazzo Caprarola, to which Proust never made up his mind to move, was the reason the writer asked Hauser to realize 10,000 francs on the sale of some securities.[6]

At long last, in November 1913 *Swann's Way* saw the light, but Proust's joy, mitigated by the shame of having paid the costs of publication, was wholly stifled by the flight of Agostinelli, who deserted his apartment to join his father in Monaco. Proust gave instructions to Albert Nahmias to find Agostinelli and make sure at all costs that his secretary/chauffer came back to him in Paris—even if it took bribing the young man's father with cash.[7] So begins the series of episodes that best defines Proust's very personal way to love, desire, yearn for the object of his lust, and be racked with passion.

As he described the most torturous sides of the amorous experience, Proust tried also to explain why a majority of people find it impossible to renounce. There was nothing trivial in Proust's love experience, as I have intimated, nothing ordinary; least of all sex. This is perhaps the darkest side of his novel's mysterious power: since its publication, *In Search of Lost Time* has initiated many of us, its readers, into a new mental faculty of sorts, an unsparing capacity for deep introspection, which keeps our inner eye constantly focused, wide open, on the core of our unfathomable longings.

The significance of this legacy was unintentionally muddled by André Gide, who, after paying a few visits to Proust in the next-to-last year of his life, transcribed their conversations on the author's homosexuality—faithfully, one would presume—in his private journal. Ten years later, in 1931, Gide became belatedly aware of a perspicuous trait of Proust's personality: "He manipulated everybody, owing to that maniacal need of his to serve anybody his or her favorite dish, with utmost unconcern for truthfulness."[8] Gide's journal entries were based on admissions by Proust which, seemingly honest and straightforward, were in all likelihood deliberately instrumental in serving Gide the reassuring dish of homosexual conformity. Had Gide realized earlier the duplicity in the circuitous manner whereby Proust earned the trust of friends and acquaintances, perhaps in 1922 he would not have committed to the pages of his journal—not with the same candid literalism, I mean—remarks and observations that were eventually very influential in creating the image of Proust as an artist utterly committed to his homosexuality.[9] It is early in the book to tackle this issue head-on, but not too early to foreshadow some of our forthcoming discussions regarding it.

We have Agostinelli on the threshold. Let us figure out the stage he is stepping onto.

It was mainly the entries from Gide's journal that encouraged many readers through the years to read *In Search of Lost Time* as a roman à clef, in which Albertine's little uplifted breasts, tenderly described by Proust, are ridiculously transposed to the hairy chest of a young chauffeur.[10] Throughout the entire history of reception of Proust's novel, this allegedly ciphered transposition has displeased many readers and critics and gratified a few. Even if Proust denounced (rightly for some of his readers and wrongly for others) homosexuality in the character of Charlus, so has gone the prevailing opinion for a very long time, his own homosexual proclivities got the upper hand over his authorial intentions, and he ended up showing us, with his "girls in flower," the spectacle (awkward to some readers and charming to others) of pretty boys in drag. Faced with such often unwitty deconstructions of intentionality, I wonder: Why not just give credit to Proust for having accomplished exactly what he meant to accomplish in the portrayals of his many characters?

This is a position argued as early as 1980 by J. E. Rivers in *Proust and the Art of Love*. "If we transpose and retranspose the sexes [of Proust's characters] in an attempt to force Proust's work to make sense in conventional sexual terms," Rivers writes, "we miss the point."[11] What is the point to which Rivers alludes? Owing to the thirty-five-year gap between his book and mine, in order to answer this question I need to bring Rivers's views up to date with our contemporary bio-evolutionary debate. In his novel, I submit, Proust engages in a search of lost time that takes on a couple of guises, respectively existential and evolutionary. We usually debate and focus only on the former. The evidence regarding the evolutionary or Darwinian thread in Proust's novel is overwhelming and I will not try to go deep into its documentation for now; I am persuaded that Proust grew increasingly coy about this thread, even diffident, to the point that he avoided making explicit mention of it.[12]

According to Darwin, the presence in the anatomy of male and female vertebrates of rudimentary sexual organs proper to the complementary gender indicates that our progenitors were hermaphrodite or androgynous. If Proust peppered his novel with Darwinian metaphors that harp on this theme a great deal, it must be because, side by side with the reversal of existential time, a subject strictly related to the workings of our individual memory, he meant for his novel to adumbrate also the reversal of evolutionary time, a subject related instead to something which had no clear-cut name in Proust's days, and which, as a shorthand, we could label as our embodied memory of the species. Are we optimally adapted to the reproductive functions that evolution has assigned to us, do we fully identify with self-satisfied specimens driven to the annihilation of competitors and ultimately to the domination of the planet? Or are we rather caught up in an unfinished process of sexual evolution, prototypes of an animal whose genital features, unhinged from the dialectic of domination and submission conventionally inherent in sexual roles, will one day consist perhaps of identifying attributes as little antagonistic as, say, eye color? This is one of the many logs that feed the fire of a speculation which, I'm persuaded, was very close to Proust's original concerns.

In an extant draft of Gide's 1914 letter of apology to Proust, mentioned earlier, there is a passage that was deleted from the final text mailed to Proust. In it Gide wrote that one day in 1912, having opened Proust's submitted manuscript in a listless state of mind, his attention had been unfortunately caught by a couple of dissatisfactory passages, one about "a cup of chamomile" (*sic*) and another containing the one phrase in the novel which he found inexplicable to that day, as it "spoke of a forehead where vertebræ showed through."[13] The incriminated passage appears near the beginning of *Swann's Way,* in the episode of the young Narrator's Sunday visit to his aunt Léonie: "I would not have been with my aunt five minutes before she would send me away for fear that I would tire her. She would hold out to my lips her sad, pale, dull forehead, on which, at this morning hour, she had not yet arranged her false hair, and where the vertebræ ["vertèbres"] showed through like the points of a crown of thorns or the beads of a rosary" (*Swann's Way*, 53).[14]

In a text as rich with Darwinian allusions as Proust's novel is, one can legitimately picture metaphorical vertebræ transpiring from the bald cranium of an ancient vertebrate whose sexual functions have long since followed the path of her hair. But if you consider that, in spite of his initial rejection of Proust's manuscript, Gide was certainly among his most insightful readers, you can easily grasp what Proust was up against, in trying to pair up the experience of existential and evolutionary time in the characters of his novel. How easily could the fans of his supposed boys in drag confuse him, as, in fact, some did and many others keep doing to this day, with someone staging a cross-dressing masquerade à la Rachilde—to mention, quite à propos, this famous (and famously unsupportive, as we will see) fellow writer of his.

Although he was a fervent Proust admirer, Jocelyn Brooke argued in 1961 that to enter the ranks of heterosexuals, as Proust slyly tried to do, he "would have to show us that he 'had complete sexual intercourse with a woman [and] enjoyed it.'" Rivers objects to Brooke's view that we miss that sort of evidence even regarding Dante and Petrarch, yet it does not seem to affect our appreciation of their portrayals of men and women.[15]

It is a fact beyond dispute that Proust's sex life, however far from a conventionally heterosexual one, remains quite difficult to sort out. It consisted of a tangle of homosexuality, more latent than proactive in my opinion, and of aggressive heterosexuality.

As to the men who stole Proust's heart for a time, there were "several" of them, to use a modest expression adopted on one occasion by Albert Nahmias. It so happens that most relevant to Proust's sexual life were the same men who played the major role with respect to the subject of the book you are reading, namely, the relationship between squandered time and money on the one hand, and artistic creation on the other. These men were, in order of relevance: Alfred Agostinelli, Henri Rochat, and Albert Nahmias. Reynaldo Hahn's steady loyalty to Proust is beyond dispute; but the discrete and tactful manners of its long evolution shielded this relationship from all money-related matters, with the one exception

I mentioned in the beginning, namely, Proust's first sentimental investment, relevant to my story because it inaugurated Proust's long-lived affair with Royal Dutch securities.

As to the array of stupendous women with whom Proust became infatuated, it would make the subject for a captivating book. Proust could hardly conceive of a heterosexual attraction immune from pecuniary considerations or liberal sacrifices of personal time, as we will see in our subsequent discussion of Hélène Soutzo's surgical operation and of the Russian Marie Scheikévitch's Bolshevism-induced financial straits. The role played by these two women, the former one especially, in the relationship between squandered time and money on the one hand, and Proust's artistic creation on the other, is not indifferent. But even a partial list of Proust's most relevant female infatuations is longer than that: it includes Jeanne Pouquet, whom we have already met as Madame Gaston de Caillavet, and who, after Proust's death, claimed credit as the model for the character of Gilberte Swann; Marie Bénardaky, daughter of a Polish nobleman and playmate of a fifteen-year-old Proust in those Champs-Élysées where his novel's Narrator used to play with Gilberte; the "delicious" Hélène d'Ideville, deliciously tolerant of Proust's illness, whom he wanted to marry (more on it soon);[16] Madame Straus, one of the two main models for the character of Oriane, Duchess of Guermantes; Madame de Chevigné, the second model, and the object of a self-flagellating love, the most often and most persistently mentioned love by Proust in his correspondence; and three of the four relevant models, listed by Proust's biographer George Painter, for the character of Albertine, namely: Marie Nordlinger, whom we have met a few times already; Marie de Chevilly, addressed by Proust as the "indolent traveler," from a verse by Alfred de Vigny, on the night in 1899 when they shared a carriage ride; and, finally, Louisa de Mornand, as explained above, in "Premise."[17]

For the sake of evidential common sense, Céleste Albaret must be added to this list of models for Albertine. Having entered Proust's service in 1914, precisely the year when he started writing on Albertine, Albaret, a twenty-three-year-old beauty from the country who, as she put it, "went to bed with the hens and rose with the roosters," soon learned to "live at night," and for the next nine years not only did she scrupulously respect but also even enabled all of Proust's needs and whims—which meant devoting all of her waking hours to him (and her sleeping hours as well, as we shall see). "Twenty-four hours a day and seven days a week I lived entirely for him," she wrote. "I have nothing to do with the book [which

Proust] called *La Prisonnière,* but [the prisoner] would have been a good name for me."[18] Just as, may I add, a mere three-letter permutation makes her surname, Albaret, a good fit for the prediminutive feminine "Alberta."

In light of my frequent usage of the term *infatuation* in this book, I should briefly qualify it, as it applies to Alfred Agostinelli as well as to several other prominent actors on stage. I am persuaded that to be properly grasped in its true nature, Proust's amorous universe must be apprehended in its own terms; one must climb up to it, if you will, rather than pulling it down to one's own sentimental drives and sexual orientations—which latter option was the one practiced by the patriarch of Proust's biographers, George D. Painter, and by Georges Duchêne as well. This explains to a certain extent the nature of my book.

As I said in "Premise," Proust's lifelong quest for an unconditionally requited love moved him to engage in dramatic financial speculations, aimed at earning the money needed, in his view, to finance such a quest. Hence, the better one understands Proust's love and sex life, the better can one explain his dealings with Lionel Hauser. This is why the theme of Proust's sexuality is woven, thread by thread, throughout the whole texture of this book, before it culminates in chapter 25, "A Relativity Theory of Sex."

Now, to keep this digression short: when I identify in Marie Nordlinger an "infatuation" of Proust, for instance, I do not necessarily disagree with Jean-Yves Tadié, when he declares that the writer was not in love with her; he saw in her, writes Tadié, "a cousin, a sister, a mother substitute, a colleague, yes; but no more."[19] Aptly enough, as I showed above in discussing one of Proust's 1908 letters to Reynaldo "Bibibuls" Hahn, Proust could imbue even a most innocent term such as *cousin* with amorous innuendoes if not sexual undertones. So, there you are. There is an all-pervasive sensuality to Proust's inner life, a pansensualism of sorts, comparable not only in reach, but also in its perennial procrastination, with the one that informs the medieval tradition of the *amour courtois.*[20] Which explains why the list of infatuations above is significant even if Proust was not, technically speaking, "in love" with all of these women.

Louisa de Mornand's threefold, superlative contribution to Proust's novel deserves its own niche. She was the actress whose scenes of jealousy with Louis d'Albufera provided Proust with the character of Saint-Loup's domineering lover, the actress Rachel. Before learning that Rachel is Saint-Loup's lover, the novel's Narrator meets her in a brothel, just as Proust had first met Louisa de Mornand in that sort of establishment.

In the decade after Proust's death, she had a rewarding acting career in the movie industry, managing successfully the transition from silent to talking pictures. A highly unconventional woman, on at least one occasion she allowed Proust in her bedroom to see her fall asleep while reading a book, providing thereby the model in the flesh, in his novel, for Albertine's slumbering under the Narrator's eyes and caressing hand. The only evidence we have of the concrete way Proust and Mornand may have shared her bedroom is indirect at best, and comes from several scenes in *The Prisoner,* all dealing with Albertine's sexual narcolepsy. Albertine falls asleep more than once under the Narrator's eyes, at times in his own bed, occasionally semi-naked. The Narrator can touch her body, move it this way and that, and she keeps sleeping like "a watch that doesn't stop . . . like a creeper that keeps stretching its branches regardless of the available support." Lying by her side, his lips on hers and his hand exploring her body inch by inch, Proust's Narrator is gently rocked up and down by the wavelike motion of her regular breathing. He touches her lips with his, and feels the pulse of her life against his tongue. He is "embarked on Albertine's sleep," as if she were a swaying ship and he the captain in full, fuller possession of her. As always, his libido is inseparable from "the marks of wealth and social prestige," as noted by the literary critic Edward J. Hughes, and he thereby reflects that this sort of intimacy is well worth the money that Albertine's cohabitation costs him. The theme of trading money for physical intimacy is greatly amplified in one of the latest additions to Proust's novel, with reference to the fictional writer Bergotte, who in his old age, as discussed in the chapter "Turning Caresses into Gold," draws original inspiration out of such undignified trade. Finally, also Albertine's equestrian accident, suffered while staying at the house of her aunt in the town of Châtellerault, and crucial to the spiraling down of her lover's existential parable, was inspired by an analogous accident suffered in 1905 by Louisa de Mornand in the vicinities of Trouville, not far from Cabourg.

Incidentally, the metaphor of the Narrator's sailing of Albertine's sound asleep body as if she were a ship lulled by sea waves is quite a daring enhancement of the metaphor used long before by Proust, if you remember, in praise of Hauser's friendly heart. In a letter to Hauser, mentioned earlier, Proust had alluded to a poem by Sully Prudhomme about the wives of some soon-to-take-ship seamen, whose anxious hearts were dragged up and down by the swaying ship at harbor; analogously with the poem, Proust compared Hauser's mental disposition to a high-sea vessel swinging up and down with the price fluctuations of a sea-shipping company's shares. We, literary critics, often talk of the anxiety of influence felt by the younger author who borrows or steals an idea, a character, or a figure of speech from the master. But in the case of the wavelike motions of Albertine's breath gently rocking her bed companion up and down, I cannot help reversing the picture, if only to guess the sort of anxiety the late Prudhomme would have felt, had he pictured to himself the oceanic distance that his original idea would cover before making landfall in an admirer's novel.

There was nothing ordinarily straight and nothing conventionally gay in the sex life of a man who, at the age of thirty-eight, came to fear that it would be "a crime" to ask a young woman to share with him his "awful life" as an invalid[21]—and not *any* hypothetical young woman, but, mind you, the Leonardesque beauty whom one of Proust's friends, Maurice Duplay, identified as Hélène d'Ideville, a friend of Duplay's family whom Proust met in Cabourg in 1908, saw frequently in Paris the subsequent year, and to whom, according to both Duplay's recollections and Antoine Bibesco's reticent ones, as well as to Proust's letters to Georges de Lauris, the writer was on the verge of proposing.[22] In the eyes of the Parisian society of this time, two men (like Proust and Agostinelli, for instance) could share their living quarters with each other without being supposed to be sharing their bed too; a man and a woman, if they belonged to Proust's social class, could not. Only by resorting to marriage, that very bourgeois institution about which Proust wrangled, three years after this time, with Hauser, calling the banker Love's Bookkeeper—only by resorting to marriage with Hélène d'Ideville, I am saying, could Proust have experienced a cohabitation of the sort shared by his Narrator and Albertine.

Of course, one must not forget Proust's cohabitation with Céleste Albaret. Critics and biographers tend to consider it irrelevant to his inspiration or unproblematic to his (and her) social standing since she was a servant, but this is far from true. It was scandalous in the eyes of Albaret's social peers that this just-married twenty-three-year-old woman should live alone in Proust's apartment. Left with no male servant by France's declaration of war in 1914, the writer himself defined their arrangement as "improper" and temporary. It lasted till the day of his death. Soon after Albaret found herself sharing Proust's apartment (her husband Odilon was serving in the army), the concierge from the ground floor took to making her unseemly proposals, on the presumption that she was a promiscuous kind of woman. Proust took care to set things straight with this man and his wife; his reputation too was at risk.[23] An indication of this may be seen in the irritation betrayed by Proust's lady friends when they received a phone call made by Albaret on his behalf. Like a young lover would do, Albaret spoke in Proust's exact inflection and tone of voice, so much so that the woman at the call's receiving end was under the impression that she was speaking with the writer himself. I have no doubt that there never was the slightest hint of sexual intimacy between Proust and Albaret. But when she remarks that even if he woke her in the middle of the night to discuss some trifle, she could not help walking into his bedroom with a smile on her lips, I cannot help thinking of the down-curved lips of many a married and sexually active couple.[24] "Ah, voilà la Joconde!" ("Here comes la Gioconda!"): when his call woke Albaret up and she came into his bedroom with her long hair undone, Proust would welcome her arrival with these words, just as though he was framing the mental picture of an ideally submissive and complicitous Albertine[25] (see illus. 4).

Proust's sex life was extraordinary in the literal sense of the word: often unenviable, at times tragic, occasionally pathetic, rarely happy (amiably so, when circumstances allowed), but unfailingly extraordinary and unclassifiable.

I am not denying that we could legitimately call Proust's sexual orientation bisexual. We could just say: "Proust was bisexual: end of story." But would we gain much from this label? Aside from the comforting sense of closure one gets from labeling or classifying or christening what was previously an unknown entity, we would still be left with the mystery of Proust's sexuality intact.

We will have further opportunities to discuss this matter at length. As I said, one cannot fully grasp the nature of Proust's financial dealings with Hauser without grasping the impact that his amorous life had on them. For the time being, I limit myself to reiterating that the pseudo-biography contained in Proust's novel is our best source of virtual insights into its author's sex life. Framed by the Narrator's distinctive penchant for osculation, exemplified in his devotional reception of his mother's goodnight kiss as a child and, later on, of Albertine's French kiss before sleep (*Swann's Way*, 13; *Prisoner*, 4),[26] in this novel we encounter over and over again an evasive sexuality swaying between opposite poles: abstinence on the one hand (which was probably the mainstay of Proust's day-to-day sexual regimen), and, on the other hand, a "something" unnamable and too "troublesome" to tell, *quelque chose de pénible* which the Narrator leaves deliberately out of his story (*Prisoner,* 163).[27] What seems clear to me is that to Proust's Narrator, yearning for the people who strike his fancy is more rewarding than winning their carnal intimacy, just as traveling toward a yearned-for city is preferable to sojourning in it (*Prisoner,* 155).[28] The object of desire, be it a city, a man, or a woman, is a feast of imaginary pleasures only as long as it is not attained. And when it is attained, as Albertine's bodily possession is secured in Paris, or as the Narrator's long-lived dream of visiting Venice is realized shortly after Albertine's death, this pleasure is made lopsided by stupor—be it Albertine's near-unconsciousness in bed, which makes her unresponsive to the Narrator's sexual release, or the Narrator's grief-induced mental numbness in Venice, which reduces him to an obtuse sex tourist.

Ah, voilà la Joconde! (Céleste Albaret). Collection Céleste Albaret–cliché Sartony (with the authorization of Éditions Robert Laffont, Collection Documento.)

We shall get to the bottom of this issue in due course, as it deserves a whole chapter to itself. I am reluctant to skip forward to this chapter right away, though, since we must sift more anecdotal evidence before taking the final leap into Proust's sex world. As you know, this is a book about opportunity costs, and, more specifically, about the symbiosis in Proust's life between creative fantasy and financial reality. Measuring with accuracy the economic costs of Proust's major infatuations, as it is done for the first time in these pages, is only the first half of my chore. The second half consists of gauging these costs' full pay off. When it comes to patterns of sexual desire, I believe that their costly implementation helped stretch Proust's creative imagination far beyond that of his contemporaries, Gide included.

Chapter 8

A WING'S WILD BLOW

> My dear Lionel,
>
> [T]he "Lesson of things" I'm being taught is as rough as a Biblical punishment. My money worries would almost be welcome, if only they helped me not to think of the poor friend I lost, who fell into the sea with his airplane. But I realize as well as Bergson does that the field of consciousness has several levels and one can think of many things at once, since my sadness doesn't wane at all when I think of my debts. (COR XIII, 156)

With these words, written in July 1914, Proust asked for Hauser's help and solidarity two months after the fateful day, May 30, when both his love life and his economic safety collapsed. He admitted his financial troubles with an opening in Latin, "I am *in profundis*," alluding to Psalm 130, the psalm of contrition. And then he detailed the list of his debt exposures.

The opening of this confession is a masterpiece of allusions. Psalm 130, used in funerary rites and prayers for the dead, suits the mournful tone Proust adopts in telling Hauser of the demise of his "poor friend" Alfred Agostinelli. Moreover, *De Profundis* ("From the Abyss") is the title of the letter-confession written by Oscar Wilde in 1897 from the prison of Reading. In both these texts, the person making amends is in desperate conditions. The "abyss" to which Proust refers is the trough of his cash deficit; he finds himself ensnared at the same time, though, in the numbing abyss opened up by Agostinelli's death.

The twofold allusion to the Bible and to Wilde's letter would not go unnoticed by Hauser, who in his correspondence with Proust kept revealing his firm aspiration to be a man of learning. A third facet, however, typical of the wealth of allusions implicit in all of Proust's writings, was likely to evade Hauser's grasp. Wilde had addressed his *De Profundis* to the young man, Alfred Douglas, for whose love he had been put on trial and sentenced to jail; the text of his letter-confession had been published posthumously without mention of the identity of its addressee. Now, Proust was familiar with Wilde's judicial odyssey and could not have missed the bitter coincidence that the object of his mourning had the same first name, Alfred, as Wilde's beloved.[1]

The funereal beginning of Proust's letter is followed by a list of forwards contracts, and subsequent obligations to pay at settlement date, whose magnitude would be enough to make a less seasoned banker than Hauser fear the worst. Ironically, as I said, the outbreak of World War I bailed Proust out for the time being, by bringing about the suspension of trading on all the stock exchanges and enabling thereby Hauser to intervene and rescue whatever was possible. To Hauser, it was no longer just a matter of looking after a client's interests: a few months later, the value of Proust's Warburg portfolio, which at its peak in 1911 was worth 241,000 francs or $1,087,000, would go down to a mere 37,000 francs or $159,000. It was a matter, rather, of making up for the mess caused by the recklessness of a dear and unfortunate friend. Suffice it to say that Proust's patrimony in real terms lost close to 350,000 francs or $1,500,000 in 1914; and the following year, owing partly to an 18 percent inflation rate, it amounted to no more than 640,000 francs or $2,400,000. Proust's personal fortune was cut by almost half in two years, from 1913 to 1915. To us, though, as we probe Proust's economic wisdom from the perspective of a time span that includes subsequent generations of heirs and publishers, it is also a matter of evaluating the longer-term repercussions of the fabulous opportunity costs with which the writer burdened himself, both in their literary and financial aspects.

So what exactly happened to Proust on the fatal day of May 30, 1914? Let us follow the events in an orderly fashion. The end of the previous winter and the beginning of spring saw Proust benefiting from a certain inner peace. We do not know what the immediate effects of Albert Nahmias's intervention in Monaco were, but from a letter written in that period by the writer to Alfred Agostinelli, the only one extant from their correspondence, it looks as if a gradual reconciliation was in progress. This seems to be the reason why Proust, as a compensation for Nahmias's efforts on the French Riviera, asked him to forwards purchase no less than

75,000 francs in securities on his behalf. These included partly securities of mining companies from the Caucasus Mountains and the Carpathians and partly securities of a French furnace company (COR XIII, 37). Not being legally entitled to operate on the stock exchange floor, Nahmias charged David Léon with these contracts. Proust's forwards contracts with this brokerage firm, and with Wellhoff & Neustadtl as well, were now in the order of 170,000 francs.

Even before the positive or negative results of these transactions could become manifest, though, Proust was suddenly in urgent need of large amounts of cash. On May 6 he asked Hauser to realize 10,000 francs quickly from the sale of securities. On May 7 Proust told Hauser that he had just withdrawn 20,000 francs from his account at the Rothschild Bank and did not dare to face Léon Neuberger for more money. On May 28 Proust sent Nicolas Cottin to Hauser's offices to find out about the sale of his securities and learned that the proceeds would be available on June 2. He demanded that this money be delivered to him on the morning of the same day. Now, however, rather than 10,000 francs, he asked Hauser for twice this sum. On May 29 Hauser wrote to Proust that he would be willing to advance him the money he needed, adding, "I won't hide from you that I'm a bit worried about your recent withdrawals" (COR XIII, 99, 100, 101, 120, 121).

Hauser's tone may appear strangely conciliatory, considering the financial quicksand his friend had recently stepped into. One must take into account, however, that Hauser was still unaware, in all likelihood, of the debt his friend had contracted the previous year with the Crédit Industriel in the amount of 218,000 francs. He was also ignorant of the fact that Proust had just embarked on a spending spree of luxury items and new forwards contracts on the stock market, both triggered by the whims of his heart. Proust sent his new housemaid Céleste Albaret to Hauser's offices, asking that he give her 3,000 francs in cash right away and that a further 18,000 francs be delivered to her, also in cash, four days later. Hauser gave the smaller sum to Albaret, but being loath to handle large sums of cash, he wrote to Proust that a check in the amount of 18,000 francs would be ready for her in four days. He also asked if this was the exact amount his friend wanted to withdraw: would he not rather cash the proceeds from all the sale orders he had given to the Warburg firm in the last few weeks? On June 3 Proust confirmed that he wanted to cash all of the proceeds, parceled out in three checks: one payable to himself, one to Wellhoff & Neustadtl, and one to David Léon (COR XIII, 122, 123, 129).

The day of May 30, in short, was the settlement date for forwards contracts at the Bourse de Paris, and as a consequence of growing international tensions, Proust's speculations had given rise to negative results. But what also happened on the same day is that, before writing the sole letter to Agostinelli that has come down to us—the impact of which on the development of his novel was to be of capital importance, as I have intimated—Proust bought an airplane worth 27,000 francs from Ferdinand Collin. Collin was the director of the flying school in the town of Buc, four kilometers from Versailles, where the writer had recently paid the fees for the flying lessons of Agostinelli (known to Mr. Collin as Marcel Swann). The airplane was meant as a gift for the fugitive chauffeur-secretary. The same day, Proust bought another item at the same price, probably a Rolls Royce, according to Philip Kolb, also intended for Agostinelli.[2]

As if to spite Proust, on the very day of these conspicuous expenses, the stock exchange sent him an unequivocal signal that no easy gain, suitable to offset them, was in sight for him. On the contrary, further debts were in the cards. Last, and most tragically, having bought the airplane and the British car, while Proust wrote a long and poetic letter to his beloved Agostinelli (in which he had no qualms in mentioning the pecuniary value of one of the gifts ready for the young man in Paris), in a fatal twist of fate, the airplane Agostinelli was flying over the Bay of Cannes plunged into the sea.[3] Proust was promptly notified of the accident in a telegram sent by Anna Square (COR XIII, xvi, 124).

All of this in one day—and, very likely, in the succession of events I just described. If only for a moment, let me put myself in Proust's shoes. It is Saturday, May 30, 1914. I start out my day after a few fairly sleepless hours of rest; I go through my daily "fumigations," then I send out instructions for the purchase of an airplane and a Rolls Royce, then I learn that my finances are in total disarray, then I write a sentimental letter of reconciliation to my beloved, and, finally, a telegram tells me of my beloved's tragic death. I have known people who have lost grip of their mental sanity for much less than that.

If Proust had been superstitious or a religious believer (he was neither), he might have worried that his citation from Stéphane Mallarmé's poem "Le vierge, le vivace et le bel aujourd'hui," inscribed at the heart of his letter to Agostinelli, had played a premonitory or even a maleficent role in the accident: "This virginal, long-living lovely day / Will it tear from us with a wing's wild blow. . . ."[4] The "wing's wild blow" ("coup d'aile ivre") struck his friend Agostinelli the same day that Proust was writing him these words. Along with Agostinelli's young life, it took away one of the most promising prospects for happiness in Proust's adult experience.

In the letter in question, Proust began by thanking Agostinelli for his last letter to him: "A sentence in it was *splendid* (*crépusculaire* etc.), and I thank you also for the telegram preceding it, which was an additional amiability." Then he apologized for his reluctance to accept an undefined "initiative" that Agostinelli had volunteered to undertake on his behalf. Agostinelli probably meant to cancel the order for the Rolls Royce, which Proust had placed in his name. In the following paragraph, in what reads like a confirmation of this hypothesis, Proust explained why he could not allow Angostinelli to cancel the order for the airplane. Two days earlier, on his way to the Russian ballet, Proust had met Monsieur Collin. Collin acknowledged Proust's right to cancel this order, but he did it with such kindness that the writer did not feel up to causing him such an inconvenience. "Please do not think that Monsieur Collin has a personal interest of any sort in this sale. He does not earn *a cent* out of the 27,000 francs that the airplane costs me." Proust then declared that if he kept the airplane, in all likelihood it would end its days in a hangar, and he would have the lines quoted above from Mallarmé inscribed on its fuselage.

The letter to Agostinelli then moved on to discuss a recent financial scandal involving Henri de Neufville, the bankrupt brother of a personal friend of Proust. It seems that Proust was jealous of one of Neufville's menservants, with whom Agostinelli had been on intimate terms in the past—this is, at least, what the tone of this passage in the letter suggests.[5] In his conclusion, Proust mentioned the two previous letters he had mailed to Agostinelli. The writer would like to have them back, and he asked Agostinelli to mail them in a sealed envelope, to protect them from indiscreet eyes (COR XIII, 124). It is likely that in making this request, Proust was already planning to use his sentimental experience with Agostinelli in the narration of the love story and cohabitation of his novel's Narrator with Albertine. Agostinelli's death, which occurred in the few hours preceding or following the moment when Proust wrote this letter, could not have been foreseen; nor could Proust have foreseen the way Agostinelli's death would affect the unfolding of his Narrator's love for Albertine.

Chapter 9

ENTER ALBERTINE SIMONET

In 1914 Proust wrote the first fifty pages or so devoted to the character of Albertine, and later on developed her story in a manuscript, completed in 1922, that fills two of the seven volumes of *In Search of Lost Time:* the fifth, *The Prisoner;* and the sixth, *The Fugitive.* The narrative cycle centered on the character of Albertine is the fourth and most ambitious section in the tetralogy-within-the-novel that Proust devoted to the theme of jealousy. The first section of this tetralogy is devoted to Charles Swann's love affair with Odette de Crécy; the second to Saint-Loup's love affair with Rachel; the third to the Baron de Charlus's entanglement with Charlie Morel, an opportunistic musician; and the fourth, as I said, to the Narrator's love for Albertine.

To my knowledge, nobody has unveiled yet the reason, if there is one, why these three couples include four times the name *Charles,* namely: Charles Swann, Charlie Morel, Charlus, and, by anagram, Rachel. Nor will I try to solve the riddle in this book; some scholars have toyed with it before me.[1]

It is only in *The Fugitive* that we discover more about the tenor of the "splendid sentence" that Alfred Agostinelli wrote to Proust. We know from Proust's letter to Agostinelli that the pivotal word in this sentence was the adjective "crépusculaire," French for "crepuscular." The same adjective is used in a letter from *The Fugitive* that contains a likely paraphrase of Agostinelli's letter to Proust; this letter is penned by Albertine after having abruptly ended her cohabitation with the Narrator. She writes to him: "I am very touched that you should have kept such a nice memory of our last outing. Please believe that for my part I shall never forget this doubly crepuscular excursion ["deux fois crépusculaire"] (since night was falling and we were destined to part) and that it will never be erased from my mind until blackest night finally invades it (*Fugitive,* 435).

In his recent English translation of *The Fugitive,* Peter Collier renders the term *crépusculaire* with the conventional "twilight." It is a poor word choice on two counts, in my opinion. By failing to do justice to the elegance of Albertine's chosen expression, the term *twilight* does not underscore, as the highbrow term *crepuscular* does, the intellectual advantages of the sentimental education that Albertine receives from the company of the Narrator. He regarded her, at the beginning of their cohabitation, as little better than an uneducated brat, but in time her vocabulary, erudition, and sensitivity show evident improvement—so much so that, in the last outing mentioned in Albertine's letter, while their carriage drives under a full moon and she comes to the secret decision that the time has come to break up with her companion, he recites poetry about the moonlight to her, counting on her appreciation of the changes in the hue of the moon, from silver to blue to yellow, according to this or that author's whim. Moreover, the term *twilight* occults the biographical parallel between the fictional letter and the two letters exchanged by Proust with his chauffeur, since a key term in all three of them—that is, in the extant, the lost, and the fictive letter—is the predicate *crepuscular.* I find it hard to define the term *twilight* as "splendid," which is precisely the predicate used by Proust to praise Agostinelli's adoption of the term *crépusculaire* (*Fugitive,* 435).[2]

The elegance of Agostinelli's word choice, as may be plausibly reconstructed from Albertine's letter, justifies the high regard in which the writer held the sensitivity of this young man —documented in letters to several friends—who was poorly educated yet evidently eager to write in the fine French of his former employer. The likelihood of Albertine's letter being a paraphrase of Agostinelli's is heightened by the following detail: Albertine declares she is ready to cancel the order of the Rolls Royce, which the Narrator wanted to give her as a gift. The Narrator answers her by transcribing almost verbatim the significant sections of the letter, just discussed, written by Proust to Agostinelli on May 30, 1914. One noteworthy difference is that, in the novel, Agostinelli's airplane is turned into a yacht (*Fugitive,* 421–24).[3]

Albertine's letter to the Narrator is written just a few days before a telegram from her aunt, Madame Bontemps, informs him that her niece just died in an equestrian accident. But owing to different speeds in delivery, the letter and the telegram reach the Narrator at the same time. (The same thing happened with Agostinelli's last letter to Proust, in which he proudly announced having gotten his pilot's license: it reached Proust after the telegram announcing his death.)[4] Mimicking Agostinelli's intentions in the days before his death, as Proust seems to have sensed them, Albertine's letter begs her lover to take her back: "Would it be too late for me to return to you? . . . I shall be bound by your decision, which I beg you to let me know without delay, since you can imagine how impatiently I await it. If it were favorable, I would take the next train. Yours with all my heart, Albertine" (*Fugitive,* 445).[5]

At this stage in *The Fugitive,* the typical phases of Proustian love, four in all, follow one another in rapid succession, as if in a flowchart. The death of the beloved—Agostinelli in Proust's case, and Albertine Simonet in his Narrator's case—brings to light, in this flowchart, Proust's conception of love's innermost essence:

1. First comes the obsession about the longed-for, yet inaccessible, person—obsessively longed for insofar as he or she is inaccessible. And who is more inaccessible than a dead person?
2. In the wake of this obsession, comes an unrelenting jealousy, an inner torture without which love does not endure in Proust. And this torture is more tenacious when it involves a dead person than when its object is a living one, since the memory or suspicion of any betrayal on the beloved's part triggers an immitigable jealousy that, at the same time, brings back to life the lover's *moi,* the loving self that suffered most acutely from the beloved's actions (COR XIII, 179).
3. In the wake of jealousy and obsession comes a state of denial, which pertains to the incomprehensibility of one's falling out of love—or pertains, in the case of death, to the even less comprehensible extinction of the beloved.
4. Last, the state of denial is completed by the demise of the self that was in love: entombed side by side with the memory of the loved one, this self leaves its place to a new self that, however able to recall the past love, does not feel it anymore and is ready therefore for a new one.

Obsession, jealousy, denial, and death of one's own enamored self: the pain caused in Proust by Agostinelli's death unfolded through these four phases. They are the same ones that the Narrator goes through in Proust's novel after Albertine's death.

Defining the Proustian meaning of the term *love,* they are also the same phases neatly articulated in a letter addressed by Proust to Reynaldo Hahn shortly after October 24, 1914 —which shows the writer's ability to practice the discipline of introspection even in the grip of the deepest pain. One year later, we find an illustration of these four phases in a letter to Proust's good friend Marie Scheikévitch, the daughter of an influential Russian lawyer. Four months before Albertine made her first appearance in the drafts of *In the Shadow of Young Girls in Flower,* this letter describes her as the character playing "the greatest role" in the novel. Confusing the fiction of Albertine with the reality of Agostinelli—as he did more than once in his letters—Proust writes Madame Scheikévitch of his jealousy for Albertine, of his desire to marry her, of their separation, and of "the great intermittent force [of forgetfulness] that in the end will prevail" over his pain and his love for her (COR XIV, 136).

The economic costs of Proust's love for Agostinelli were significant. But their advantages to Proust's artistry were not indifferent: in an eight-year span, from 1914 to 1922, they gave Proust the opportunity to revolutionize and greatly enrich the thematic thrust of *In Search of Lost Time.* With Gaston Gallimard, who took Bernard Grasset's place as the novel's publisher after the success of the first volume, Proust boasted that his talent was expressed at its best in the volumes devoted to Albertine, and especially the second one, *The Fugitive* (COR XXI, 310).

As to the concrete scale of these opportunity costs, first of all one must factor in the 54,000 francs paid for the airplane and the Rolls Royce meant for Agostinelli; it should be kept in mind, however, that either Proust himself or his heirs, later on, must have recovered some money out of the sale of these two vehicles, a consideration that the writer's biographers never make in their tirades against his economic improvidence.[6] Second, one must factor in the luxury gifts and above all the liquid cash which Proust gave Agostinelli when he and Anna Square were living with him in Paris. There were also the 5,000 francs probably given by Proust to Agostinelli's family, to pay for the divers who fished his corpse out of the Bay of Cannes and the costs of his funeral. Last, there was the money that Proust had to spend after Agostinelli's death to cope with the needs (rather instrumental and opportunistic) of the young man's family and his companion, Anna Square.

But we should also factor in the collateral expenses Proust underwent shortly before May 30, 1914, namely, the financial speculation which he was drawn into by his gratitude for Albert Nahmias's role as in-between in Monaco. Even the possible losses from this 75,000-franc investment must be treated as a specific sort of opportunity cost pertaining to Albertine's saga, since they eventually translated into a specific instance of literary creation on Proust's part. Nahmias's mission to Monaco provided in fact the outline for an analogous scheme undertaken in *The Fugitive* by the Narrator's friend Saint-Loup.

As I said earlier, Proust's sources of inspiration were multiple, indirect, and never precisely allusive to this or that individual. If in this specific instance, Nahmias figures as the prominent model for the character of Saint-Loup, in most parts of the novel this character is based on two other friends of Proust: Louis d'Albufera, who, as we saw, provided the blueprint for Saint-Loup's tormented relationship with Rachel; and Bertrand de Fénelon, who, like Saint-Loup during World War I, died on a battlefield. Robert de Billy, as I explained earlier, added minor sartorial touches to the character of Saint-Loup.

A further element in our cost-benefit analysis of the role played by Nahmias regarding Albertine's saga comes from the consideration that his role was distinctly multifaceted. In addition to contributing to the characterization of Saint-Loup in the trio made up of the two estranged lovers of *The Fugitive* and the middleman charged with their reconciliation, he contributed his own first name to the character of Albertine. And even the fluid unresponsiveness of Albertine's personality, who transitions in time from the irrepressible beach nymph of Balbec to the secretive woman of fashion in Paris, may be a trait she inherited from Nahmias. You may remember the letter that Proust wrote to Albert Nahmias from Cabourg, at the time when he was genuinely infatuated with his secretary/editor,[7] in which he accused Nahmias of being made of water, "perpetually inconsistent, as quick in streaming away as . . . swift in plunging into oblivion." We have no way of knowing, certainly not any better than Proust's Narrator himself, whether Albertine is unfaithful to him, but the novel makes absolutely clear that just by being a tiny bit less insouciant, less oblivious of her lover's gnawing insecurities, she could assuage most of his heartaches. Borrowed probably from Nahmias, her waterlike shiftiness extends to her facial features, where her beauty spot winks at the Narrator from the least expected angles—now the cheek, now the nose, now the groove between the nose and the upper lip (*Young Girls in Flower,* 455).[8]

To complete the picture of Albertine's saga in terms of costs and benefits, I must finally mention the far from negligible contribution given to her character, later on, by Henri Rochat, a Swiss member of the

Grand-Hôtel's staff in Cabourg. We shall spend some time in the company of this disquieting figure later on, after he makes Proust's acquaintance, since ultimately he spent much longer in Proust's company than Agostinelli himself. Suffice it to say, for now, that in 1918 Rochat took money from Proust with the greed of a leech, providing in return other important facets to Albertine's characterization.[9]

Years later, when Nahmias was asked whether he considered himself the model for Albertine, he aptly replied with the phrase mentioned earlier, "There were several of us."[10]

Chapter 10

WARTIME FINANCE

Since the long-term opportunities inherent in his mind-boggling waste of money were not immediately evident to Proust, who was at one and the same time the victim and the beneficiary of his own amorous transports, we should hardly expect Lionel Hauser to appreciate the hidden advantages of Proust's losses. The writer's portfolio was going to the dogs, and fortunately for him, Hauser was capable of appreciating only one thing in this ruinous situation: that he had a decisive role to play in salvaging whatever could be saved.

On June 28, 1914, the grand duke of Austria and his consort were assassinated in Sarajevo; on July 23 Austria-Hungary issued to Serbia an ultimatum. The day before the ultimatum, *Le Figaro* reported panic at the Vienna Stock Exchange:[1] the prices of securities were in free fall. On July 26 Proust replied to an urgent phone call from Hauser with a letter, promising he would do his best to reduce his financial exposures abroad (COR XIII, 154). Two days later, as we saw, he declared himself *in profundis* and confessed to Hauser the extent of his financial exposure. Trading at the Bourse de Paris had been suspended on the day of Hauser's phone call to him.[2] The most recent trades were canceled and future trading was forbidden.

"I don't think that such a harsh avowal was ever wrested from any sinner at the confessional," Proust wrote to Hauser. "If I tell you this, it is just for my mortification since it's naturally too late to sell anything" (COR XIII, 156). Too late indeed, and lucky for him: another twenty-four hours of this nightmare and he would have been left with only his personal belongings to sell.

Based on the details from the confession that Proust wrote him "from the abyss," Hauser probably drew the following conclusions regarding his friend's patrimony. Before trading was suspended at the Bourse de Paris, Proust paid about 50,000 francs in additional collaterals he owed to the Crédit Industriel, David Léon, and Wellhoff & Neustadtl. Proust's portfolio with the Crédit Industriel held 300,000 francs in securities, 122,000 francs in forwards contracts, and a 218,000 franc debt. In turn, Proust's portfolios with David Léon and Wellhoff & Neustadtl entailed a commitment of 205,000 francs in forwards contracts. Warburg & Co. had sold a block of securities on Proust's behalf and sent him two checks, both drawn on the Comptoir d'Escompte in Paris: one in the amount of 20,000 francs, which he cashed and spent; and a second one in the amount of 30,000 francs, impossible to cash after the initiation of conflict with Austria-Hungary.[3] At present, Proust's frozen portfolio in Hamburg held securities that amounted to only 37,000 francs. In the first half of 1914, Proust's extraordinary expenses amounted to about 106,000 francs or $455,000! To cover these expenses, he withdrew 20,000 francs from the Rothschild account and 71,000 francs from the Warburg account; at least 21,000 francs had been advanced by Hauser, who paid himself back eventually with the sale of further securities from the Warburg portfolio.

In 1914, including all bank accounts and portfolios, and with all debts accounted for, Proust was left with a personal fortune amounting to about 790,000 francs or $3,400,000. Hauser wrote to Proust: "I've read your confession with great interest. I refrain from reproaching you any further, as you have been punished enough by current events." He suggested that Proust should make an inventory, assigning zero-value to his forwards contracts (since they could not be traded as long as markets remained closed), and then calculate whether the remainder was enough to live on (COR XIII, 159). Three days later, Proust answered him: "I know that [your letter's] sweetness is devoid of indulgence but its harshness is not devoid of friendship." Then he added that he had just escorted his brother Robert to the train station, where he had joined the soldiers of his company embarking for Verdun. Hauser replied in the same sober tone, sharing with Proust a kind of dread that was bound to push their common financial concerns to the backstage: "War has touched me too and very closely, since my wife's brother, who got married eighteen months ago and already has a baby child, just left for Verdun too. . . . I'd be truly grateful if you spoke of him to your brother" (COR XIII, 161, 162).

No more than three weeks later, though, financial concerns took the upper hand again because of a false rumor spread by *Le Figaro* on August

19, stating that the London Stock Exchange would soon reopen trading on forwards markets. Proust's portfolio with David Léon included Ural Kaspian securities, forwards purchased in the amount of 13,000 francs, which were traded on the floor of the London Stock Exchange (COR XIII, 156). Proust wrote to Léon that if forwards markets were reopened in London, he would not be able to meet his obligations.[4] Léon answered with oddly exquisite politeness: "Monsieur Proust must not lose his sleep on such a trifle. Nobody will be charged collaterals in London until one year has passed after the end of the war and M. Proust least of all. I won't deny that I'd like it better if he had the cash at hand to be sent to the broker. But since he does not, I will pay on his behalf, linking his account to my own, and I will do my best to sustain his market position and not upset his peace of mind" (COR XIII, 170).

Is there irony in these words? Or bad faith? As an investor, Proust had lost some of his initial candor. He commented on Léon's words in a letter to Hauser: "[Here is how he answered my letter,] causing me not only deep surprise but also keen anxiety, because I fear he must be hiding something" (ibid.). Léon was probably not hiding much, except for the fact that a skilled broker does not draw back from any opportunity to make a profit, even when this comes at his client's expense. He was not a "sentimental financier" like Hauser, that's all. Luckily for Proust, the London Stock Exchange did not reopen till November 18.

The second half of 1915 coincided with an intense stage of financial apprenticeship not only for Proust, but for Lionel Hauser as well. The banker, too, admittedly with greater aplomb, had to learn to navigate the treacherous waters of wartime finance. In Proust's case it was not simply a matter of tough sailing; he would also discover that he did not have a thorough knowledge of the battered boat of his own making—the "boat full of leaks," as Hauser would call it in 1916 (COR XV, 59)—that he had taken onto the open sea of high finance. First of all, the writer would have to learn how to deal with inflation, the Leviathan of all wars (See Figure 2).

Although quiescent, or almost so, during the prewar years, the inflation rate grew to colossal proportions during the war and postwar years, totaling a compounded 150.3 percent increment in six years, starting in 1915 and ending in 1920. It then went down to almost minus 9 percent in 1921. Personal fortunes larger than Proust's were washed away under such massive erosion.

Proust also had to acquaint himself promptly with certain subtleties of the forwards markets to which he had neglected to pay attention until then. Even during the suspension of forwards markets, the principle of *escompte* (discount) allowed the holder of a forwards contract to trade it for cash over the counter (OTC), owing to the fact that, even in markets operating under normal conditions, this sort of contract was not traded on the floor of the stock exchange. Proust would have liked to have had recourse to this expedient in August, after he heard a rumor that the settlement of forwards markets—put off in Paris with a moratorium since July 1, 1914—might be set to start again before the end of 1915. An ordinance published in the *Journal Officiel* eventually decreed that obligations on forwards contracts had to be met by September 16, 1915, and interest amounts accrued on the payments suspended by the moratorium had to be paid by October 2, 1915.[5] Proust was right in trying to protect himself, then, as he racked his brains on how to raise the cash needed to face up to his obligations.

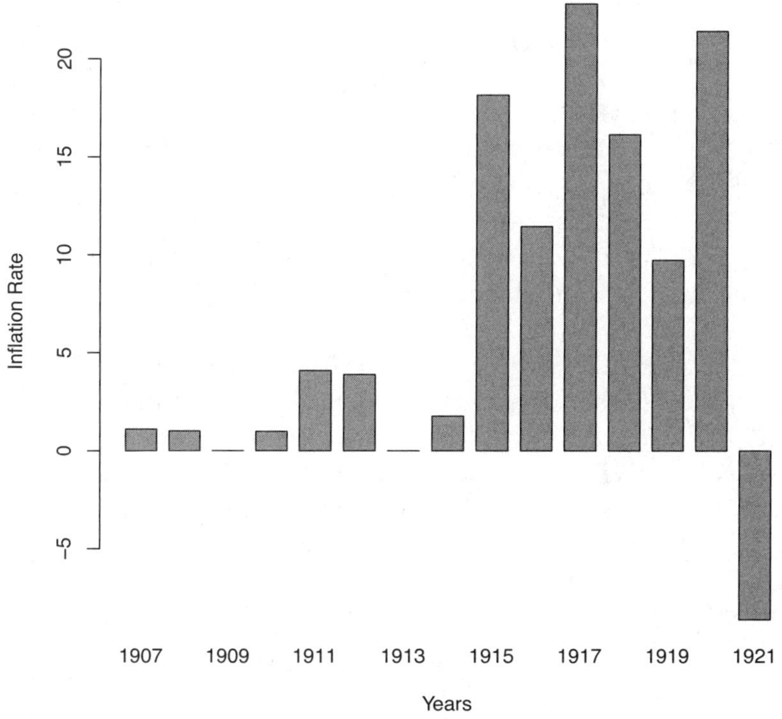

French inflation rate (1907–1921). *Source*: Gian Balsamo, "Proust and His Banker: Numerical Documentation," Item 5.

Proust learned the simple but strict principle of *escompte* after a failed attempt to close his forwards contract on one hundred Malacca Rubber shares, held in his portfolio at the Crédit Industriel. Hauser had to instruct him on the detail that often neither the buyer nor the seller of a forwards contract actually had at hand the securities they were trading. But since forwards markets were officially closed at this time, and Proust had therefore to sell his Malacca Rubber securities for cash OTC, he needed to have them at hand. And to have them at hand, he had to "discount" the original seller; that is, he had to pay him the settlement price. A preferable alternative procedure was the "deferred payment," a variant on what contemporary traders call "short sell." A short sell entails selling a security with the agreement that it will not be delivered immediately but at a later date. The difference between a short sell and a sale at deferred price is that, in the former case, the seller does not know the future price at which he will have to buy the security in order to deliver it on the agreed-upon date, while in the latter case, the seller, who holds a forwards contract on the security he is selling, knows the future settlement price which was agreed on at the signing of his forwards purchase. Hence, if Proust were able to find a buyer for his Malacca Rubber at a satisfactory "deferred" price, he would be able to sell these securities right away, and then wait to receive the payment and deliver the securities, which were not in his hands for now, at the end of the moratorium, when he would pay their settlement price. This seemed to be the best option (COR XIV, 68).

These financial maneuvers began in the summer of 1915. Before the summer, Proust's financial concerns and ambitions went into hibernation, though, buried under the black mantle of much greater fears. War took the life of his good friend Bertrand de Fénelon, reported missing at first, who was one of the major models, as I mentioned, for the character of Saint-Loup in Proust's novel. War also took the life of Gaston de Caillavet, Jeanne Pouquet's husband, and that of Marie Scheikévitch's brother. Besides Proust's brother Robert, both his closest friend Reynaldo Hahn and his trusty part-time chauffeur Nicolas Cottin were at the front. Proust wrote to Robert de Billy:

> Ever since the war started, I have lived in a constant state of anxiety for all those I love (I mean, deep down also for those I do not know and whose distress I envisage very vividly), but I can't help feeling especially hag-ridden with regard to my brother, who has run into great dangers in Argonne, and

> especially hopeless about the disappearance of Bertrand de Fénelon. . . . In the next few days I must face an army committee and random chance is now so much the rule in everything that I risk being reported fit for military service while so many fellows in good health take their leisurely strolls [in Paris]. (COR XIV, 26)

Proust would have to face the same conscription committee twice, and in August his unfit status was temporarily revoked. This news allowed Hauser, whose pragmatic nature made him suspicious of Proust's hypochondriac lassitude, to make an ironic comment: "I was delighted to hear that after a medical examination, the army committee's Major found you fit for military service, and if in six months he'll be still of the same opinion, I wouldn't be surprised if one of these days I saw your chest adorned with the Cross of War" (COR XIV, 102, 103).

Chapter 11

THE COBBLER *&* THE BANKER

In working out the fine details pertaining to the character of Albertine, Proust seemed driven either faithfully to duplicate reality in his fiction or scrupulously to mold his real life on fiction. It is hard to say which comes first, in his very personal brand of realism.

He charged Maurice Rostand, whose recent words of praise for *Swann's Way* were, in Proust's own view, a "ridiculous exaggeration," to investigate what kind of life Alfred Agostinelli had lived on the French Riviera in the weeks preceding his death.[1] On Proust's recommendation, Rostand's father Edmond Rostand, the celebrated author of *Cyrano de Bergerac,* had hired Émile Agostinelli, Alfred's younger brother, as a driver, so Maurice could take advantage of this young man's cooperation and play detective. In the first part of *The Fugitive,* it is Aimée, maître d'hôtel at the Grand-Hôtel de Balbec—the sea resort where the Narrator had met Albertine Simonet for the first time—who takes up Rostand's role. Shortly after Albertine's death, Aimée goes to Châtellerault in Center-West France; this is the city where, after leaving the Narrator's Parisian apartment, Albertine had taken shelter, at the house of her aunt Madame Bontemps. Aimée is tasked with investigating the young woman's sexual habits. Earlier on, Aimée had conducted the same investigation in Balbec. His task is to find out once and for all if Albertine was a promiscuous lesbian (*Fugitive,* 490–91).[2]

We have no reliable sources about Rostand's reports to Proust, but it is not difficult to imagine their gist. In romantic matters pertaining to jealousy and betrayal, even an amateur private eye like Rostand would have easily guessed that innocence can never be proven, only guilt can; a verdict of innocence is usually taken as evidence of the detective's ineptitude. For their part, Aimée's reports to Proust's Narrator leave little room to imagination. The pretty laundry girl who, according to Aimée, was sexually intimate with Albertine in Châtellerault, used to lick with her tongue Albertine's neck and arms, and even the soles of her feet. Remarkably ingenious in his improvised role as detective, Aimée goes to bed with the laundry girl better to interrogate her; and this is where he sees with his own eyes the marks of the bites which, in her sexual convulsions, Albertine left allegedly on the arms of this young woman, who reveals herself "very skillful" at sexual games.

Although Aimée's investigation gives positive results, it does not so much confirm the Narrator's suspicions as show him the pathetic irrelevance of his urge to know the truth. As remarked by Antoine Bibesco, the renegade friend who wrote some unfair and lucidly cruel words about Proust almost thirty years after his death, nothing good can come from this doubling of "the role of Sherlock Holmes with that of Othello."[3] First of all, the Narrator is well aware that his amateur detective Aimée is too well paid to afford to come back empty-handed from his mission, and probably has no scruples about giving credit to dubious evidence, if not making it up altogether. Second, Albertine would be the only person able to confirm the evidence; or, faced with the evidence, she would be the only person likely to either betray some revealing reaction or adopt an attitude apt to stir up or extinguish the fire of the Narrator's passion. But she is gone forever! Moreover, if Albertine had been disloyal to the Narrator with women lovers when she was alive and he had known about it right away, he realizes that this would have triggered the first two phases in the transports of his love, pricking his jealousy and unchaining his obsession for her. But if the young woman were to emerge as guilty of the same betrayal now that she is dead, this evidence would not change in the least his own need to love her. At worst, it would delay the granting of his posthumous pardon to her, slowing down the modification of the mental image he holds of Albertine in his own memory. In adding the predicate of homosexual promiscuity to the contours of her persona, the revelation of her secret would undoubtedly create an additional obstacle to her spiritual profile fitting snugly the figments of the Narrator's remembrance of her.[4] However enduring an obstacle, though, her homosexual secret would not be impossible to overcome. He remarks: "The infinite extent, or the egoism, of love causes us to love people whose intellectual and moral features are the least objectively defined for us, we readjust them endlessly according to our desires and our fears, we cannot separate them from ourselves, they are no more than a vast and vague terrain where we externalize our affections" (*Fugitive,* 462).[5] Even if the immense sentimental vacuum left behind by Agostinelli's death was destined to become crowded with the misapprehensions and bad faith created by too many intrusive biographers, his absence filled the pages that Proust devoted to Albertine with some of the soberest reflections on love to be found in twentieth-century literature.

But with the coming of August, the shadows of real and imaginary mourning were pushed aside by the severity of financial emergencies. Only Hauser could save Proust from ruin. After four months of procrastination, owing probably to the reluctance of a banker as skilled as Hauser to bother with a case as desperate as Proust's, Hauser got down to work. The two friends engaged in a very intense exchange of letters, and once more Hauser demonstrated his own disinterestedness by putting all his skills at his friend's disposal, as well as the material and human resources of his firm.

David Léon wanted to know Proust's intentions about the securities of oil and mining companies which he had forwards purchased at the overall cost of 30,000 francs. Overwhelmed by the current dynamics of forwards markets, Proust did not know what to do and asked for Hauser's advice. Should he renew the contracts, hoping in the rise of these securities' prices, or should he pay the additional collaterals he owed Léon and close the contracts? He was afraid of doing the wrong thing and finding himself forced to "discount" these positions and buy the securities. Proust added that his account manager at the Crédit Industriel recommended that he sell some of his securities right away and be prepared for any surprise the market might bring. The securities he held in his portfolio with the Crédit Industriel, such as Nitrogen Company, Waters Company, and Egyptian Preference Bonds, were not too strong on the market at the present time. The influential economist Raphaël-Georges Lévy, a far relative of the writer,[6] was of the opinion that Proust ought to sell solid bonds whose prices had not dipped much thus far. Proust owned quite a bit of these solid securities: French Government, Suez Canal, and Jutland Bonds. But they were held in his Rothschild portfolio and the writer did not dare to confront Léon Neuberger about their sale. What should he do? (COR XIV, 102)

Hauser answered that he could not possibly advise Proust without knowing the exact composition of his various portfolios and the nature of his exposures with brokerage firms. He did not know what interest rate

Proust paid on his debts, the amount of the additional collaterals he owed on his forwards contracts, or the value of the coupon payments he would receive in the near future.

Proust must have been under the impression that Hauser was reluctant to get involved any further in his financial mess. So, at the same time that he complained about the Crédit Industriel, for selling off his Egyptian Bonds, Swiss Railways, Tunisian Bonds, and other securities at discounted prices, he sent Hauser an illustrated copy of his book *Les Plaisirs et les jours* (*Pleasures and Days*), published in 1896. Yet, while he did so, he thwarted this act of kindness by declining Hauser's offer to take a look in his turn at a manuscript that the banker had been working on during these war days of forced inactivity. Proust's unintentionally wounding excuse was that he did not have the time and did not sleep enough "to give this pleasant reading the attention it deserve[d]." But, he added, he would make sure to remember the manuscript's title to enjoy it "later on" (COR XIV, 103, 104). I doubt he remembered this title when Hauser, in 1918, made him a present of his just published book.

A few days later, puzzled by Hauser's lack of cooperation, Proust renewed his assault on the banker with another proof of esteem, in a form that would become more and more typical of the writer: that is to say, so clearly adjusted to his own advantage that it might suggest a coldhearted form of flattery to a less tolerant temperament than Hauser's. Proust wrote Hauser that as a writer, he was afraid to strike too materialistic an impression in the eyes of his friend the banker by talking finances to him. There was material for a fable in this. It is true that the fable "The Cobbler and the Banker" had already been written by La Fontaine, but it did not tell their entire story. Not that Proust would disdain the humble role of the cobbler in his relationship with Hauser. But La Fontaine's cobbler spent his days singing, without giving a moment's thought to money-related matters, and then slept like a log at night. Proust would soon be left with nothing to sing about—certainly not money—and as to sleeping, his sleep had little to do with the quiet of the night because he spent his nights either writing or ailing.

Enraptured by the manifold facets of this literary allusion, only too late did Proust realize that he had lost sight of the reason why he started this letter, which was to provide Hauser with a detailed description of the composition of his portfolios. He would do it in his next letter, he promised. Before taking leave, though, he still wanted to share one of his worries with Hauser. Near the sites of military conflict in Russia,

Proust owned or held in forwards contract 300,000 or 400,000 francs in securities of mining companies: Spassky Copper, North Caucasian, and Doubowaïa Balka. Was there a chance that the German or the Russian army might destroy these mines or their adjacent factories, causing their values to nosedive to zero? (COR XIV, 106) Hauser did not seem to have an answer to this question.

Meanwhile we learn that Proust's second guardian angel, the laconic Léon Neuberger, had suggested that Proust should stop paying a monthly rent to his landlady, aunt Amélie, with the pretext that the breakdown in financial relations with German banks made it impossible for him to cash the Warburg check in the amount of 30,000 francs. The writer was going to follow this advice. However undignified, it was a way to make ends meet in these hard times.

Proust put, if not all, most of his bookkeeping into Hauser's hands. Assisted by his accountant, Hauser went to work on these materials and tried to clear up the confusion. While Hauser was busy at this task, Proust told him of his intention to continue making speculative investments; apparently, he had not forgotten the U.S. Steel Corporation and the favorable tips that he could get about it. Hauser reacted with a firm paternalistic rebuke:

> Allow me to clear up a mirage to which you have unfortunately fallen victim. You imagine, like many others, that the gains one makes at the Stock Exchange depend mainly on the securities which one buys. Well, even if it may appear paradoxical, I assure you that they depend above all on the person who does the trading. I've known people who got rich at the Bourse by trading tenth-rate securities, and others who ruined themselves with blue-chip securities. . . . There are people born to do this job and people born to get their fingers burnt with it. I don't think I'm exaggerating when I classify you in the second group, but if you disagree with me, feel free to prolong the experience, I'd be happy to be persuaded that I am wrong. (COR XIV, 123)

Proust would act wisely in taking a break from speculations as he waited for Hauser's verdict about his finances. He persevered instead in confirming Hauser's bad opinion of his financial competence. In his next letter, he told Hauser that the 40,000 francs in Tramways de Mexico securities that he held a forwards contract on at the Crédit Industriel had risen in value. Since, for once, he was not the one who owed additional collaterals to the bank, but it was rather the bank that owed him, why didn't they refund him the difference? Of course, this is not how forwards contracts work: the rise in prices would earn him a profit the day when he paid the securities at the lower settlement price. Decidedly, the concern of Proust's parents that their son would have a hard time deciphering a simple business letter was sadly turning out to be correct (COR XIV, 124).

Chapter 12

A RUINED MAN

Hauser's verdict reached Proust on October 29, 1915. The writer's Rothschild assets yielded a yearly income of 23,000 francs, and his assets at the Crédit Industriel yielded a yearly income of almost 10,000 francs. As for the additional collaterals owed on his forwards contracts, added to the interest charges, quarterly commission, and moratorium interests he had to pay by the end of that month, Proust had an overall negative balance of 274,000 francs, a figure that did not include the fees owed to his brokerage firms.

Hauser suggested that Proust should get rid of his debt with the Crédit Industriel as soon as possible, and to that end provided him with a list of securities that would extinguish the debt if they were sold at current prices. By selling them, Proust could earn the money needed to extinguish his debt and pay off all other outstanding amounts; this operation would cost him only a loss of 5,400 francs in yearly income. As things stood, Hauser explained, he was losing 22,000 francs a year by paying a 6 percent interest on his debt and a 2 percent yearly fee on bank commissions. Since his gross yearly income totaled 33,000 francs, his net income was a meager 11,000 francs, while Hauser's strategy would more than double it. Let me stress this: *Compared to 1907, Proust's personal assets had lost 58 percent in value, and his solvency depended more and more on small change.*

Hauser's strategy aimed at shrinking Proust's capital, and, in so doing, shrinking his debts and passive interests as well, thereby increasing his income. Agreeing to both Hauser's verdict and the plan he suggested, Proust went to work on a new episode for his novel that would be based on this very financial predicament.

He was currently writing the first drafts of *The Fugitive,* in which the Narrator takes a holiday in Venice shortly before World War I.[1] He was thus antedating the episode by more than one year with respect to biographical reality. In Venice, the Narrator learns from his *coulissier* that the values in his portfolio have collapsed. He had made risky investments to "have more money to spend with Albertine," but after the girl's death, had not paid them any attention. To get rid of collateral debts and passive interests, the Narrator decides to "sell everything," and in the end finds himself owning "barely one fifth of the wealth that [he] had inherited from [his] grandmother and had still possessed while Albertine was alive" (*Fugitive,* 604).[2]

Keeping in mind that Proust did not have at hand the accounting evidence used in the composition of this book, and that he was moreover inclined by temperament to gauge his "ruin" on an emotional rather than an objective basis, the proximity between the novelistic loss (amounting to four-fifths or 80 percent of the Narrator's wealth) and Proust's loss (amounting to close to three-fifths or 58 percent of his wealth) confirms the strong autobiographical elements behind the financial details of this episode. These autobiographical elements are further confirmed by the following consideration: my estimate of the 1915 values of Proust's patrimony derives from a rather optimistic calculation, principally aimed at understating Proust's financial success in the postwar years, preempting thereby the suspicion that my calculations may be biased in favor of my own thesis about Proust's affluence on the longer term. A less forgiving application of my algorithm would indeed output for Proust's remaining patrimony in 1915 a ratio very close to the novelistic "one-fifth" or 20 percent of his previous patrimony, just as declared by his Narrator.[3]

But Hauser's plan was not easy to execute, and in fact it would be completed in stages: in 1915, it prevented Proust's income from disintegrating; in 1916, it brought his income up to 15,000 francs in real terms; in 1917, it kept it to the same amount in spite of a punishing 23 percent inflation rate; and in 1918, it raised his income to 18,000 francs.

Proust was not exactly impoverished. In comparison with the sum of 60,000 francs or $280,000 that his patrimony could potentially yield at the time of his earliest business contacts with Hauser, though, his situation was close enough to how he defined it in a letter to the banker, dated October 31: he was "a ruined man" (COR XIV, 130). In 1911, the year of his fastest plunge into debt exposure, his patrimony had been worth more than 1.5 million francs in real terms—a Gargantuan figure, compared with the 640,000 francs to which his patrimony shrank in 1915, when he found himself on the brink of economic disaster.

Proust did not give in, though. Although he accepted Hauser's reproaches and criticisms, he could not resist reciprocating with a bit of mischievousness. He wrote to Hauser: "Auguste Comte said that we have the Morals of the Theology we profess. I don't know much about your theology, but your morals are those of the Church, those of Sin. You wouldn't refrain, I fear, from advising me to sell assets at harmful conditions, so as to turn my punishment into a more expiatory rite of purification" (COR XIV, 130). Since Proust was on the verge of selling securities in the amount of 300,000 francs ("insignificant though it is for a great financier like you, . . . a considerable sum for a ruined man like me"), he would appreciate it, he wrote, if Hauser would take charge of the sale of the securities that were to be sacrificed from his Rothschild portfolio.

At the beginning of the war, the Rothschild brothers had moved all the securities in their custody to the French Midi. One must not forget that, at this time, the ownership of stocks and bonds was exclusively proven by the possession of paper certificates, as easily lost or stolen as they were likely to be destroyed by a bombing from the air—nowadays most of us own or trade in digital securities, with a digital backup encrypted in a cloud somewhere. The Rothschild Bank was now transferring back to Paris the securities that Proust and Hauser had decided to put on sale. Hauser was reluctant to take this part of the sale into his hands, though. The beginning of his reply to Proust displayed disarming honesty. Proust could not ignore, he wrote, that in circumstances similar to his present ones, a banker's interest is generally opposite to that of his client. "It's not at a time when your resources are reaching rock bottom that I would want to make this operation juicy for myself." Hauser's "delicacy of feelings" called to Proust's mind the exaggerated reactions of many of his friends on the day when he "trumpeted his own ruin." Aside from the extreme case of Louis d'Albufera, who immediately sent him a stash of banknotes, the others did their utmost to make their houses and castles available to him, without of course expecting the payment of any rent in return (COR XIV, 133–35).

In the end, considerations of a patriotic order were added to considerations of a friendly one, and Hauser's unwillingness to be involved more than he already was in the restructuring of Proust's finances grew fainter. The Ministry of Finance announced the issue of new National Loan Bonds that earned an advantageous yield. Moreover, subscribers to the previous loan were given the privilege of subscribing to the new one at a reduced price. By returning the bonds of the National Loan in his portfolio to the Treasury Department, Proust would earn the privilege to subscribe to the new bonds for up to 121,000 francs. The additional cash necessary to cover this subscription would come from the sale of other securities, in addition to those that Proust and Hauser were planning to sell in order to pay off his debts and collaterals. The yearly revenue from these Treasuries would be substantial. In the event that Proust could not raise all of the 121,000 francs needed for the entire subscription, Hauser could still perform the transaction by selling fractions of Proust's subscription privileges to his own clients or even to himself (COR XIV, 149).

At first, the prospects of this possible new strategy were explained to Céleste Albaret by Hauser's accountant, who was sent to report about it at Proust's apartment in Boulevard Haussmann. There he was met by the housemaid while her master, as usual, was asleep in the middle of the day (COR XIV, 145). A few days later, Proust, vexed by this mishap, contrived a tortuous way to keep in closer touch with Hauser: he wrote him that every day, there came a moment when his physical pain became too hard to bear, and he was forced to ring the bell to get some help from his servants. If Hauser sent his most urgent messages to Proust's apartment early in the morning, by the time the first crisis struck and Albaret came to his aid, she would at the same time bring him Hauser's new message. This way, even if the asthma attack made him unable to talk, Proust could still read Hauser's message and answer him in writing, or even have his housemaid call him by phone. "Since I haven't got out of bed in fifteen days and my bedsheets are in bad need of being changed as soon as possible, it's certain that tonight I will gulp down enough drugs to kill a horse so as to manage to get up tomorrow, or, if the drugs don't work fast enough, [the next day]" (COR XIV, 150).

Since the end of 1914, incidentally, Proust had had phone service discontinued in his apartment, officially because of its cost, more likely to make it harder for friends and acquaintances to interrupt his writing; whenever he was taken by the sudden fancy to get in touch with somebody, which happened mostly in the heart of the night, Albaret would go place a phone call down at the nearby Café d'Anjou, where they kept very long hours. It seems, as mentioned earlier, that Albaret made an excellent if unconscious imitation of Proust's voice and inflection; many a lady, Princess Soutzo among them, complained with the writer he should not allow his housemaid to be so cheeky—which amused him no end.[4]

When he woke up after the accountant's visit to his apartment and Albaret updated him on Hauser's new strategy, Proust was delighted by the banker's initiative, and especially by the friendly devotion he saw in it. He translated these feelings into one of the amiable metaphors he liked to draw from La Fontaine: "I seem to understand that Fortune came to me in my sleep," he wrote to Hauser, in an allusion to the fable of the two men courting Fortune, one by running after her and the other by waiting for her in his bed.[5] Then he added that the securities they had agreed to sell from his Rothschild portfolio were already back at the bank's headquarters, in Rue Lafitte. As for the sale of the securities meant to extinguish his debt with the Crédit Industriel, the bank itself would handle it. But, asked Proust, would Hauser be so kind as to handle the sale of the securities for raising the cash needed to subscribe to the new National Loan? (COR XIV, 145)

Proust laid down only one condition along with this request, seemingly a mere whim: if Hauser accepted this task, he must please abstain from "touching his Royal Dutch." In the long run, this apparent quirk of our ruined man's would turn out to be more farsighted than many of Hauser's clever strategies.

The transition of Proust's novel from Grasset to the *Nouvelle Revue Française* (NRF) was an important move for the future of Proust's literary career as well as for Gaston Gallimard, the NRF's director, who secured future credentials for himself as the most illustrious among modern French publishers. Proust was a tough nut to crack, though. This transition was preceded by a most disarming letter from Proust to the publisher, dated May 1916. It consisted mainly of a long and detailed list of factors and considerations that ought to have dissuaded Gallimard from publishing the next volumes of *In Search of Lost Time*. There could be serious drawbacks in his move from Grasset to the NRF, wrote Proust: "My novel . . . includes a volume which, after a verse by Alfred de Vigny ('Woman will have Gomorrah and man Sodom'), I title *Sodom and Gomorrah*. . . . Now, although innocent of any immoral intent, it is a completely truthful and audacious fresco [of sexual mores]" (COR XV, 57). Its "pictorial authenticity" could disturb or offend several readers, including homosexual individuals who would find themselves portrayed mercilessly in the character of Monsieur de Charlus. It could even expose Proust himself to retaliations that the NRF might prefer to avoid. Proust went on:

> After I have left Grasset, I won't be able to go back if at the last minute you refused to publish me or asked for changes that I

> could not make. . . . In a word, dear friend, if I feel a greater obligation toward you than toward Grasset, I feel . . . an even greater obligation toward my work than toward you. [With Grasset] I found a home for my novel, I do want to try to leave it, but I want to make sure first of all that the new home you offer me won't suddenly crumble away. (COR XV, 57)

A further reason why Proust was trying "to discourage" Gallimard was that certain controversial aspects of the current war were going to figure in the final parts of his novel; he was referring both to the well-informed conversations on war strategy held by the novel's protagonist and his friend Saint-Loup, who was, as we know, a junior cavalry officer,[6] and to Charlus's transformation of Paris—crowded with soldiers like certain paintings of Vittore Carpaccio—into a hunting field for his sexual exploits.[7] "All of this, I don't need to tell you," he concluded, "is not anti-militarist in the least. But newspapers are so idiotic (and treated very roughly in my book). They could cry scandal. I anticipate all your possible objections" (COR XV, 57).

Needless to say, Gallimard's professional instinct, zealously advised this time by André Gide, Jacques Rivière, and other collaborators, was far from dissuaded by Proust's words of caution. The transition of Proust's novel from Grasset to the NRF was energetically undertaken. Three years later, in 1919, after the end of the war, Gallimard would publish the novel's second volume, *In the Shadow of Young Girls in Flowers.*

The war had already been going on for two years. Robert Proust was a doctor with the troops on the battlefront; he kept his chronic dysentery a secret, for fear of being discharged from active service. Louis d'Albufera had been promoted to second lieutenant of heavy artillery after working as chauffeur for the chief of the army. Alexandre de Neufville, the brother of the bankrupt financier alluded to earlier—as we saw in Proust's letter to Agostinelli—was in Rouen, writing letters to Proust on the letterhead stationary of the British staff officers. Reynaldo Hahn was fighting (and writing new music as well) in Argonne.

One day Proust paid a rare visit to the Countess Adhéaume de Chevigné (the model who provided the character of Oriane de Guermantes with superb dresses, a birdlike face, and the gravelly voice of a chain-smoker)[8], as she was entertaining Countess Élisabeth de Greffulhe; the latter had been overwhelmingly attractive and much photographed in youth, and in fact contributed, it seems, a beautiful neck and posture to Oriane de

Guermantes's head.[9] The two women chatted with each other, recalling anecdotes from the recent past; yet, "so deep [was] the gap between the years before the war and the formidable seismic quake [caused by the war]" that their words called to Proust's mind a conversation from the Ancien Régime of early modern France (COR XV, 18, 18 [note 16]).

Bertrand de Fénelon was still reported missing. Proust wrote about him to René Blum, the person responsible for expediting the writer's transition from Grasset to Gallimard.

> Dear friend,
>
> [T]he uncertainty, by now a practical certainty, about Bertrand's fate is as sorrowful to me as I imagine it is to you, I mean, inconsolable. What makes it endurable is that I hadn't met Bertrand in ten years: memory feeds the heart and the heart wanes together with memory itself. Not long before the war I had the same experience when I lost the person I loved the most. (COR XV, 62)

He is alluding to Agostinelli, of course, and to his own theory of the dissipation of the loving self, which would be articulated in the volumes of his novel devoted to Albertine. After Agostinelli's death, as we discussed, Proust realized, at first with fright and then with acquiescent relief, that his amorous *moi,* the self that had been in love with the young man, was gradually being worn out by the depletion of remembrance; and it was gradually replaced by a new individual who, if not fully oblivious of the beloved companion, was mildly indifferent to his memory. The letter goes on:

> Nonetheless, since Bertrand has gone missing I find it impossible to stay in bed without taking heavy doses of drugs, so cruel is my anguish (not the anguish of uncertainty anymore, but that of my memories of him clashing with a reality that contradicts them). . . . I find it impossible to bear the thought that no sweet emotion or affectionate feeling subsists for him anymore, and because of it, just as we keep making the movements that hurt us, I can't help thinking of it over and over again. (COR XV, 62)

Chapter 13

OPIUM & DYNAMITE

The misery described in the letter to René Blum is of a sort that Proust could not share with Hauser, for the simple reason that virtually they had no friends in common. As a banker, or more precisely, as a provider of investment services, Hauser shared a small affinity, and a huge disaffinity as well, with the character of Charles Swann. This slight affinity stems from the fact that as a young man, Swann, coming from a family of stockbrokers, was expected to practice Hauser's trade instead of becoming an art collector and would-be art critic. But this is where their similarity ends. Just like his real-life model Charles Haas, Charles Swann is the dilettante by definition in Proust's novel: a man incapable of applying himself to anything with constancy, and least of all to the interminable essay he dreams of writing on Johannes Vermeer, the Dutch painter. And this capricious work ethic makes a brilliant man of the world of Swann, welcome in aristocratic circles that are well above his family's standing. From this perspective, Hauser was the opposite of Swann: he was as tenacious in applying himself to his professional obligations as he was scornful of fashionable people and their pathetic lackeys—the snobs, whom Proust, too, had harshly scourged in his youthful writings.[1]

Regarding personal temperament, one could say that Proust stood midway between Hauser and Swann. Proust was as brilliant as Swann in high society. He was welcome in Paris's aristocratic circles—more warmly welcomed than his novel's protagonist, by the way, who by Proust's own admission was a snob, or, more exactly, a poet of snobbism (COR XV, 65). Proust's acquaintances from the Faubourg Saint-Germain did not see the writer as a climber or an arriviste, but rather a peer whose superior intellectual gifts and unique esprit made up for the inferiority of his social origins. But in the long run Proust proved to be immune from Swann's dilettantism. When it came to excelling in his chosen profession, he was as tenacious and indefatigable as Hauser: not even his endemic condition as a bedridden invalid could undermine the completion of his seven-volume novel, a milestone in the history of world literature.

The closer Hauser got to Proust, the better he understood that the friendship of this refined, pallid artist was not readily granted; it came at a huge personal sacrifice. In Hauser's case, it would never be as unconditional as the friendship that Proust seemed to bestow on people of higher birth and lesser merit. Although Hauser put all his professional talent into the service of Proust's damaged finances, he was never invited to meet the writer for a friendly chat.[2] On certain occasions, the banker was under the impression that Proust's seclusion was less inflexible than he led his acquaintances to believe, and that it was actually interrupted more often than not to allow the writer to meet people he regarded as close friends.

In this regard, Hauser was both right and wrong. As we discussed earlier, Proust argued in later writings that, however intimately sought after, friendship is a dead weight for a writer, as it takes time away from artistic work. He soon began to apply this precept to his own everyday life, making himself inaccessible, as we will see, even to princesses and queens. Yet, as his seclusion grew stricter and stricter over time, he gradually developed a friendly affection of the most genuine kind for Hauser.

A gradual approach of this sort takes time, though, and not even a dedicated theosophist like Hauser was able to tolerate the impression of being cut off or even snubbed for too long. In March 1916 he flew off the handle. "My dear Marcel," he wrote, "you accuse me of being hard and ironic toward you":

> You surround yourself with sweet and sympathetic people who treat you the way you like to be treated. . . . Unfortunately you live in an idealistic world where you find, I'm sure, infinite joy of a kind you could hardly find on this earth. . . . This is where all your misfortunes come from. Though you have grown up since childhood, you have not grown old, you are still the child who does not accept any reproaches, even when he has misbehaved. . . . You complain with your entourage that you are ruined—which is an exaggeration, by the way—and, blind to the fact that you are the sole author of your ruin, you want everybody to feel sorry for you, and reject the heart-piercing

> response of a member of your entourage in the same brutal way by which I dare to shake you, as I do my utmost to plug the leaks which you have made in your own boat. I fully agree with you that man is not the unchallenged master of his own destiny, but this observation should not encourage you to let go of the helm when your spirit, lulled by seductive dreams, leaves your languid body behind. . . . I'll do all I can to wake you up, which explains why I'm not using opium but dynamite. (COR XV, 59)

Hauser's exasperation was also owing to the grueling work he had done on Proust's behalf. After stemming the worst damage caused by debts and interest charges, he had to arrange a drastic change in the composition of the writer's portfolio. As war was on everybody's mind, it comes as no surprise that the two friends soon found themselves using and abusing war metaphors to define Hauser's financial tour de force.

"Your skillful campaign was crowned with success," Proust wrote to Hauser in July 1916, in response to Hauser's sale of 102 of his 502 Doubowaïa Balka securities at an interesting price. He referred to the banker as "My dear Lionel Broussilof," using the surname of the methodical strategist at the head of the successful offensive carried out by the Russian army in the Ukrainian region of Galicia. He was only regretting that—like the prisoners of General Evert, another senior officer of the Russian army in Galicia—he could not count in the thousands "the growing amount of coins that you snatch every day from the hands of an implacable enemy." Two days later, Hauser adopted a similar tone: "I was forced to discontinue my offensive on the front of the Doubowaïa Balka." One month later, Proust's military similes became more refined. Alluding to the first line of "Letter to the King," written by Nicolas Boileau in 1675, he remarked that "Broussilof does not suffice anymore and reviving Boileau's flatteries of Louis XIV, I tell you: Great King stop winning, or I will stop writing" (COR XV, 102, 102 [notes 2 and 6], 104, 119, 119 [note 3]).

Day after day, Hauser's disinterested altruism opened a breach in Proust's heart, in spite of the fact that, over the course of this year, the banker's dynamism clashed often, and rather harshly, with the writer's indolent candor. In fact, with the exception of a thank you note to a recent new acquaintance, the young diplomat Paul Morand, dated January 1, 1917, the only letter Proust wrote to express season's greetings, included in the pertinent volume of his *Correspondance,* was the one he sent to Hauser:

> My dear Lionel,
>
> I write you these few words at the end of this terrible year, which together with my share of universal sorrow has brought me, thanks to you, the consolation of sweet emotions and spiritual joys; it is you who gave them to me with your good-heartedness, with the vibrant and pure gratitude you awoke in me. In this sense I can say (but do I dare to define my own simple, insignificant sorrow as distressful, compared with the dejection of the whole world?) that 'there is a silver lining to every cloud.' Without it, how could one experience the affectionate tenderness of a hand reaching out to help? I shake yours, my dear Lionel. (COR XV, 162)

The previous year, Proust and Hauser had agreed on a strategy of debt reduction, and Hauser was still working on it, with a remarkable outlay of personal resources. In March, he called Proust's attention to a new opportunity that was both profitable and patriotic. The Treasury Department had invited the share and bond holders of foreign companies from nonhostile countries to lend their securities to the state, in order to raise money for the war effort. In exchange, the state would pay a 25 percent increment over the regular yields or coupon payments accruing to the subscribers to the loan. Proust held some of these securities in his portfolios, such as Egyptian Preference shares and Suez Canal Bonds. By subscribing to this national loan, he would make an extra 1,300 francs a year. Some of these securities had been moved to the Crédit Industriel as a warranty for the line of credit opened by Proust in 1912. They would have to be replaced, therefore, perhaps with his new National Loan Bonds of France's Treasury Department, which were still held at the recently founded firm of Hauser et Cie, headquartered in Rue des Petits Champs. This operation was carried out expeditiously (COR XV, 32).

Proust's dealings with the Crédit Industriel were the thorn in the side of his finances. Hauser paid a personal visit to the director of this bank to ask for a reduction in the interest Proust owed on his debt, which, added to the bank's regular commission, amounted to a burdensome 8 percent. The director took his time to decide, but Hauser was unwilling to wait. He told Proust that the London County & Westminster Bank—which for brevity's sake I will call London Bank hereafter—would be willing to take over his debt at 5.5 percent interest and no commission costs. In order to transfer his debt, Proust would have to transfer substantial blocks of his most reliable securities as warranty replacement. Hauser further advised him to reduce his debt by selling the Doubowaïa Balka securities held in his Crédit Industriel portfolio. If he made a total of 100,000 francs out of this sale, he could reduce his debt of the same amount, and his interest charges with the London Bank would shrink by 5,500 francs a year. As we saw above, Hauser soon started working with some success on the sale of the Doubowaïa Balka securities. Meanwhile, bearing some further loss from the additional collaterals he owed David Léon, Proust closed his remaining forwards contracts with this brokerage firm. The Crédit Industriel, where Proust had two open accounts, was the only firm with which he still had active brokerage dealings (COR XV, 35, 36).

At the end of March 1917, Hauser made a list of the reliable securities that he advised Proust to transfer to the London Bank as a warranty for the line of credit he would open in order to extinguish his debt with the Crédit Industriel. As far as Hauser was concerned, Proust ought to liquidate all his open positions at the Crédit Industriel, and even close down his accounts altogether (COR XV, 51).

This idea triggered the crisis that led the banker to write the letter, cited earlier, in which he said that he preferred to be a dynamiter rather than an opium dealer. Proust was dead set against cutting all bridges with the Crédit Industriel, and his reply to Hauser's advice gave three reasons: the first was that even after his debt was extinguished, this bank would still hold many more assets of his than Hauser seemed to be aware of; second, while the London Bank was willing to accept only first-rate securities as warranty to the line of credit, the Crédit Industriel had kindly accepted as warranty less-solid securities as well when Proust had asked for a line of credit in 1912; third, and this was the most cryptic of Proust's reasons, but also the least disputable by Hauser, the writer declared that "family obligations" prevented him from severing his dealings with the Crédit Industriel (COR XV, 52).

Hauser answered him on the same day, and received in turn Proust's response in less than 24 hours—which brought the number of letters exchanged on this subject by the two friends to a total of five in three days. The emotional climate was getting overheated and the terms of confrontation grew sour. Hauser wrote: "I know my classics well enough to be aware of the kind of trouble one asks for by meddling with a man and his battered wife, I abstain therefore from trying to persuade you" (COR XV, 55). Proust replied in a wounded tone: "You compare me with a woman who likes to be thrashed, a comparison that would be correct only if my motives . . . concerned the Crédit Industriel. I told you instead that they have nothing to do with this bank, and depend on family matters. . . . A gentle word from you, of the kind you often have in store for me, would have done me more good than your sarcasm" (COR XV, 56).

In spite of these squabbles, Hauser-the-dynamiter worked full speed at rescuing Proust's finances. It was the writer who raised obstacles: "Whether an intermediate treatment between what you wittily call opium and dynamite exists for sensitive subjects [such as I] is a psychotherapeutic issue which I leave to the neurologists to sort out" (COR XV, 60). Hauser could not avoid replying to this new provocation, even if it diverted his attention from the financial goals that figured high on his list of priorities. He protested that the true nature of his friendship should have been evident to Proust. And to the extent that Proust proved he could handle his finances by himself, he would be glad to get out of his way. But when circumstances made his intervention indispensable, he had no choice but "to shoulder the role of a medical doctor." His diagnosis was that Proust's case had turned out very serious, which explained the extreme measures he had taken, opposed by the writer's "restrictions of a sentimental order"—such as his stubborn refusal to close his accounts at the Crédit Industriel. "If I submit to your restrictions in spite of seeing no rationale behind them, be so kind as to at least not expect me to encourage you with words that would be devoid of conviction" (COR XV, 61).

Understandably enough, Hauser could see no rationale behind the cryptic "family matters" because of which Proust refused to close his accounts at the Crédit Industriel. But there is a solid chance that such matters were not as whimsical as they appeared to be. The fact that neither Adrien Proust's nor Jeanne Proust's Rothschild portfolios included certain shares inherited by their son Marcel, such as his stash of seventy or eighty de Beers shares, discussed previously, suggests that these shares came to him via a different source[3]—the most likely source being a semiclandestine portfolio that Jeanne Proust held at the Crédit Industriel. I submit, in sum, that, before his death, Louis Weil must have held his de Beers shares as well as others at the Crédit Industriel, and that his heir Jeanne Proust kept them there as well, till they were split in her two sons' separate portfolios after her death. Needless to say, this was a delicate matter of family discretion, since the Rothschild brothers would not have appreciated it, had they come to know that they were not the sole provider of financial services to Louis Weil and his heirs. In this light, Proust would have certainly had plenty of good reasons to feel a special attachment to the Crédit Industriel, even if he was not at liberty to disclose them to Hauser.

The time had meanwhile come to finalize Proust's new line of credit with the London Bank. After Proust signed the contract, Hauser would deposit at the London Bank 31 Suez Canal Bonds, 63 Tunisian government bonds, 50 bonds of the French Railways company in Santa Fé, besides French Treasury notes and French Registered Treasury notes. Furthermore, Hauser would withdraw from the Crédit Industriel the Egyptian Preference and Suez Canal Bonds needed for Proust's loan of securities from nonhostile countries to the Treasury Department (COR XV, 67).

Proust seemed to take Hauser's laborious creation of his new instruments for granted, even though their complexity was detailed for him by the banker in a letter dated June 3, 1916. The next day, rather incongruously, Proust's answer ignored Hauser's efforts altogether and harped instead on the banker's indifference to his feelings.

> My dear Lionel,
>
> . . . Since my eyes get strained easily, I failed to follow up on our recent academic debate about the comparative efficacy of sweetness and violence. The medical area within which you confined yourself supplied my memory with some similarly topical arguments (a patient cured of nervous paralysis by the fear of a rabid dog, a patient killed by the abrupt interruption of morphine, etc.). For the same reason I haven't objected to something that deserves the simple reproach of being incorrect. Example: 'You complain of your ruin to force your entourage to pity you.' I do the exact opposite. And when I talk of my ruin, it's on such a merry tone that a few days ago I found a letter signed by Lionel Hauser who said that I spoke of my material situation with such gaiety that he wondered whether I was well aware of its gravity. My dear friend, I grumble about people dying [in the war], about their sufferings. As to my money losses, the effects of my own stupidity, I regret them very much, but don't talk of them in the elegiac mode. (COR XV, 68)

Hauser could not even find the time to show his disappointment with Proust. He kept shuffling Proust's various portfolios as if they were multiple decks of cards, moving securities to the London Bank, evaluating what forwards contracts Proust could afford to close at a loss in order to decrease his exposure on the market, and instructing the Crédit Industriel not to sell securities owned by Proust, when they could instead liquidate the forwards contracts he held on the same type of securities (COR XV, 69).

Proust is not at his best in these confrontations with his benefactor. Two different personalities begin to emerge out of the correspondence exchanged by him and his banker— increasingly distinct from each other. It is almost as if their respective letters conformed to two canonical types: on the one side, the artist secluded in his ivory tower, ready to sacrifice not only his present well-being for his future artistic work, but also the advantages he could derive from the appreciation and assistance of a friend such as Hauser; on the other side, the pragmatic banker of impeccable integrity, so altruistic that he is willing to disregard his own personal advantage, but who wants to gauge the results of his work in the present moment. From the viewpoint of the artist, who lives in a world of metaphors and aesthetic values, there are intangible duties, responsibilities, and priorities that have absolute precedence over common sense, ordinary decency, and equanimity. In spite of many appearances to the contrary, it would be inaccurate to mistake the behavior informed by this viewpoint with that of an egotistical personality; we know all too well the degree of self-abnegation imposed on Proust by his muse. From the banker's viewpoint, who—even when donning his theosophical hat—lives in a sphere of literal values that are closely adjacent to the sphere of accounting records, a person's decency and equanimity are easy to gauge: "Every man should constantly try to have an open account with . . . his fellow human beings." Every received service ought to be compensated with a service rendered, if we want to break even and pay off all our debts (COR XV, 75).

Having completed the transfer of Proust's debts to the London Bank, Hauser focused his attention on the rest of the writer's finances. Why not get rid of securities whose yield was uncertain in the long run? he asked. This would extinguish another portion of the debt that Proust had just contracted with his new bank. After all, even at a lower interest rate, its cost still weighed considerably on his balance sheet. By getting rid of more of this financial ballast, the shrinkage of Proust's patrimony caused by the sale of securities would be amply compensated by the shrinkage in his interest charges, bringing about a significant increase in his yearly income.

As he made these suggestions, Hauser remarked in passing that Proust held 3.5 Royal Dutch shares in his Rothschild portfolio. The company's new issue (corresponding to a 49 percent capital increase)[4] would therefore give him the right to buy a further 1.1 shares, for a total of 4.6. As if endowed with a momentum of their own, Proust's Royal Dutch shares had been growing slowly yet steadily. This aspect of Proust's Rothschild portfolio must have gone virtually unperceived by Hauser until this point, although he did get a hint of its importance to the writer the previous year, when he had been advised not to "touch" the Royal Dutch shares while consolidating the portfolio. As we noted earlier, by the end of the war, Royal Dutch securities would become the glue holding together the patrimony that Hauser was presently trying to salvage.

Proust learned from Robert de Billy, who queried the managers of the Mirabaud Bank on his behalf, that the Doubowaïa Balka had excellent prospects. The experts predicted a speedy economic recovery in Russia after the war, in spite of the current political turmoil. (We know, of course, that the current turmoil would lead instead to the Bolshevik Revolution and a type of socialist economic growth that eventually undercut the profitability of East European companies). Hauser's farsighted reaction was that Proust's stock of Doubowaïa Balka ought to be sold right away, and, as we saw above, he sold 100 shares by July 21 at a good price. In order to sell Proust's Tramways de Mexico securities, which were currently traded only in London, Hauser came out with one of his fine stratagems: a financial-services firm based in London and affiliated with Hauser et Cie owned a quantity of Tramways de Mexico shares; they would be willing to sell 100 of them on Proust's behalf if he delivered an equal number to their French branch. There was a problem, though: the quotation of Tramways de Mexico was low in London. Instead of making the expected amount of 24,000 francs, Proust would barely earn 15,000 francs from this transaction. He also had to subtract from this sum the cost of the English stamp to be attached to the 100 securities that he would deliver to the financial-services firm in Paris. Hauser's opinion was that Proust ought to sell at the current London price, and the writer agreed (COR XV, 92, 99). This is when the two friends took to congratulating each other using war metaphors.

At the beginning of August, Proust asked Hauser to divert 1,000 francs from the money earmarked for the London Bank; he wanted to send this sum to his landlady, Aunt Amélie. To reach its declared goal, his letter takes a curious detour, indicating that Hauser must have warned Proust from time to time to stay away from the salons of his friends, the demimondaines, and from brothels—two distinct social settings which the banker would have lumped together. If Hauser did not trust him and feared that he might waste this money "on a prostitute," Proust wrote, he could simply transfer the money directly to the current address of his aunt: Madame Denis Weil, Hôtel Splendide, Aix-les-Bains, Savoie. Proust told Hauser that for reasons that would take too long to explain, from time to time he contravened Léon Neuberger's advice not to pay his rent and sent a down payment to his aunt. Like many other members of her social class, Amélie Weil was currently the guest of a vacation resort, far from the dangers of war, and was probably in need of ready cash to pay her hotel bills (COR XV, 112).[5]

In this same letter, as if transfigured into a character worthy of Voltaire's *Candide,* Proust described Providence's munificent ways. He had just signed a letter prepared for him by the Rothschild Bank, addressed to a Monsieur Jordaan. In this letter, Proust instructed Monsieur Jordaan to deliver to the Rothschild Bank "the certificates for 1,100 francs of nominal shares which he had subscribed on Proust's behalf from the Royal Dutch's new issue." This letter, Proust remarked playfully, did not even indicate the quantity of nominal shares that Monsieur Jordaan had purchased on his behalf, not to mention that it had never occurred to him to order this purchase. Moreover, Proust's letter to Monsieur Jordaan asked him to deposit 615 francs, credited to him as a result of this transaction, in his Rothschild account. Proust tried to guess what was behind this mysterious bounty. Perhaps the Royal Dutch shares in his portfolio entitled him to purchase the new issue at a discounted price? Perhaps Monsieur Jordaan was the agent asked by Léon Neuberger to subscribe to the new issue on Proust's behalf? Perhaps Monsieur Jordaan was instructed to keep only a fraction of the new shares acquired by Proust, and to sell the rest at market price to finance the entire transaction? Perhaps the net result was that the Royal Dutch shares in Proust's portfolio had increased to 4.6 shares without the least cost to him, not to mention a profit of 615 francs? It is evident that the answer to all of Proust's guesses was yes. And this was not thanks to a miracle from Divine Providence, as his marveled tone might suggest, but simply the result of Neuberger's sense of timing. Like Hauser, Proust's second guardian angel worked hard, although more discreetly, at safeguarding his interests. "Take the money and don't try to understand," was Hauser's unusually superficial reply. Faced with the Rothschild Bank's all-powerful proficiency, even a brilliant operator like Hauser took shelter in the buoyancy of providential fatalism (COR XV, 112, 113).

Thanks to Hauser's untiring campaign and bright maneuvers (if I may borrow the two friends' flair for war metaphors), by the end of 1916

Proust's patrimony had indeed grown smaller, but his yearly income had increased significantly. His debt with the Crédit Industriel had been fully extinguished. At present he had a credit worth 80,000 francs from his loan of securities to the Treasury Department. And his portfolio with the London Bank held 265,000 francs in first-class securities, most of which were in warranty to the 200,000-franc debt he had contracted a few months earlier, half of which had already been paid off. The bottom line is that Proust's 1916 yearly income amounted to 15,000 francs. In terms of American dollars, during a year that had been disastrous for the finances of most Frenchmen, Proust's income had grown from $49,000 to $52,000.

It was with good reason, then, that in August, Proust complained about the "Lilliputian" commission that Hauser charged him. The following month he compounded this allusion to Jonathan Swift's *Gulliver's Travels* with an allusion to François Rabelais. "I rejoice for the results and regret your very minuscule fees, so that I'm at once smiling and weeping like Rabelais's hero, who is happy thanks to his son Pantagruel and sad because of his wife Badebec. You are a skilled strategist but of a merciless generosity." Disarmingly honest as always, Hauser answered that he would never charge his friend higher tariffs than the ones he charged his other clients. If Proust truly cared to show his gratitude, why did he not put in a good word for the Hauser et Cie firm with those of his friends who were "burdened with a discreet number of millions?" (COR XV, 122, 127)

Proust's answer was sagacious. He explained to Hauser the hardships he had already faced several times in trying to recommend his firm to his wealthy friends. "As you well know, Israel is often at the roots of personal fortunes that are quite eager to forget their own origin." Louis d'Albufera's patrimony came mostly from his wife, a relative of the Heine family, Jewish bankers. The patrimony of Proust's friend Gabriel de La Rochefoucauld also came from his wife, a relative of another branch of the Heine family, who were also bankers. And the mother of Armand, the duke of Guiche, was born a Rothschild. Several members of French aristocracy owed the solidity of their wealth to alliances with Jewish heiresses. If certain families of Jewish high finance consented to make alliances with the Catholic nobility, the Catholic nobility in turn gave up its own financial autonomy in return for greater wealth. In sum, each one of Proust's wealthy friends was tied hands and feet to the bankers of his wife's family. This explained his difficulty in persuading them to become Hauser's clients (COR XV, 125).

Chapter 14

THE CRY OF THE VALKYRIES

War simplified Marcel Proust's world. Provisions and fuel were scarce; firewood was not to be found. Unable to heat up their splendid mansions in Paris or provide themselves with adequate light and food, several of Proust's favorite ladies from the world of high society turned to the Ritz Hotel, where they entertained their party guests. Some of them moved into the hotel altogether while waiting for better times. The worldly epicenter of the Faubourg Saint-Germain, the aristocracy's neighborhood of choice—saturated with invitations, receptions, and soirées—shrank to the parlors, reception rooms, and dining rooms of Paris's most exclusive hotel and restaurant. To Proust, it was like a transition from a bewildering maze, chock-full of possibilities and alternative paths, to a small playground where all routes were fixed; and, above all, where the men and women he sought out to fulfill his need for affection, or those who were the targets of his satirical vein—often the same individuals—were unable to sneak off at his appearance. It was these circumstances, perhaps, that explain the very intense nightlife which filled up a good deal of the year 1917 for the writer.

It is hard to say how Proust was able to find the energy to go out so often, seeing as only a short time before he had been living a cloistered life as a captive to illness, or rather, a captive to a complex and elusive syndrome that no medical diagnosis was able to label in a satisfactory manner. In spite of his intense nightlife, Proust complained endlessly about the poor condition of his heart. He wrote to Hauser about cardiac crises that pushed him "between life and death," and of asthma attacks that turned his breathing into a spasmodic "barking"—so much so that his neighbors thought he must have "bought a church organ or a dog," unless a lady friend of his had given birth in his apartment to "a baby sick with whooping cough" (COR XVI, 25, 33). At this time, he was working on the galley proofs for the novel's second volume, the publication of which was destined to be delayed until the end of the war.

Nonetheless, he was indefatigable in his quest for nocturnal company. He often met with Antoine Bibesco, Reynaldo Hahn, Paul Morand and his irresistible lover, Princess Soutzo (Hélène, née Chrisoveloni)—a woman he met for the first time in March 1917, and whom he immediately put under siege with awkwardly passionate love letters.

His entourage at the Ritz Hotel also included Bibesco's lover, Princess Marie Murat (née de Rohan-Chabot), the woman whose ridiculous claims to a rank superior to blue-blooded nobility (as opposed to her imperial or Napoleonic title) Proust would mock in his pastiche "From Saint-Simon's *Memoirs*."[1] Marie Scheikévitch, a Russian exile in financial straits, whom Proust—the eternal Candide—wanted to help with the proceeds from the sale of some bits of old furniture and carpets, also figured prominently among the friends with whom the writer frequently associated. Scheikévitch was eleven years his junior, which added to her attractiveness (COR XVI, 21, 164). His cardiac crises came punctually after his soirées at the Ritz, and at times he would leave abruptly for fear of a sudden attack.

In December 1917, Paul Morand was assigned to the French embassy in Rome. His lover and future wife, Hélène Soutzo, was thus poised to suffer the pains of separation. Proust applied the flowchart of waning love that he had been refining since Agostinelli's death—and which would be applied to Albertine's death in his novel—to Soutzo's changed situation. As you may recall, there is a progression of phases to this schema. First, the absence of the beloved (owing to death, separation, or abandonment) is accompanied by the lover's obsessive grief. Then comes jealousy, followed by the gradual diminution in the lover's fondness for the beloved. Later on, love's incremental depletion goes hand in hand with the progressive extinction of the lover's enamored *moi,* or self. And last, the demise of the enamored self brings about the emergence of a new self, whose remembrance of the loved one has biographic rather than affective significance. For Proust, in sum, we cannot help but reconcile ourselves to the ending of all love affairs, regardless of how passionate and tempestuous they were; slowly but surely, we console ourselves for our loss and eventually engage in a completely new affair.

Proust attended Morand's farewell party at the Ritz, but soon had to take his leave, overwhelmed perhaps by the inexorable verdict of his vision for the future: Hélène Soutzo would get over the pain of separation from Morand and then start looking around for a new lover. Who would this fortunate mortal be? Proust himself, perhaps?

The day after the farewell party, Proust wrote a letter to Soutzo, expanding on the inescapable withering of our affections whenever they are worn out by distance or absence. "A Proust unknown to himself" will soon see the light, he wrote, and this new man "will easily learn to do without Morand." He left the princess the simple task of applying this parable to herself and drawing the due consequences. "The Proust of today is not like that yet," he reassured her, laying it on thicker with an implied analogy between a friend's heart and a lover's heart: "I have never loved Morand as much as I love him today."[2] The rest of his letter consisted of a clumsy declaration of love: "My affection for you has become a pain whose intensity only my Céleste has been able to gauge" (COR XVI, 170). (As Proust's closest friends were by this time aware, Céleste Albaret had also come gradually to perform the role of confidant.)

It was not the first time that Proust had become openly infatuated with a woman who was intimate with one of his best friends. The same thing happened to him with Bibesco's lover, Princess Murat (in spite of her misplaced aristocratic pretensions). It also happened in his youth with Jeanne Pouquet, the girlfriend of one of his best friends at the time, Gaston de Caillavet, who married her in 1892. Jeanne Pouquet was underage at the beginning of her relationship with Caillavet, and Proust helped to shield the two illegitimate lovers from attention by enacting a pretended courtship that soon became suspiciously intense.[3] Moreover, we have evidence of Proust's persistent courtship of the mothers of two of the boys with whom he had been infatuated at the Lycée Condorcet: Léontine de Caillavet in Gaston de Caillavet's case, and Geneviève Straus in Jacques Bizet's case. It would seem as if Proust was more comfortable playing the role of the lovesick suitor than being the man in charge[4]—an attitude not unrelated to that "troublesome . . . something" mentioned above, a constitutive element of Proustian sexuality which the novel's Narrator passes deliberately under silence, and which we shall grapple with later on.

Near the end of July 1917, on the 27th of the month according to *Le Figaro*, the first enemy fighter plane was sighted in the Paris sky. Until then, the German army had only used dirigibles—the infamous zeppelins—in raids on the French capital. The anticraft artillery went on attack and Proust, the night owl, who was taking part in a spiritualist séance at the Ritz, did not miss the opportunity to watch the spectacle from a balcony. He described it in a letter addressed the next day to Geneviève Straus.

> Madame,
>
> . . . I couldn't tell you whether [the fighter planes] took to the right or the left of Cassiopeia,[5] I only know that I caught a cold[6] because I went out on the balcony and lingered outdoors for longer than an hour to see this admirable Apocalypse in which the airplanes going up and down shuffled and reshuffled the constellations in our sky. If this had just had the effect of making us lift our eyes to the sky, it would've been quite beautiful in itself, so wonderful it was. What was extraordinary is that, as in the painting by El Greco which shows the heavenly scene in the upper part and the earthly scene in the lower part, while from the Balcony one could look at this sublime "Crowded Sky," downstairs it looked as if the Ritz Hotel (where all of this was going on) had become the Free Exchange Hotel.[7] There were women wearing their nightshirts and even their bathrobes who wandered through the 'vaulted' passageways under the weight of pearl necklaces which they clasped against their breasts. (COR XVI, 97)

Proust's reference to El Greco's painting should persuade even the more obstinate reader of the writer's eye for scathing social satire. Proust's letter is referring to the 1588 *Burial of Count d'Orgaz* (COR XVI, 97 [note 13]), which is split in two sections by a vaulted arcade of clouds; in the upper heavenly part, preparations are made for the arrival of the soul of the saintly man, the Count d'Orgaz, while in the lower earthly part, the count's funeral is overseen by the incarnated souls of Saint Augustine and Saint Stephen (see illus. 5). Proust has no qualm in comparing El Greco's picture of paradise with the clash of flying war machines in a Parisian night sky which, pierced by searchlights, he calls "sublime." And he compares the corridors of the Ritz Hotel, which the curfew makes as dark as a gloomy Spanish funeral of the sixteenth century, with the squalid stage for *Free Exchange Hotel,* a comedy of mistaken identities; from his elevated vantage point, the writer may observe, unobserved, the hotel's rich clients who, wandering abashedly under the hotel's vaulted passageways, fearful of looting, show their true colors.

El Greco, *Burial of Count d'Orgaz* (1588),
Parroquia de Santo Tomé, Toledo, Spain. Alinari / Art Resource, N.Y.

Nothing was lost in the catalogue of accidents and events that punctuated Proust's social life. The episode of this attack from the air found its place, duly adapted, in the pages of *In Search of Lost Time*—in the last volume, to be exact, *Finding Time Again.* This detail belies the critics who reacted to the appearance of the first few volumes of Proust's novel by accusing him of lacking control over the freewheeling impulse of his disorderly recollections. The contrary evidence is instead that, at the time when he was correcting the galley proofs of his first two volumes, in which he set down the principles for his philosophy of existence, Proust had already been working for years on the last volume, in which all these principles are taken to their logical conclusion.

In *Finding Time Again,* the attack from the air occurs one year earlier, in 1916. The airplane described in *Le Figaro* of July 28, 1917, is substituted by the fleet of zeppelins that in 1916 made fierce raids on Paris, and only in January 1918 were systematically replaced by the German fighter planes called *gothas* (COR XVII, 34). From his balcony at night, the city of Paris appears to the novel's Narrator as an enormous moving beast, shapeless and black. Woken by the screams of the anti-aircraft sirens, the city becomes fully alive, aims the piercing eyes of its searchlights at the sky, and unleashes squadron after squadron of fighter planes. The aviators scour the sky, suddenly more crowded than the city streets, like a wild band of Valkyries. The Narrator gives a description of this spectacle to his friend Robert de Saint-Loup, soon to die on the battlefield, who is taking a short leave in Paris. Saint-Loup remarks that there is something Wagnerian to the sound of the alarm sirens—which is only to be expected, he adds, since they meet the German invader with their cries.[8] Owing to the anti-German sentiment prevalent in Parisian artistic circles at this time, Saint-Loup concludes wittily, "obviously the Germans have to come before we can hear Wagner in Paris" (*Finding Time Again,* 66).[9]

Proust's nightlife did not slacken in the least in spite of curfews and air raids. At the beginning of the war, the mobilization of Parisian men "had . . . created a vacuum in Paris," but in 1917 the streets were crowded with soldiers from all armies and all nations. This was especially true at night, when ordinary citizens kept to their houses or took cover in air-raid shelters, and the streets and boulevards were full of exotic soldiers of many ethnic groups, their colorful uniforms turning Paris into "a town as cosmopolitan as a port." The French capital became the Sodom of homosexual individuals, an ideal cruising ground for Proust's character, the Baron de Charlus. This is perhaps another reason for Proust's restlessness at night. Compounded metaphors taken from the classics abound in the fictional transpositions of his nightly sallies: Paris is the biblical Sodom and Socrates' Athens, and it becomes Pompey, city of sin, whenever a new air raid forces people perfectly unknown to one another to take shelter in the pitch-black passageways of the métro: tunnels "as dark as catacombs," where "darkness . . . has the effect, irresistibly tempting to some, of suppressing the first stage of pleasure and allowing us immediate access to a realm of caresses which normally we reach only after some time" (*Finding Time Again,* 71, 108, 142).[10]

Most of the strange and unreliable rumors that have come down to us about Proust's monstrous sexual perversions, having to do with caged rats, exhibitionism, and what not, sprout from this period in the writer's life. I will have to say a little more about this later on, but, be reassured, it will not be much; this is not that kind of book. What we know for certain, from many of Proust's letters, is that he scorned the safety of his own apartment, and did not even know how to reach the cellars of his apartment building, which had been turned into a bomb shelter. He often spent the night walking through this strange new nocturnal world, no less fantastic and outrageous than the one described in his great novel.

The fervor of Proust's nightlife increased in inverse proportion to the slowdown in civilian life. Work was languishing at Hauser et Cie, which army conscription had emptied of all its male personnel. Lionel Hauser could thus afford to devote some of his time to his passions for theosophy, philanthropy, and the arts. Since the offices of his firm were partly unoccupied, Hauser gave permission to René Schwaller, a leading figure among Parisian theosophists, to conduct his alchemical experiments there; Hauser even financed these experiments with a regular money allowance. And when Hauser's friend José Villegas Cordero, a Spanish painter and the director of the Prado Museum in Madrid, opened an exhibit of paintings on biblical subjects at the Jeu de Paume on May 9, 1917, the banker promoted it on his behalf. He wrote of it to Proust (COR XVI, 6, 53), who answered in equally enthusiastic terms, not so much because he was taken with Villegas's work (he confused the painter with a sculptor, proving that he did not bother going to the show), as because he was thrilled by the tenor of Hauser's letter, which dealt with aesthetic rather than financial matters.

> My dear Lionel,
> . . . Pascal spoke of the pleasure we feel when we are in search of an Author and we find a man instead. The pleasure is no less vivid in finding out that behind the banker there is an artist, and an artist-philosopher on top of that. . . . This is to tell you how well I understand that Michelangelo's *Moses* interests you more than currency exchange, and how I think more highly of you for thus being the *homo duplex* who does not keep within the narrow confines of his job, but roams in that space which opens

> onto infinity, and to which Montaigne assigned the excessively modest name of backshop. (COR XVI, 60, and 60 [note 5])

Faithful to the game of learned allusions that patterned their correspondence, Proust was referring here to the thirty-ninth essay by Michel de Montaigne, "On solitude" ("De la solitude"), in which the essayist argues that "we must have a private laboratory, wholly unencumbered ["*franche*"], for our private use, where we can establish our true liberty and our main site of retreat and solitude."[11]

No sooner did Proust hear rumors about the war's positive effects on the value of shipping-company securities than he started planning new financial speculation. In a letter that was bound to leave Hauser speechless with surprise, Proust produced out of his magician's top hat a long list of maritime insurance companies, whose securities, inherited from his father Adrien Proust's Rothschild portfolio in 1904,[12] were held in his own Rothschild portfolio. From this we can deduce that, until this time, Proust had not shared the composition of his Rothschild portfolio with Hauser in its entirety. The most significant names on the list were Sécurité, Équinox, Comptoir Maritime, Mélusine, and Prévoyante. Proust wanted to know what he should do with these securities. Should he take advantage of the favorable market and sell them? (He sold part of them eventually; illus. 6 shows what was left of them at Proust's death.) In the same letter, which dates to about the beginning of May 1917, Proust resolved to make available to Hauser all his bank statements from his Rothschild account, because he needed the banker's help in filing the new complex tax return.

Hauser was hesitant at the prospect of taking up a new initiative involving Proust's Rothschild portfolio, since, less than two years earlier, Hauser et Cie had orchestrated the withdrawal of 160,000 francs in securities from it. To the protocol of nonintrusion, which the Rothschild Bank's officers forced Proust's bankers, Hauser included, to carry out uncomplainingly, must be added the consideration that his uncle Léon Neuberger was close to retirement age, causing a reshuffling in the ranks of the bank's executive officers. If Proust was slow in grasping the reason for Hauser's hesitancy, soon he promoted it nonetheless with an infelicitous remark: perhaps Hauser was not well acquainted with these securities? Perhaps "his trans-oceanic gaze [swept] over much too wide an expanse to notice these sea-bound companies?" If this was the case, Proust would have the alternative option of consulting Léon Dubois-Amiot, his brother Robert's father-in-law, for whom "anything related with speculation ha[d] no secrets." Instead of putting Hauser's back to the wall, these words enabled the banker to excuse himself from an unpleasant task. He would never dare compete with an expert of the caliber of Robert Proust's father-in-law, he wrote sedately to Proust. However, he would be glad to take a close look at the unexpurgated list of Proust's holdings in the Rothschild portfolio, he added.

From this letter, we learn that two months previously Proust had not pursued his original plan to file his tax return with Hauser's help, which would have required that he show the banker his statements from the Rothschild Bank. Proust explained that he had been afraid of "bothering" Hauser with the triviality of these fiscal matters; and in fact he even neglected to ask Hauser to update the fiscal data concerning his own assets at Hauser et Cie. He resorted instead to the solution of sending his Rothschild statements to the tax inspector, failing to mention his account at Hauser et Cie altogether. He did so on the presumption (more fanciful than delinquent, since his Warburg portfolio was indeed tiny) that his utter transparency with regard to the assets held in his Rothschild portfolio would offset his omission with regard to those in the Warburg portfolio (COR XVI, 5, 59, 79).

The previous March, Proust had notified his "Spiritual Father for Financial Matters" of an important development, apologizing for a delay that was due to a cardiac crisis that, he added in a composed tone, cut his weight down to 99 pounds (or 44.9 kilos: the greatest living writer is gradually reducing himself to a creature of pure thought, the ectoplasm from a spiritualistic séance!). This was the subject of Proust's letter: after a lottery draw, 20 Chinese Treasury securities, held in his Rothschild portfolio, had been redeemed by China's Treasury Department at their initial cost of 500 francs each; the sum of 10,000 francs had been credited to his Rothschild account. "Is this a good thing or a bad thing?" Proust asked (COR XVI, 25). It was indeed a stroke of luck: according to the *Journal Financier,* these bonds were traded at 460 francs each, so Proust had just earned an extra 800 francs on their market value (COR XVI, 25 [note 4]).

In wondering what he should do with this money, Proust said that he would not mind giving it all to his aunt in order to pay off his overdue rent. Hauser's opinion was that he should deposit it all at the London Bank, thereby saving 550 francs a year on interest charges. But then Hauser noticed a negative balance in the statement from one of Proust's accounts at the Crédit Industriel, so in the end, they decided that these

10,000 francs would be split between this bank and the London Bank, and Proust's Aunt Amélie would still be left waiting for the money owed her. First though, Proust wrote, he would have to pass "under the caudine forks of the Rothschild Bank," where the money still resided. As a rule, the Rothschild brothers never transferred money out of their safes, so as "to make it clear that they [were] not a lending institution but a bank, and a bank, on top of it, that [had] only friends among its clients" (COR XVI, 25–27, 29, 31).

The unexpected news of Proust's negative balance with the Crédit Industriel exacerbated Hauser's annoyance about the two accounts that remained open there. It had become clear to him by this time that nothing positive would come of insisting that Proust completely shut down his dealings with this bank. But he saw no harm in watering down all of the writer's engagements with the Crédit Industriel, one by one, as a way of reaching the same goal by different means. A tactic that may remind us of certain marital conflicts, in which a spouse who agrees to a sequence of apparently unrelated decisions, is eventually brought face to face with the accomplished fact of his or her defeat. At this stage in their epistolary and financial relationship, Proust and Hauser had indeed carved out the space of an idyll at a distance, one that was structured around all the conflicts and reconciliations typical of conjugal life. Which explains why Hauser could not possibly prevail. Who does not count among their acquaintances one of those litigious married couples in whose quarrels, no matter how tenaciously and persuasively a sound point of view is put forward, it is the obstinacy of temperament that carries the day in the long run? In spite of Hauser's determination, then, we should not be surprised to learn that at Proust's death in November 1922, the Crédit Industriel still counted the writer among its faithful clients.

But at this point, Hauser wanted to chip away at the holdings: it was imperative, he wrote Proust, that he get rid of "the acrid aftertaste left by [his] financial orgies" and unload the contract on the 100 Tramways de Mexico shares which he held at the Crédit Industriel, even if it sold at a loss (the further 100 units of this stock in his portfolio had been bought cash-down). Proust's answer reminds us that he was at work on the galley proofs of *In the Shadow of Young Girls in Flowers,* the second volume of his novel, and particularly on the theme of Charles Swann's amorous disillusionment: "Traded securities are like old mistresses," he wrote to Hauser. "We love them precisely because of the fits of anger they have given us, and we live in the hope of better days to come" (COR XVI, 35, 36).

In the novel's first volume, Charles Swann at first experiences indifference toward Odette; later he succumbs to infatuation—she is a work of art to this art appreciator, as gorgeous as a portrait by Botticelli; then he yields to excruciating suspicion about her unfaithfulness and unreliable apathy; finally he goes down on his knees, eager to devour the crumbs of meager devotion that Odette is willing to pass down to him.

In the second volume, *In the Shadow of Young Girls in Flowers,* Swann finds peace at last in his marriage to Odette, through which he auctions off his longing for the impossible possession of Odette's heart, and secures in return the contractual possession of her physical being. An analogous de facto possession intervenes in the relationship between Proust's Narrator and Albertine, when she moves in with him in Paris. Soon the mystery of her abrasive sensuality, desultory and overpowering at once when he first met her in Balbec, gets deflated and domesticated—sweeter in its reliable steadiness, true, but depleted at the same time of its original cravings, even frankly boring at times. In the end, their caged mistresses less and less causative of the sexual longings they used to inflame, both Swann and the Narrator acquiesce to living, in the words of Proust's letter to Hauser, "in the hope of better days to come."

Proust lived fully immersed in the fantastic world of his characters and drew practical lessons from their fictitious experiences. The defaulting pathos of both Swann's and his Narrator's unhappy loves taught him that there comes a moment when the lover, or—sticking to his simile between mistresses and securities—the stock-exchange trader must accept defeat and cut his losses. Hence, he acknowledged with Hauser that his Mexican securities had to go. "Some time ago I gave up hope of ever seeing a golden sun shine again over the land of Ferdinando Cortez [the conqueror of Mexico] and 'new stars emerge from the depths of the ocean.'" Proust and Hauser had been debating for years about the likelihood of Mexico's becoming a stable U.S. ally or even a state in the U.S. federation, thereby causing an automatic rise in the value of Mexican securities. In the elegant phrasing Proust used to express his sacrifice of this hope, Hauser was probably able to recognize an allusion to "The Conquerors," a poem on Columbus's journey to the Americas by the Cuban-born French poet José-Maria de Heredia:

> Bent on the prow of white caravels,
> They watched new stars leave the depths of the Ocean

And make their way up into a sky unknown. (COR XVI, 36, 36 [note 6])

At the end of June, Hauser "unchained a violent offensive"—the last of 1917—and sold 65 shares of the Banco Español del Río de la Plata and 19 of Doubowaïa Balka, both at decent prices. Proust reacted with a tribute, as he wrote, to "the special virtue you are endowed with, whereby no sooner do you touch my Doubowaïa Balka than they rise in value, just as the heat of the sun has the virtue of making the level of mercury rise in a tube (and in the same way, the friendly zeal you show in these kind actions makes the warmth of my gratitude rise too)" (COR XVI, 85).

Evidence of Proust's warm feelings toward Hauser is found in the New Year's card he sent him at the end of 1917, the only such card we find among the writer's collected letters. On January 1, 1918, Proust sent a letter to Hélène Soutzo, congratulating Paul Morand's lover for her return to good health (after an appendectomy), and a letter to Morand as well, rejoicing in the successful surgery and the return of the princess's flourishing beauty. But one finds no traces of conventional season's greetings in the 1917 volume of Proust's *Correspondance*—except for the one card he sent to the discreet and dutiful man who kept him on the safe side of financial ruin, thereby sheltering him from the ostracism of high society. Without the work of Hauser behind the scene of Proust's worldly life, the sincerity of the writer's high-ranking friends would have been put to a harsh test (COR XVI, 194; XVII, 1, 2).

At the end of 1917, thanks to Hauser's restructuring of his debt and portfolios, Proust's patrimony held out well in spite of the war. The fact must not be overlooked, however, that inflation had risen to 23 percent, undermining Hauser's effectiveness and gnawing away a huge slice of Proust's income, which in real terms remained the same as one year earlier. In the meantime, the French currency had lost 42 percent in value with respect to the American currency, so Proust's real income decreased from $52,000 in 1916 to $30,000 in 1917. These were hard times even for somebody who enjoyed the protection of a guardian angel of Lionel Hauser's standing.

Chapter 15

THE MISTRUST OF FRIENDSHIP

This is what Proust writes of friendship in *Le côté de Guermantes*:

> It has never failed to surprise me that a man [such as Nietzsche] whose degree of self-honesty even led him to cut himself off from Wagner's music out of scruples of conscience could have imagined that truth can be attained by the mode of expression, intrinsically vague and inadequate, represented by . . . friendship. . . . [Friendship] is totally bent on making us sacrifice the only part of ourselves that is real and incommunicable (except through art) to a superficial self that, unlike the other, finds no joy on its own; what it finds instead is a vague, sentimental satisfaction at being cherished by external support, hospitalized in the individuality of another person, where, in gratitude for the protection afforded by this, it radiates approval of its well-being and marvels at qualities it would castigate as failings and seek to correct in himself. . . . But, whatever my view of friendship, to mention only the pleasure it procured me, so mediocre in quality that it seemed to fall halfway between fatigue and boredom, there is no potion so deadly that it cannot in certain circumstances become precious and restorative by providing us with just the boosts and the warmth we are unable to muster of our own accord. (*Guermantes Way*, 390–91)[1]

How badly Proust needed the strength of purpose that he found in his friends rather than in himself! The friendships he cultivated during the war years were at one and the same time an inspiring spur and a demanding obstacle to his work. Every night he spent at the Ritz, every visit he received in his bedroom, every letter he wrote widened the neck of the sand-glass through which ran the fistful of months, years at most, that were left him to complete his masterpiece—as he foresaw clearly by this time. He wrote to Gide in January 1918, apologizing for being unable to receive him: "In my state of health I must not waste any time, all the more given that my manuscripts are hard to decipher . . . and if I died, nobody would make head or tail out of them." He was still working on the galley proofs of the second volume of *In Search of Lost Time.* For more than a month the printing press had told him that they could not send him any new proofs because they were short of typographers; they then changed their tune, claiming that they had already sent him all the proofs. Proust had entrusted them with a copybook with more than one-third of the next volume in it, and kept sending them copybook after copybook. There were no fair copies for any of these writings. Could he trust the people at the printing press? What if his work got lost? (COR XVII, 17)

Four months after this letter to Gide, he confided to a friend, the writer Lucien Daudet (son of the author of *Tartarin de Tarascon,* and brother of Léon Daudet, the dedicatee of *The Guermantes Way* in 1920), that he "kill[ed] himself" working on the galley proofs, and then sent the corrected proofs to the printing press; the typographers made new proofs from his corrections, erasing whole chunks of text that had been inserted into the previous proofs. "And I must start all over again!" (COR XVII, 64)

Friendships had a debilitating effect on Proust. Hélène Soutzo's illness had forced him to adapt to the visiting hours prescribed by her doctor, conflicting with the punishing timetable imposed on him by his daily intermittent seizures. And his own illness "took its revenge, like the swing of a pendulum." While the princess had recovered, it was now Proust who had become unwell (COR XVII, 6, 17). Over time, he learned that in moments of mental or physical discomfort, he should not expect to be treated with equal attentiveness by Hélène Soutzo, whose closeness had become precious to him. A little later, by the month of October, a break occurred in his friendship with the princess. The pretexts she came up with, in order not to meet with him, Proust wrote her in a letter, were no less predictable than the German army's tactic for surrounding their enemy, unfailingly adopted at every battle. Although Proust had more than one reason to criticize her lofty disposition, their break was not provoked by him, but rather by Soutzo herself and her lover Morand, both of whom had grown tired of Proust's company. However, in the winter months, Proust's correspondence with Soutzo was still frequent and brilliant. He wrote to her near the end of winter, on March 9, 1918:

> Princess,
> . . . I do not talk of the war with you. Alas, I have absorbed so much of it that I cannot pull it away from myself anymore: I cannot talk of the hopes and fears it fills me with any better than one can talk of feelings that are so deeply rooted that one cannot distinguish them from oneself. War is not so much an object for me (in the philosophical sense of the word) as a substance standing between me and the objects. Just as [in days of old] people used to love in God, so I live in the war." (COR XVII, 66, 174)

And to stay on the safe side, in case Soutzo was not too fluent in theological jargon, he added right away: "You know, those neuralgias one never stops being aware of while talking of other things, even while sleeping."

In July 1918, Hélène Soutzo left Paris for her holiday in Biarritz without giving Proust her address there,[2] and Proust's lonely dinners at the Ritz became "the ridiculous and aberrant form" of his worship for her. He sensed the cooling off in their friendship, and tried to remedy it by means of the one skill at which he excelled like no one else, that of exquisite writing. In one of his letters, he told her of the pinnacles of love towering over the wreckage of his heart. "It's as if certain feelings—like certain illnesses—had the inherent power to cling to certain stones. There are also feelings for which this comes very naturally, such as jealousy, for instance. I had no idea I was my own prophet when I described Swann after the end of his love for Odette." In his begging for the princess's benevolence, Proust could not threaten her more openly than by means of this analogy between the extinction of Swann's love and the agony of his own. Proust went on: "[Swann finds himself] suffering a new spell of jealousy, not exactly caused by Odette, but rather by his suspicion of what she might have done in a certain house [on a certain day]." He is alluding to the house the door of which Swann knocks at repeatedly in vain one afternoon, fearing that Odette might be hiding inside in the company of Monsieur de Forcheville. Several years after this episode, Swann still rediscovers "the surviving figments" of his late persona as Odette's lover, in the jealousy triggered by his recollection of that faraway day, that hour, and that house. He will die without knowing that his suspicions were correct.[3] "To put it more simply," Proust concluded, "I keep going to the Ritz like a cat that rubs itself every day against the chaise longue which his mistress used to lie on in the past" (COR XVII, 135).

Yet, for all her lofty fickleness, Hélène Soutzo did not use up a disproportionate amount of Proust's time and health, since the writer himself volunteered to sacrifice some more of both to one of her avatars, Marie Scheikévitch. One year previously, a small yet steady stream of funds from Russia had enabled Madame Scheikévitch to give the cold shoulder to Proust's offer of economic help—admittedly, a clumsy offer, based on his unrealistic and still pending project of selling some carpets and furniture. But at this time, her funds had dried up after the advent of the Bolshevik Revolution; she must have been in quite a tight spot when Proust learned, to his great dismay, that she was considering finding herself a salaried job. This was an unthinkable idea in Proust's opinion, who contrived to find a solution for his friend that was both generous and ridiculous. "Decidedly, Lenin's regime is not conducive to your personal comfort," he wrote to her. Decidedly, after the efforts and social chameleonism it had taken him (even if he would never admit it) to gain admission to the exclusive circles of the Faubourg Saint-Germain, he found it unacceptable that 129 years after the French Revolution, the heads of another great branch of European aristocracy would fall again—even if, strictly speaking, Scheikévitch's family did not belong to Russian aristocracy.

This was the bright idea Proust came up with, as a remedy for the damages which Vladimir Lenin had caused his attractive friend. Since Scheikévitch had close ties with the editorial offices of *Le Temps,* he suggested that she should ask them to entrust her with a daily column. Proust was envisaging something simple, a column devoted to sundry facts, such as "road kills or things of the sort." Then he would write her daily column in her stead, so that on top of getting paid with no personal involvement, she could keep "meeting her friends and dreaming in front of her flowers." For his part, Proust would enjoy the reward of knowing he was "working on her behalf" (COR XVII, 21, 22).

Even when distant and unengaged, the affectionate regard of a beautiful woman friend must have had a tremendously stimulating effect on Proust. It seemed to give him the energetic strength of purpose that he was not always able to find within himself. Overburdened by his interminable novel, ensnared by the interminable jumble of his galley proofs, and incessantly diseased, he still had the courage and imagination to come up with such self-destructive ideas as the plan to write Marie Scheikévitch's daily column for free, or to sacrifice the fragile balance of his daily and nightly schedule to the pretensions of Hélène Soutzo. Furthermore, Proust was painfully aware that his altruistic deeds would benefit people whose virtues, were they his own, he might choose to consider shortcomings and do his utmost to eliminate. This was the onerous yet animated role that friendship played in the writer's life. Like "old mistresses," like addictive stocks and bonds, a few rare friends gave and gave, asking little in return (as was the case with Lionel Hauser and would soon be the case with Jacques Rivière, his energetic and enthusiastic editor at the NRF), while most others made intrusive, insolent claims on Proust's time, money, health, and sense of personal identity (COR XVI, 36). Which leads us to Henri Rochat.

Chapter 16

ENTER HENRI ROCHAT

Proust's *amitié particulière* for Henri Rochat began about the end of 1918. Born in Switzerland, Rochat was a staff member at the Ritz, where Proust met him. Rochat, who soon moved in with Proust, did not have the intellectual finesse or the spiritual refinement of Alfred Agostinelli. Along with sensual fulfillment, he brought emotional turmoil to Proust's life. In a December 1918 letter to Jean Cocteau, who had solicited an article from Proust for the journal *Sirène,* the writer described "the awful spiritual and material life" that had taken the place of "the calm illness I loved." To Geneviève Straus he wrote of "dead-ends and joyless sentimental matters, perpetual sources of fatigue, pain, and absurd expenses" (COR XVII, 204).

Rochat was a leech on both his soul and his wallet. For example, the same month of his letter to Cocteau, Proust bribed the hotel manager at the Ritz with 200 francs ($525) in exchange for closing his eyes on a day of unjustified leave that Rochat had taken. The previous January, Proust still felt he could find the time and energy to write a frivolous daily column on behalf of Marie Scheikévitch; twelve months later, his friend Rochat had managed to drain his meager strength to the point that he found himself unable to comply even with Cocteau's request for a few extemporaneous pages. Notice that this is the same writer who in later years, once rid of Rochat, would excel at placing all his recent and not-so-recent articles in journals and newspapers, and in some cases even manage to have the same piece published simultaneously in more than one venue.

Proust's letters to Hauser during this period swarmed with references to the dinner parties he attended "here and there"; or at least this was

Hauser's impression. Understandably for someone who was unaware of the writer's tortuous relationship with the experience of friendship, the banker wondered why he and his wife were not included in Proust's inner circle of friends. "Why them and not us?" Hauser asked Proust in December 1918. Proust had but to give them a day, a time—and even a menu in case he was on a diet—and he and his wife would gladly comply with his instructions (COR XVII, 213).

In his answer, Proust made it clear that his letters did not list society gatherings that he attended, but rather the invitations he received, and which he duly declined. He made only one exception. He was well known in "certain hotels," where they served him any night he made an appearance, and the waiters waited patiently for him to be done with his "six cups of coffee," even if the lights had already been turned off. He was referring to the Ritz, of course; but also to the Crillon Hotel. Patronized especially by American expatriates, the Crillon did not enforce the curfew as rigorously as the Ritz, which stood right in front of the Ministry of Justice. After dining at the Crillon, Proust was able to stay on and work on his galley proofs until very late, with nobody around to bother him, since his friends were all at the Ritz. As mentioned earlier, the Ritz Hotel was where some of his lady friends had elected to stay as wartime residents: when they gave dinner parties, Proust explained to Hauser, they sent him an invitation to join them, because they were well aware that he would probably take his meal out in any case. Such social occasions were therefore the opposite of attending dinner parties "here and there." By all means, Proust added, he would be more than ready to compromise and dine with Hauser. But the cliché he adopted to express his eagerness was rather worn-out: "By doing a favor to you, I would do myself a greater one." As soon as he felt a little better, he would have Céleste Albaret give Hauser a call to invite the banker to join him at 8:15 in the evening at "whichever Ritz may suit them." (There was only one Ritz in Proust's Paris, of course.) The invitation would be only for Hauser, though, and not for his wife Jeanne, Proust specified awkwardly, since he would not dare to subject a lady to "such an impromptu rendezvous." If he and Hauser met from 8:45 to 10:30 P.M., they could have a nice chat, and afterwards Proust could still go back home to do some more writing or work on his galley proofs (COR XVII, 215).

Hauser's answer was a courteous masterpiece of negative diplomacy. Pretending not to notice his wife's exclusion from Proust's plan, he replied they would be glad to receive his phone call.

> My dear Marcel,
>
> . . . Since we dine at seven in the evening and are therefore done by eight, I don't find it very practical to start eating again at eight thirty nor would I want to postpone our meal until then, because, since our meeting is meant to be a chat together, I don't see how this pleasure would be enhanced by ingesting some victuals cooked in a more or less artificial manner (as is the case with the fare served in restaurants patronized by chic customers). . . . This won't stop the two of us from keeping you company and tasting a cup of tea as we listen to you, on condition however that this does not take place at the Ritz or a similar establishment, where I haven't set foot since the war began, except when I found myself forced to do so. (COR XVII, 218)

Or even better, he added, why should they not make things easier for themselves by meeting at his place—actually not at his residence, because his apartment was on the fifth floor and he would not want to impose five flights of stairs on Proust, but at his office, where Proust could join him and his wife after dinner? "While we talk, we might end up discovering an ordinary restaurant in the neighborhood, where they serve modest dishes no more than twice as expensive as before the war" (Ibid.). Entrenched like two regiments on their respective positions, needless to say, the two friends did not carry out this plan to meet in person.

By this time, Proust could not be unaware of the fact that Hauser's attitude toward friendship went against the stream as much as his own did. As we saw, on December 31, 1917, Proust had sent a greeting card to Hauser. Three days later Hauser had reciprocated Proust's good wishes in a rather unusual way: "I've often wondered about the origin of New Year's wishes and come to the conclusion that this venerable institution must go back to a time when human beings were so virtuous that they had a considerably positive balance in the checking account given them by God." For this reason, when they wished happiness to a friend, it was as if they signed a check in his name, and this check was immediately honored. "Unfortunately things have changed," he went on. Everybody was now heavily indebted to God, and their checks bounced, with rare exceptions. Hauser was in any case pleased that Proust had taken advantage of the New Year to express his affection, all the more so since Hauser had done the same thing with his three hundred or so friends for twenty years in a row. He had stopped sending cards at the beginning of the war, but no more than half a dozen friends had noticed his silence and attempted to find out if he was still doing fine. Had he still nourished any illusions at that point on the meaning of friendship, this indifference would have wounded him. "By my great luck it's been many years since I gave up expecting anything good from anybody except myself" (COR XVII, 5).

Promptly, Proust borrowed Hauser's idea of the impalpable "checking account" and twisted it his own way for *In the Shadow of Young Girls in Flowers.* We read here of the "professional mannerism of a lady of the Faubourg Saint-Germain [such as Madame de Villeparisis, who] takes full advantage while she can of any opportunities to have the account books of her friendly relation with [certain middle-class people] record in advance a credit balance," so that when she is rude to them, "it shall be without qualm" (*Young Girls in Flower,* 304).[1]

If there is a bland form of misanthropy, self-protective to an obvious extent, in Hauser's spite for his friends' bouncing checks, I find it more deplorable than the misanthropy which Proust had embraced at least ten years earlier, in defense of his artistic integrity. In a passage from *Contre Sainte-Beuve,* destined to remain unpublished in Proust's lifetime, we read:

> In reality, what we give to the public is what we write in solitude, for ourselves; we do indeed become our own work of art ["l'oeuvre de soi"]. . . . What we give to intimacy, I mean, to conversation . . . is the work of a much more superficial self, peripheral to the deep self that we can only encounter by keeping away from everybody else and from the self who knows them as well, the self that we wait for while we are in the company of others, and which we know for certain is our only real one, the only self that artists end up living for, like a god that they part from less and less, and to whom they have sacrificed a life whose only aim is to honor it. (224)

Hauser sees friends as permanently indebted to one another. To Proust, we are indebted only to our own truest self, which is totally unknown to our closest friends, or even to the people who will eventually benefit from our labor and efforts.

And where does this leave us, the admirers of the misanthropic writer, as we learn to respect his misanthropic banker's integrity of character? I feel an oppressive sort of disquiet, of restiveness, in front of the endemic lack of communication between these two friends; they both long for a tangible, however tiny, sign of mutual affection, and yet are prepared to squander whimsically enormous amounts of the same sentiment. While Proust lavished his love on an unworthy partner like Henri Rochat, who gradually took center stage in his life, Hauser wasted generous amounts of his time in the maze of Proust's bookkeeping, only promptly to lose his way and give up hope in the uneven yet more hospitable windings of the writer's heart.

Proust never managed to reconcile the duties of his art with the outbursts of love and friendship he experienced in his short life. On the one hand, he felt the urge to translate "the fabulous world of his memories into a world of truth," as he writes in his aborted novel, *Jean Santeuil* (397). He had to be unconditionally honest with the "deep self" ("moi profound") of which he writes in another aborted novel, *Contre Sainte-Beuve,* the self which drove him toward the accomplishment of his artistic work, even if this honesty to himself entailed living in the solitude of misanthropy (225). On the other hand, he also frequently succumbed to the opposite urge to come to terms with the "external support," the external scaffolds of companionship and insincerity, which he describes in *The Guermantes Way* (391).[2] He had to adjust to this sense of dissociation, forced on him by the company of friends and acquaintances, because it was out of them that sprang forth the raw materials that nurtured his inspiration.

In between these opposite drives toward truthfulness and insincerity, we find Lionel Hauser: an embarrassment to Proust the writer, insofar as Hauser's brand of altruism and generosity undercuts the catalogue of human types depicted in his novel. As a man of simple and unquestionable duties, Hauser was unfit to provide Proust with creative materials for his writing. The banker lacked the essential attribute that would allow Proust to disguise him as one of the characters in his novel: he was not burdened, that is, with the self-deceiving hypocrisy that puts Proust's fictional creatures under the strain of Lost Time, a trait which they all display in their own sensational way. Aside from the obvious specimens of snobbery like Monsieur Legrandin, through whose Bohemian pose the social climber shines through, or Madame Verdurin, who only stops climbing the social ladder in her old age, the day when she wears the tiara of Princess of Guermantes, most characters from *In Search of Lost Time* move imperceptibly from the elegy of early beginnings or youthful promise to the squalor of adult complacency or old-age obtuseness. An outstanding example is found in Gilberte Swann, the Narrator's first flame, who disowns her father's Jewish name to take on the aristocratic one of Monsieur de

Forcheville, her mother Odette's old lover and second husband. Gilberte even spreads the rumor that Monsieur de Forcheville is her biological father. Another outstanding example is the Baron de Charlus, whose flaunted virility and Don Juanism—behind which is hidden his unflagging homosexuality—in the end hold up the incorrigible and pathetic masochist to public scorn.

A rare and delicate gem in the turmoil of Proust's myriad sources of garish inspiration, Lionel Hauser was loyal and devoted to his friend Marcel Proust—too literally devoted perhaps, even narrow-mindedly so at times, to the extent that one does not really pity him when he falls into the metaphorical claws of Proust's letters to him. Nonetheless, as loyal and devoted as he was, Hauser expressed these sentiments in such a self-abnegating way that the ferocious satirist which Proust was becoming would not know what to do with him as a fictional character.

Chapter 17

A FAIRY-TALE PRINCESS & AN AMERICAN TENNIS PLAYER

In 1918 Hauser's role as Proust's confidant and spiritual censor grew in importance, while his influence on the writer's financial decisions grew proportionally weaker. Too many incompetent advisors deprived Hauser of his authority. Two of the occasions when Hauser's place was usurped by a circus of amateurs stand out: the litigation subsequent to the accidental sale of 100 Tramways de Mexico, which were still in Proust's portfolio at the Crédit Industriel; and the attempt to cash Proust's Warburg check in the amount of 30,000 francs, which, as you may recall, was drawn on the Comptoir d'Escompte. Aside from a colossal waste of time for all parties involved, both cases dragged on with no tangible results: the former until the end of 1919, and the latter until 1920, when it was precariously solved by another providential intervention of Robert de Billy—as you may recall, Billy had rescued Proust once before in 1912, when the writer was burdened with more than half a million francs in obligations to buy with his stockbroker David Léon, and his friend bought out some of these forwards contracts in the amount of 100,000 francs.

Aside from the competent economist Georges-Raphaël Lévy, who tried to cash Proust's 30,000-franc check after the writer endorsed it to his name, and no sooner than this attempt failed, endorsed it back to the legitimate owner, the two people most actively engaged in usurping Hauser's role were Walter Berry and Hélène Soutzo. The financial premises they drew on were very different from Hauser's. We are acquainted with the princess: after a period of lethargy and irritable saturation, her interest in Proust was promptly revamped by the prospect of paying haughty visits to various vice-directors at the Crédit Industriel on behalf of her defenseless, talented friend. We are meeting for the first time Walter Berry, who is destined to become one of Proust's closest friends in his late years.

A close friend of two famous American expatriates, Henry James and Edith Wharton, Berry was a descendant of the influential Van Rensselaer family of New York. He had been educated at Harvard and Columbia University. After serving as judge at the International Tribunal of Egypt, which oversaw a variety of courts created for the trial of civil cases arising between natives and foreigners or between foreigners of different nationalities, Berry settled permanently in Paris, where he had been born in 1859. He became a strong advocate of France in the United States after World War I broke out, which earned him deep gratitude and admiration from Proust, who in 1919 would dedicate *Pastiches et mélanges* to him. In 1916, the year when he first made the acquaintance of the writer, Berry had been elected president of the American Chamber of Commerce in Paris.[1] Taller than the average Parisian and more athletic, blue-eyed, elegant, and "très sec," he had a taste for Proust's languidly nocturnal elegance; yet he was known for rising early in the morning to play tennis at the Bois de Boulogne, a practice which Proust looked frankly at as an eccentricity.

If nothing else, the incompetence of these two new impromptu agents should have helped Hauser's professionalism stand out by contrast in Proust's eyes. Hauser made it a rule to work in a manner that was as judicious as it was effective: in June, in the heat of Proust's clash with Charles Martin, the director of the London Bank in Paris, which was fueled by Berry and Soutzo, Hauser would pay a tactful visit to the director. He would manage to extract a 20,000-franc advance on Proust's loan, money that would come handy in case war-related events forced the writer to leave Paris. After Berry and Soutzo's first infelicitous moves, Hauser found himself asking Proust if he meant to undertake a frivolous lawsuit against the London Bank, so as "to shoot [his] last few bullets in order to heighten the affluence of the Order of Lawyers in Paris" (COR XVIII, 45).

Proust's Tramways de Mexico shares had been handled at first by Hauser et Cie, in coordination with the Central Bank of France, which had the authority to trade them on the London Stock Exchange, where they were listed. But in April 1918 Hauser, who was a British subject, feared he might be drafted into the British army. He had therefore entrusted these securities to the London Bank, which from then on acted as intermediary with the Central Bank of France. In April and May, a misunderstanding or lack of coordination between these two banks resulted in the sale of the Tramways de Mexico shares at a price lower than the limit set by Proust on Hauser's recommendation. Hauser thought that Proust ought simply to demand the return of his securities. In October the war seemed close to an end; it was likely that Mexico would become allied with the United States, and hence the price of Tramways de Mexico shares was expected to go up. However, the London Bank was willing to acknowledge its mistake and refund the difference between the proceeds from the sale and the limit price asked by Proust, but refused to buy the securities back on Proust's behalf.

Hauser suggested that Proust should ask for arbitrage; it was at this stage that Walter Berry came in. Proust wanted to have Berry as the arbiter between himself and the bank. In December the London Bank refused to go into arbitrage. While Hauser tried to persuade Proust that the mobilization and subsequent turnover of the bank's personnel, together with the emergency transfer of stock certificates away from Paris, may have played a role in the whole affair, Hélène Soutzo, enticed by Proust's artful rendition of the affair, declared she was ready to take charge of it. "A woman friend of mine . . . good at business and who enjoys some personal influence," Proust wrote to Hauser, has volunteered to put pressure on the London Bank (COR XVII, 216).

At this point in the story we must briefly skip forward to 1919. On January 10, 1919, Hauser wrote to Proust: "I'm pleased to see that a young and charming princess has taken your interests in her hands. This is not a novel anymore but a true fairy tale." Hauser seemed to understand that Soutzo's aggressive arguments did not differ at all from those adopted till then by Berry, and since the latter's views did not persuade the London Bank, it was evident that the princess deemed "her powers of persuasion or even of suggestion greater than the force of good old-fashioned logic." Proust should just wait and see, while attempting to share her optimism (COR XVIII, 5).

From February 4 to February 5, 1919, Proust successfully performed the strange feat of writing in one day two letters of opposite content. He wrote to Hauser that the princess's intervention had no results at all and that he feared he might, on top of it, also lose his line of credit with the London Bank. To Berry, he wrote instead that his bad state of health made it impossible for him to have a preliminary meeting with Mr. Martin, the director of the London Bank, and therefore he agreed that it was time "to declare war" (COR XVIII, 27, 29). Nothing would come of it, of course. Neither Berry nor Soutzo had the stamina to handle such a gratuitous lawsuit. By the end of 1919, the Tramways de Mexico affair ran aground and faded away from the correspondence between Proust and Hauser.[2]

In September 1918 Hauser alerted Proust to a new initiative from the Ministry of Finance. The ministry was giving the owners of securities loaned to the Treasury Department the authorization to swap them against ten-year National Defense Bonds with a 4.27 percent discount on the market price. The Egyptian Preference Bonds, some of which Proust had loaned to the Treasury Department against yearly revenue of 2,363 francs, figured in the list of the swappable securities. Assuming the exchange rates would go back to normal after the war, by the time the loan expired Proust's bonds would go back to their after-tax revenue of 1,810 francs. In order to persuade Proust that it was advantageous to swap these bonds against the new National Defense Bonds, Hauser embarked on an ingenious mathematical disquisition, whose prolixity was probably meant to remind Proust of the difference between professionals and amateurs, when it came to financial matters.

A forewarning is in order before I transcribe the salient passages from Hauser's letter. The banker's actions on Proust's behalf were in this case a small masterpiece of financiering, and his pride was bitterly wounded when, the following year, on the advice of yet another one of the writer's new extemporaneous financial advisors, Henri Gans, Proust remorselessly undid all his efforts. Nonetheless, we have epistolary evidence that Proust gave careful consideration to Hauser's disquisition, with a blend of meticulous attention to the financial minutiae and tolerant detachment from the wearying details. If you have ever attempted to make sense of your retirement fund's prospectus and the commissions you pay to the portfolio manager, you know what it felt like to read Hauser's letter. Delve into it at your own risk, or skip it right away if compounded interests on discounted prices are not your cup of tea.

> My dear Marcel,
>
> . . . Yesterday the Egyptian preference bonds were quoted at 84 francs a piece at the Paris Exchange. The Treasury Department trades them at 87 francs a piece. It is true that with the yield of these securities covering April 15 to October 15,

> you miss on five and a half months of coupons equivalent to 1½%. On the other hand, in exchange you receive National Defense bonds whose yield matures on the first of August, earning therefore two months of coupons, that is, 0.8%; your loss is therefore only 0.7%, but is largely offset by the 3% margin offered by the Treasury Department when it buys your bonds at 87 francs instead of 84 a piece. If you subscribe to the swap, you will earn: 47,850 francs—i.e., 55,000 times 0.87. If we divide this figure by the price of 95.73 which you pay for the 10-year National Defense bonds, we get about: 50,000 francs in the nominal value of these bonds, which yield 5% a year, that is, 2,500 francs. And if, as I presume, you opt to subscribe to the issue of the next National Loan with a 4% yield, you will be given the option to trade these National Defense bonds against it. Although the issue price of this new loan is not official yet, it is expected that it won't be higher than 71% of its nominal value. Hence, in return for your National Defense bonds you will receive a nominal capital of about 67,000 francs of this 4%-yield loan, yielding revenue of 2,695 francs. It seems to me that this operation is very advantageous since it gives you additional yearly revenue of 333 francs over the revenue which the State is currently increasing by 25%, and [additional revenue of] 885 francs over the 1,810 franc revenue which you would earn from your Egyptian bonds when their loan to the State expires. (COR XVII, 150)

Hauser concluded his letter by saying that if Proust agreed to all this, it was imperative to act by the end of April.

This time Hauser had outdone himself! Proust agreed to his plan of action with a splendid answer.

> My dear Lionel,
>
> I've read your demonstration over and over as though it were a page from Descartes's *Discourse on Method*. You would rightly disbelieve me if I said that I was swimming like a fish through the nets of your deductions, and when I saw that I was supposed to divide the sum of 2,200 Egyptian pounds, that is 55,000 francs, by 95.75, I paused with a sense of dejection. (COR XVII, 151)

The following month, it was the turn of the Rothschild Bank to suggest a similar transaction, regarding the Consolidated Russian Bonds in Proust's portfolio, which could be advantageously swapped with notes for the Liberation of French Territory loan (COR XVII, 172, 172 [note 3]).

On October 20, 1918, Hauser asked Proust if he still owned shares in Royal Dutch. This letter indicates that Hauser was largely in the dark regarding the writer's steady interest in the Dutch oil company (even though in 1918 the accountant of Hauser et Cie did help Proust fill out his tax forms). Hauser queried whether, in the event Proust still owned shares of this company in one of his portfolios, the banker who handled them told him that there had been a few increases in Royal Dutch capital during the last two years. They were quite advantageous to the shareholders. (Hauser was referring to the current capital increase of 78 percent and the previous year's 47 percent increase).[3] If his banker took advantage of them, Proust's capital in Royal Dutch ought to have grown "at a significant rate," wrote Hauser (COR XVII, 173).

Proust did not reply immediately to these queries for the simple reason that they were made in a letter that was otherwise openly insulting to him. Hauser had accused him of incompetence, arguing that Proust should dodge self-destruction by investing most of his personal fortune in a life annuity policy. Proust responded to Hauser's queries about his Royal Dutch shares only two weeks later, declaring that he had no idea if the banker who handled his Royal Dutch shares had taken advantage of his new acquisition privileges; but he would find out as soon as his headache gave him some respite (COR XVII, 192). Since we know that Proust's block of Royal Dutch shares kept growing, this answer does not enlighten us in the least as to whether it was Hauser's hint that alerted him to fresh opportunities for these securities—his most generous "mistresses" on the Stock Exchange—or if, on the contrary and more likely, it was Léon Neuberger who took another one of his many semiclandestine initiatives on Proust's behalf, igniting the miracle whose effects we will soon discuss.

Chapter 18

IN SEARCH OF TIME SQUANDERED

The title of this chapter sums up the main controversy between Proust and Hauser, namely, their opposing views on the best usage of time. This opposition may be better qualified in terms of the difference between the banker's zero-sum game of wasted time, and the writer's positive-sum game of time found again. In order to grasp this contrast—which boils down to the role one is willing to assign to the faculty of memory in the meaningful unfolding of one's life—we need to take a look at Proust's theory of involuntary memory.

In Proust's *In Search of Lost Time,* involuntary memory is a phenomenon occurring at the intersection of sensory experience and memory retrieval. In the novel's first volume, *Swann's Way,* the gustative and olfactory sensations from a madeleine dunked in tisane and then eaten in a moment of sadness by the novel's Narrator trigger a special, nonsensory feeling of elation in him. This feeling of elation has neither sensory content nor sensory origin, since flavor and scent are not—or more precisely, were not considered by most psychologists of Proust's time—objective conveyors of emotions.[1] Yet the Narrator has a conscious grasp of his mood swing, from sad to elated, which tells him that the madeleine has the prerogative of affecting him in more ways than he is immediately aware of. He decides to probe this experience more deeply. "I create an empty space before [the sensation that is slipping away], I confront it again with the still recent taste of that first mouthful [of tisane-soaked madeleine], and I feel something quiver in me, shift, try to rise, something that seems to have been unanchored at a great depth; I do not know what it is, but it comes up slowly; I feel the resistance and I hear the murmur of the distances traversed" (*Swann's Way,* 46).[2]

After several failed attempts, the Narrator recalls certain past events that fit his present experience. They consist of a series of long-forgotten madeleine-eating episodes associated with his sick aunt's bedroom in Combray, the provincial town where he used to spend his holidays as a child. The Narrator's remembrance brings about the "transmutation of remembrance into a directly felt reality," as Jean Santeuil, the Narrator's fictional precursor from Proust's aborted eponymous novel,[3] describes the effects of this sort of mnemonic effort (399). A memory from the past, mirrored in a current event that reawakens it, is retrieved not like a distant recollection, but rather like something experienced in the here and now. This analogy between episodes or events or sensation separated by time and forgetfulness depends on the Narrator's "escape from the present"—on his ability, that is, to tear two or more distinct moments in time away from their chronological separation and join them in a cohesive whole on the basis of a common perception (*Finding Time Again,* 180).[4]

In the novel's last volume, *Finding Time Again,* the Narrator manages to understand at long last what lies behind his "escape from the present." By heeding sensory experiences that have effects on him which are analogous to the madeleine-eating episode, and then linking these experiences to their pertinent memory, his sense of personal identity is enhanced. The analogy between present and past episodes projects his sense of selfhood into a dimension "outside of time." When distinct yet kindred experiences are bound into a cohesive whole, his selfhood feeds on two or more disjointed temporalities, but identifies with none; he becomes "an extratemporal being." While each of the Narrator's possible identities—for instance, his bereaved self after his grandmother's death, or his jealous self after Albertine's flight from his apartment—is exclusively invested in certain emotionally charged circumstances, to the exclusion of his other individual identities, his extratemporal identity is more durable, "freed from the order of time." As such, this extratemporal identity is immune from the fear of death: "the word 'death' has no meaning for him" (*Finding Time Again,* 179–81).[5]

Proust thought that this lesson from his novel could also make the word *death* meaningless to us, his readers. A discussion of Proust's creative usage of involuntary memory remains incomplete unless it addresses one last vital detail: namely, the obligation felt by Proust toward us. This is the aspect of the writer's *ars poetica,* as Paul Ricoeur defines it, that shields *In Search of Lost Time* from being classified as a self-centered or solipsistic novel.[6] This *ars poetica*, elaborated by the Narrator near the end of the novel, in the solitude of the Princess of Guermantes's library, makes explicit the tasks which Proust assigns to his protagonist on the day the latter embraces his vocation as a writer. Without the succor of artworks, according to Proust, "the qualitative difference in the ways we perceive the world . . . would be the eternal secret of each of us." And after the difference in perception brought about by involuntary memory exorcises his Narrator's fear of death, this formerly recidivous loafer feels bound to share this different manner of perception, that is, the analogy between present and past sensations, with everybody else by means of a novel. Thanks to his artwork, the way he perceives the world, which would normally be destined to remain his own "secret," will provide us, the readers, with analogous "means to read within [ourselves]." Proust does not want to encourage us into a generic sort of intro- or retrospection, but rather into the same kind of self-decipherment that both he and his Narrator practice (*Finding Time Again,* 204, 342–43).[7] Incidentally, involuntary memory has also a practical application to sexuality in Proust: it enhances and makes it wholesome, as I will show when we dig into his and his Narrator's respective sexual lives.[8]

We are now better equipped to grasp the significant contrast between the views that Proust and Hauser held on the best usage of time. From Proust's perspective, the time of our lives is not a scarce commodity, like the goods dealt with in classical economics, whose utility is maximized via rational allocation. Hauser is partial to this notion of time. To his mind, one could say, we are endowed with a given length of time to spend on this planet, and by the end of it, all of our past history, that is, the sum total of the time we have used meritoriously and the time we have squandered, equals the length of our original endowment. As I hinted earlier, this is indeed the textbook scenario of a zero-sum game. But it is also something more than that.

Hauser traded in financial securities. In his world, wealth was embodied in stocks and bonds, which were exchanged in the form of paper certificates. These certificates meant that the bearer had an equity stake or a creditor stake in some company, that is, he or she owned wealth equivalent to a certain amount of currency, the latter being equivalent, in turn, to either the market price or the face value of the certificate itself. Under the gold standard, this price or value was equivalent, in its own turn, to a certain amount of solid gold. But at the outbreak of World War I, France had broken away from the gold standard of the Latin Monetary Union. It is not difficult to imagine the effect this event had on such a scrupulous trader as Hauser. With the simultaneous disappearance of gold as the stable guarantee of market prices and the international disruption of financial obligations, the certificates traded on financial markets had become little better than unreliable scrawls on paper.

Hauser must have been acutely apprehensive when he came to realize this implication. That's probably why he channeled much of his energy, as we will discuss presently, into writing *The Three Levers of the New World,* a book on the social values and moral duties that most mattered to him, namely, competence, probity, and altruism—values and duties which, in his view, humankind had little time left to turn back to. In his correspondence with Proust, Hauser became more and more insistent on the scarce time that remained to both of them to live, on the margins of a war that was rushing toward some unimaginable and irremediable catastrophe. To this pragmatic banker, the optimal usage of time was gradually becoming the last inviolable token of human permanence on this planet.

Influenced by John Ruskin, as we know, with regard to the distinction between real gold and artistic gold, Proust took wealth to be but a means to those "urges of expansive self-expression" about which he would soon engage in controversy with Hauser. Earlier on, if you remember, I described Proust's compulsive drift from the costly quest for love to the hunt for speculative gains suitable to finance such a quest. Now I wish to add that to Proust, whether attained or not, love enjoyed a privileged relationship with Lost Time, and this is why it could sponsor his "expansive self-expression" like no other experience or predicament.

John Updike had a keen insight into love's relationship with past time. "What is it that shines at us from [the beloved's face] other than our own past, with its strange innocence and its strange need to be redeemed?" wrote Updike in an occasional piece.

> What is nostalgia but love for that part of ourselves which is . . . forever removed from change and corruption? A woman, loved, momentarily eases the pain of time by localizing nostalgia: the vague and irrecoverable objects of nostalgic longing are assimilated, under the pressure of libidinous desire, into the details of her person. . . . Perhaps it is to the degree that the beloved crystallizes the lover's past that she presents herself to him, alpha and omega, as his Fate.[9]

I do not know if Updike's succinct outlook on the relationship between love and past time was meant as homage to Proust, because he makes no explicit allusion to the French writer in this piece. Be it as it may, I have rarely found such crystal-clear description of the very way in which love, even when hopelessly coveted, provides Proust with basic materials for his novel on Lost Time.

Wealth has a role to play in Proust's self-expression in direct proportion to the role it plays in his love quest—which is an indispensable role, as we learned a while back from his imaginative treatment of Albertine's sleeping body as a vessel, of which he wants to be not only the captain in control but even, say, the ship owner. Wealth is primarily the means of acquisition for the fodder of his novel on Lost Time. And this novel, in turn, is designed to make Lost Time not ineluctable, as Hauser would have it, but rather reversible. In Proust's treatment of Lost Time, our future becomes a cornucopia of opportunities for the disjointed events from our past to become parts of a new and cohesive whole. At the end *In Search of Lost Time,* his Narrator—and we, the readers, together with him—does indeed find Lost Time again, as an occasion of self-affirmation that is forever expandable. With this understanding, we are in a better position to follow the evolution of Hauser's role in Proust's life, from financial advisor to confidant and spiritual censor.

Chapter 19

THE THREE LEVERS OF THE NEW WORLD

In February 1918, Hauser confided to Proust that wartime conditions had curtailed his business commitments, so the writer should feel free to consult him both on economic and personal matters. A few days later, Hauser's accountant queried Proust about his intentions regarding the securities, held in his Rothschild portfolio, of a meat-extract company called Liebig. Apropos, Proust had been puzzled about the recent performance of these securities. The anecdote he told Hauser about them seems devised to test the banker's patience. From time to time, Proust got coupon payments in the mail from Liebig's headquarters in England. Ten years previously, when he had moved from Rue Courcelle to Boulevard Haussmann, the payments kept coming, because the porters at the Rue Courcelle apartment building were careful to forward the letters from England to his new address. At first the war had not changed anything for the worse: certainly not the coupon payments, which had become larger and more frequent. But it had been a year since Proust had received the last payment. Either there was a new porter in Rue Courcelle, who pocketed Proust's money, or the Liebig Company was no longer paying dividends; or the United Kingdom was prohibiting earnings from financial transactions to cross the channel. Proust was considering writing a note to the porter in Rue Courcelle to warn him that those payments belonged to their legitimate owner (COR XVII, 42, 43).

He did not have to wait long for Hauser's answer:

> My dear Marcel,
>
> . . . The epic of the dividends of [your Liebig securities] is evident proof that the realm of poetry has nothing to share with

> what we, simple middle-class people, call the realm of common sense. I do not know if the book you are working on these days is the sequel to your last one and if it is intended to guide the reader again in the quest of lost time. If this is the case, you should devote a chapter to the matter of your Liebig coupon and ask each reader to gauge, roughly at least, the time you'd have gained, the efforts you'd have spared yourself and perhaps the money you'd have saved if, promptly after your old porter had forwarded you the first misaddressed letter carrying a dividend from this company, you had written a letter to notify them of your new address. (COR XVII, 44)

Proust answered in a sour tone, explaining that in his book the expression Lost Time ("temps perdu") does not signify "squandered time" but rather "the Past" or time gone by ("le Passé"; COR XVII, 46). In Proust's ears, the cutting tone of Hauser's letter must have resounded of "the sense of . . . superiority" of the busy man described by him in *Sodom and Gomorrah,* who "drafts reports, lines up figures, answers business letters, or follows prices in the Bourse," and sees in literature "the comic pastime of the idle" (*Sodom and Gomorrah,* 423).[1] It is understandable that Proust's letter went on in an ironic and vindictive tone: "Fortune, if one understands this word in the meaning of 'chance' which is preserved in the adjective 'fortuitous,' does not smile only upon the bold,[2] but also upon the slothful. No sooner did I receive your letter than the porter from Rue Courcelle sent me a coupon payment from Liebig and moreover, my housemaid . . . recovered an advance from last September" (COR XVII, 46).

It was Hauser's turn to be ironic: "The odyssey of your Liebig dividends is an amusing distraction, helping me to forget the peace treaty of Brest-Litovski." The war had taken a bad turn on the Russian front. In March 1918 the Russians were forced to sign a peace treaty without negotiating its terms, because the Germans threatened to continue the offensive until the deal was sealed (COR XVII, 47, 47 [note 2]).

The motif of common sense, introduced by Hauser in his contrast, above, between saved time and squandered time, soon resurfaced in his response to Proust's praise of "the Leonardesque versatility" of his talents. A recurring and moralistic propensity for stoicism is beginning to stand out as a dominant aspect of Hauser's personality. Common sense, he explained to Proust, was the source of all his personal gifts. God had sown common sense in the soul of every human being as a "small mirror designed to reflect divine Wisdom." Common sense had been his only sextant in negotiating many dire straits (COR XVII, 48, 49).

As a consequence of the great German offensive in the spring of 1918, the United Kingdom raised the conscription age from forty-one to fifty. There was a chance that Hauser, a British subject, would be drafted into the army. It was at this point that he entrusted Proust's 100 Tramways de Mexico shares to the London Bank, with the pernicious results we have discussed (COR XVII, 59). The letter in which Proust expressed his concern at the news of his friend's possible conscription—how would Hauser's family manage if he went to war?—contained a sample of the writer's black humor. On March 3, the projectile from a howitzer (an artillery piece somewhat between a regular gun and a mortar) hit the Church of Saint-Gervais during a Good Friday function, killing seventy-five people and wounding ninety.

> My dear Lionel,
>
> . . . I've often noticed (concerning the bombshell fallen on the Church of Saint-Gervais) that Israelites have always had a keen predilection for things and names Catholic. The names elude me a bit as I write, but in a word, the Halphen family lives at the Monastery, Madame Henri de Rothschild [lives at] the *Abbey* of the Veaux de Cernay, Madame Singer [lives at] Neufmoustiers, which means monastery too, Madame Progès [lives in] another Abbey. . . . By the same token, at the wedding ceremony of Madame Jules Porgès's daughter, I remember that there were so many crucifixes, missals, etc., that a friend of mine, very badly mannered, asked the hostess if, still being a novice [in these matters], she hadn't by chance muddled the Sacraments and confused her daughter's marriage with her First Communion. To get back to the Church of Saint-Gervais where there was a General whose name was Frankfort (who is, I think, the cousin of my aunt and landlady), as well as several Mendelsohn, a name which at times goes hand in hand with that of Mayer. . . . E *tutti quanti*. . . . In such a predicament, the Grand Rabbi's visit to the shelled church didn't simply have the character of Holy Solidarity that so moved the newspapers. And the Pope himself . . . doesn't seem to have read the list [of the victims] too closely when he especially deplores this tragedy because it fell on "particularly devout Catholics." (COR XVII, 60)

After this macabre tirade, Proust adopted a contrite tone: "In the end, regardless of whether the victims were Catholics or Jews, I am no less saddened by this hecatomb."

It looks as if Proust was determined to counter each and every hint of Hauser's moralistic stoicism with an antidote of equal and opposite strength. The macabre tone of this letter seems conceived as a sort of deterrence; and predictably enough, Proust's remonstrance against Hauser's possible mobilization inspired the banker to speak in a martyr's voice. If he went to war, his wife would do exactly what millions of other unfortunate women were already doing. If Proust, however, became a theosophist like Hauser, he would realize that "our passage on earth is just an act in a very long comedy or tragedy. From this viewpoint, death is simply the lowering of the curtain, announcing that the time has come to change the backdrop" (COR XVII, 61).

This pressure on Proust to adhere to theosophy foreshadows an impending complication in the relationship between the two friends. A few days later, in fact, Proust received "a confession" from Hauser: "Today I come to you," Hauser wrote, "in the clothes of a penitent rather those of a banker. Yes, my patient friend, I come to confess. . . . Would you believe it, I've written a book! Had I started to build something anew, one would be inclined to overlook it, but daring to write . . . at my age!" This last sentence alludes to a fable by La Fontaine, "The Old Man and the Three Youngsters," to which Proust had referred in a previous letter, where the writer expressed his hope that the old Léon Neuberger had managed to move from Paris to the country, where he would not be forced, at his venerable age, to hide in air-raid shelters. La Fontaine's fable tells of three young men watching an octogenarian plant a small tree in an orchard. "If he were trying to build something, one could overlook it," they remark, with a slightly sexual allusion which may have eluded Hauser, "but planting at his age! He must have lost his mind."[3]

Hauser's old manuscript, which Proust had politely yet firmly declined to read three years earlier, had become a 128-page book published by Émile Nourry with the title *The Three Levers of the New World: Competence, Probity, and Altruism.* Hauser wanted to hear his friend's opinion of it. In his letter, Hauser described the nature of his undertaking. Proust knew him well, he wrote: he would never pose as a man of letters, nor would he dream "of passing himself off as a stylist." Since life was short, he had devoted most of the time allotted him to the discovery of his own ideas, and very little time to reading and absorbing those of others. Such a work of introspection took him many years, after which he realized that his ideas regarding man's social life differed significantly from those of the majority of his fellow citizens, those who were reputed to constitute public opinion. He had to wonder, then, in all honesty, if truth was on his side or on theirs. The tragic events of the last few years had given him a partial answer, as they had proved that the others were wrong.

> Does that mean I am right? Not necessarily, because there can also be a middle way. . . . I don't blame you for your skeptical smile, my dear Marcel. I don't flatter myself that my voice has the reach of the kolossal Krupp kannon. . . .[4] I'm only asking one thing of you today, please read my work without prejudice and then tell me, with brutal sincerity, the impression it made on you. (COR XVII, 81)

Hauser would come off badly if he were to count on Proust's impartial judgment, because, as we saw, and as Gide would come to realize a decade too late, the writer was incapable of the "total sincerity" Hauser desired. Proust subsequently took up a wide-ranging campaign to promote Hauser's book, comparable in magnitude and wasted efforts to the saga of the accidental sale of his 100 Tramways de Mexico shares; it involved an even larger number of players (literary critics, editors, and publishers in this case), and led Proust himself to the edge of glamorous quarrels with some of his trusted friends. To no avail: because, on the one hand, ink, paper, and space on the pages of journals and magazines were scarcer and more expensive in wartime; and, on the other, because Hauser's *Three Levers of the New World* failed to convince the critics, it would seem, owing perhaps to the very theosophical fundamentalism that Proust would denounce in his response.

After showering Hauser with praise for his Kantian connection between practical prescriptions and metaphysical premises, and also for the primacy he assigned to individual self-improvement, Proust chastened him for indulging in a sort of dogmatism. Hauser proclaimed "the theosophical dogma of subsequent incarnations without providing any proof of its validity." To Proust this was "an article of faith comparable to the belief in the Immaculate Conception." Not that Proust was unequivocally opposed to the principle of reincarnation: "My constant study of interior phenomena, my constant attention to unexplainable reminiscences, would lead me to believe that our present life is not the first we live, and that the sponge of forgetfulness has not wiped away completely the memory of previous lives." This was a topic, however, that Hauser ought to have dealt with overtly, in Proust's opinion. Since, in his letter, Hauser had mocked his own scarce talent for literary style, Proust made it a point to extol the efficacy of his prose: everything he meant to convey in his book, he argued, Hauser managed to convey perfectly and exactly, which was the essence of a well-wrought style.

We must not forget how sensitive Proust was to style-related matters. A couple of years later, on the wave of his literary consecration by the Prix Goncourt, he contributed to the debate started in August 1919 by Louis de Robert's article "Flaubert Wrote Poorly" ("Flaubert écrivait mal"), and fueled in 1913 by Jules Lemaître's derogatory memoir of his literary discussions with Flaubert, with a defense of Flaubert's style in the *Nouvelle Revue Française*.[5] To Proust, the gift of the true stylistic master consisted in the ability to conjure up valuable metaphors. Flaubert lacked this gift; his style was rhythmic and uniform like a moving walkway ("un trottoir roulant"). Nonetheless, "[Flaubert's] entirely new and personal use of the simple past, the past indefinite, the present participle, certain pronouns and certain prepositions, has renewed our vision of things almost as drastically as Kant did with his Categories, the theories of Knowledge and of the Reality of the external world."[6]

Far from lukewarm or occasional in nature, Proust's response to Hauser's book unfolded in a curious blend of appreciation and polemical self-concern. Hauser's book advocates a perfect balance in the usage of our faculties, together with the nurturing of bodily health, moral integrity, and the adoption of pedagogical practices grounded on rational principles. His proclivity for combining abstract yet unquestionable norms with a meticulous guidance to practical conduct reminded Proust of his beloved Ruskin, who was similarly prone to grabbing "the fiery sword of the archangel," and dispensing, at one and the same time, careful "advice in practical matters." However, as a rejoinder to Hauser's salvo of theosophical wisdom, Proust felt under the obligation to improvise a sort of Decadent Manifesto. Although Plato's young disciples used to practice the very virtues promoted by Hauser, Proust was persuaded that an opposite attitude was more beneficial in these times. "I've seen the new word, apt to unveil a still uncharted facet of the human spirit or some concealed nuance of tenderness in it, sprout from the intoxications of Musset or Verlaine, from the perversions of Baudelaire or Rimbaud, or even of Wagner, and from the epilepsy of Flaubert." He then went on to discuss, almost openly, his own personal case. "If for nothing else than the creative value of human pain, I think that in these depraved days of ours, *physical illness is almost a condition of brilliant intellectual strength.*"

I have italicized the last clause because it reads like the lucidly existential program of a short-lived hero of the decadent arts. Unquestionably, not even his friendship for Walter Berry would ever drag Proust out of bed early in the morning for, say, a tennis match at the Bois de Boulogne.

His last remark, in turn, inspired Proust to formulate a crucial axiom regarding his notion of an artist's optimal intercourse with his or her fellow human beings.

> My dear Lionel,
>
> . . . Above all I think that our individuality, to which you justly assign an important role, acts beneficially to others not so much through the good it tries to do them as through the scrupulous performance of its duties toward itself. I am only talking of course of the highest and most ingenious forms of human activity. But, in this kind [of activity], all the good things accomplished on this planet by artists, writers, and scientists were accomplished in such a way that, without being exactly selfish (since their goal was not the fulfillment of their own desires, but the unveiling of an inner truth which they had caught a glimpse of), did not overly concern itself about others. According to Pascal, to Lavoisier, to Wagner, altruism has never entailed breaking off one's solitary work in order to undertake charity work. [Artists, writers, and scientists] have made their own honey like bees, and in reality everybody else has taken advantage of this honey. (COR XVII, 83)

The invention of concise and effective metaphors was Proust's fundamental criterion in the definition of a good style. Here Proust gives an example of it, in the simile between the industrious bee and the creative individual. This simile, derived from a verse attributed to Virgil by a fourth-century grammarian, Titus Claudius Donatus, contains in a nutshell Proust's categorical imperative: artistic creation must enjoy unconditional primacy vis-à-vis all social, political, ludic, amorous, friendly, and charitable obligations (COR XVII, 83 [note 23]).

At the beginning of summer, when the wealthy men who stayed in Paris to take care of business or war or politics prepared to join the rest of their families, sheltered in the countryside (Hauser had not been drafted after all, and would soon join his wife and two children, François and Daniel, in the town of Royat in Auvergne, central France), Céleste Albaret insisted with Monsieur Proust that they too ought to leave the Paris apartment. In anticipation of a move out of the city, which Proust's tenacious attachment to his deep-seated habits made highly improbable (and in fact they did not leave), the writer decided he needed to put together "a small or rather a large 'war chest.'" He would like to have 30,000 francs in cash at his disposal. He could withdraw this money from the Rothschild Bank; but after Léon Neuberger's place had been taken by a "Mr. Gute" (as Proust called the new Rothschild executive, Paul Guth), Monsieur and Madame Straus had acted as his intermediaries with the bank, and they were currently out of town, unable to help (COR XVII, 110).

The day before Hauser left for Royat, he paid a personal visit to the London Bank, as we have already seen. He asked for 30,000 francs on behalf of Proust; the bank offered 10,000, and a compromise was reached on the sum of 20,000 francs (COR XVII, 111). So, Proust had his "war chest" at hand, Hauser could leave for his summer retreat, and the two friends' correspondence entered a hiatus that lasted until the end of the summer months. Even in such hard times as the war years, the habit of the summer vacations was hard to die among well-to-do Parisians. In the fall season, the financial industry in Paris would spurt out of its temporary paralysis, which was partly war-induced, for sure—but undeniably also a result of the upper crust's special prerogative to take time off, while the large-scale slaughter of the masses continued on.

Chapter 20

TURNING CARESSES INTO GOLD

The summer of 1918 was over and not a single review of Hauser's book had been published yet by the critics and journalists to whom Proust had recommended his friend's work. If in the last two months he had not suffered "great torments of the heart," Proust wrote to Hauser, he would have almost lost his mental sanity after the failure of all his efforts on behalf of his friend. Since he was not a theosophist like Hauser, he existed in a broader amorous sphere than his friend's marital one. Of late, certain torments of the heart had the questionable advantage of distracting him from the sorrow of not reading, day in and day out, generous praises of Hauser's work in the organs of the press (COR XVII, 148).

Hauser replied that Proust was wrong in wasting page after page of his letter on the subject of the ignored book, while saving a single line for the torments of his heart. The two of them were excellent friends, were they not? Should they not share every concern, and especially their deepest sorrows? Our Hauser was a serious and well-meaning fellow, unaware, deep down, of the special nature of Proust's erotic tastes and amorous orientations. He could hardly anticipate the consequences ensuing from his promotion of a regime of mutual confidence with Proust (COR XVII, 149). As we know, the reason and cause of Proust's sentimental pains was Henri Rochat, who had come to live in the writer's apartment some time earlier.

Proust's response was eager and grateful, but also rather vague.

My dear Lionel,

. . . I told you that I suffered from torments of the heart. When one is not a theosophist, and moreover has not fallen

> in love with a person from his own milieu but with someone from the indigent classes, these sorts of torments are usually enhanced by remarkable financial hardships. "It's sad," La Bruyère wrote, "to be a lover without wealth." (COR XVII, 151)

The same citation from Jean de la Bruyère's "Du Coeur" (chapter 4 of his *Caractères*) appears in *In the Shadow of Young Girls in Flower,* one set of whose multiple versions in galley proof Proust started correcting in the month of April of 1918.[1] The excerpt above comes from a letter written to Hauser on September 24, 1918. This is a case of epistolary correspondence imitating art.

In the company of Henri Rochat, Proust verified that the more he spent on the young man, the greater devotion he gained from him. Rochat was a leech, but of an arithmetically predictable kind. Money has also a lot to do with the character of Gilberte Swann from Proust's novel, although she is the opposite of a leech (and with good reason, since one of the greatest fortunes in France, large enough to induce Robert de Saint-Loup to forget her Jewish origin and marry her, falls eventually in her lap from an unidentified relative's inheritance). It is during his teenage infatuation for Gilberte that Proust's Narrator discerns, yet fails to learn, that money and devotion do not always work in pairs: having delayed his afternoon visit to the girl, in order to secure for himself the preposterously large sum of money which he intends to spend in lavish gifts and flowers for her, from his carriage he sees Gilberte taking a romantic walk with somebody else, and renounces her love forever (*Young Girls in Flower,* 199–200).[2]

Under this respect, neither Proust nor his protagonist ever fully emancipated himself from the misconception that there is a meretricious side to all love affairs: their libidos are inseparable from the power and acquisitive abuse, to use Edward Hughes's phrase, "of wealth and social prestige." Money can't buy you love, but to Proust, it may earn you the gratitude of the objects of your longing, and even place you on a pedestal in their consideration, and this goes a long way in unlocking the way to their heart. Yet the protagonist of Proust's novel never faced the matching counterpart to such pecuniary management of affection that Proust had to face in Henri Rochat.

Less than two weeks after the second letter to Hauser dealing with his "torments of the heart," Proust declared himself furious about the critics and journalists among his circle of friends who had let him down, ignoring his entreaties for some decent reviews of Hauser's book. Hauser asked him not to take it personally: it is well known that friendship, when lacking theosophical altruism, is a fragile, unreliable thing. Proust was consoled by these words from Hauser. Not only did he find them to be true regarding ordinary friendships, they turned out to be even truer when applied to nontheosophical love—or, in other words, to the non-marital kind of love that afflicted Proust. Friendships of the sort that tied Proust to Hauser, of whose strength Hauser must never doubt, were rare and precious indeed, concluded Proust, completely unaware that his confidential mood would soon put Hauser's theosophical friendship to a very harsh test (COR XVII, 157, 158, 168).

Hauser was no less shortsighted than Proust on this occasion, but for opposite reasons. He did not have the slightest hint of what La Bruyère's aphorism, which Proust had cited in the previous letter, actually meant, even though its allusion to the interplay of love and money would have been enough to enlighten many another correspondent. Hence, being an incurable literalist, he asked for clarifications. What did Proust do with the 20,000 francs that Hauser had withdrawn on his behalf from the London Bank last summer, before the German offensive? What happened to Proust's "war chest"? (COR XVII, 169) Proust did not hesitate to answer. Obviously, he had misinterpreted his friend's overtures as heralding a much more open-minded and anticonformist attitude than Hauser's temperament could ever tolerate.

> My dear Lionel,
>
> . . . I thought I had already told you that although I didn't leave Paris, a love affair—non theosophical—with someone from the indigent classes, together with the philanthropic contributions pertinent to it, had turned those 20,000 francs into a banquet which I wouldn't go so far as describing as a sunny experience and whose menu included even a dessert (let's say that I was served in the guise of a pear), at the cost of an additional 10,000 francs, which I withdrew part from Rothschild and part from the London bank. All in all, 30,000 francs, not all gone, it's true, and of which I must add that they cover also my own nutrition (scarce) and my pharmacopeia (abundant). (COR XVII, 171)

We are faced here again with one of the opportunity costs that enabled the completion of the last few volumes of *In Search of Lost Time*. But

Hauser had no access to the hindsight that supports our appreciation of Proust as, if you will, a farsighted squanderer. His banker's mind was irreparably remote from such a positive interpretation.

With Henri Rochat, Proust discovered a Pygmalion-like vocation in himself. He tasted the expensive gratification of decking out his Henri with the most expensive outfits; and he eventually sweetened the pecuniary and sentimental shortcomings of this trying venture by attributing a similar kind of experience to his novel's Narrator. In *The Prisoner*, Proust's alter ego is initiated by Oriane de Guermantes to the secrets and mysteries of high fashion. He can thus take to playing with Albertine the way young girls play with their favorite doll, choosing her dresses, her shoes and slippers, even her hairdo.

Under the guidance of the Duchess of Guermantes, Proust's Narrator buys several dressing gowns and a cape for Albertine, manufactured by the incomparable Venice-based craftsman and fashion designer Mariano Fortuny y Madrazo. Born in Granada, Spain, Fortuny was admired by Proust for his fabrics in silk, cotton, satin, and velvet, decorated with motifs borrowed from famous Venetian painters such as Carpaccio, Titian, and Bellini. Proust could comfortably study these fabrics at Babani's, a store in the neighborhood of Boulevard Haussmann. At the time when, inspired by his own ambitions with Rochat, Proust wrote of his Narrator-as-Pygmalion, he took advantage of the detailed information about Fortuny's work and inspiration which he obtained from Maria Hahn, Reynaldo Hahn's sister, who in 1899 had become Fortuny's acquired aunt by marriage.

The fact that the Narrator chooses to decorate Albertine's body, both in the privacy of their intimacy and in public, with motifs drawn from the Venetian pictorial tradition denotes an ominous aesthetic choice; throughout their cohabitation, in fact, the Narrator regrets that Albertine's presence in his apartment, added to his morbid (and ineffectual) urge to quarantine her from all sexual promiscuities, is an unsurpassable impediment to his desire to visit the city of Venice. Only her death could free him to do what he wishes, thinks he, disastrously unaware of the multiple ways that her death, which will soon occur, would impact his future life. Albertine's Fortuny cape is inspired by Vittore Carpaccio's several depictions of the black mantle, embroidered with gold and pearls, which was worn, especially in the weeks preceding Mardi Gras, by the young members of various associations called Compagnie della calza.

Henri Rochat was a more voluble fellow than Alfred Agostinelli, and also more opportunistic than the Franco-Italian chauffeur and secretary, who would have never tolerated being decked out in "very dazzling pajamas,"[3] or expected Monsieur Proust to buy him thousands of francs' worth of new clothes in a single day.[4]

The fabulous Scheherazade-like elegance that embellishes Albertine at the time of her cohabitation with the Narrator is complemented by her spiritual embellishment, a consequence of the constant dialogue between the two lovers: the man's intellect is cultivated and refined, and the girl's mind, eager to absorb his Socratic method, penetrates it with no less ardor than that of her tongue, when each night it slips its rosy tip into his mouth before sleep. No such good fortune befalls Proust in his scabrous dealings with Rochat, whose spiritual embellishment is a lost cause, and who returns Proust's favors with the impersonal dexterity of a card dealer. Nonetheless, it is to the greedy malleability of this Swiss waiter, who, according to Jean-Yves Tadié, stayed at Proust's home "four times as long as Agostinelli,"[5] that we owe, in addition to the repertory of fantastical inventions which enrich the Narrator's cohabitation with Albertine, also, according to Proust himself, some of the peaks of his novel's narrative style (COR XXI, 310).

Not only does Proust turn the money squandered on Rochat into the pages describing Albertine's transformation into a "woman of fashion" ("femme élégante"; *Prisoner,* 54)[6]; four years later he also translates his bittersweet experience with Rochat into a remarkable metaphor of literary inspiration. You may recall, at this juncture, how much Albertine's stupor in bed delights Proust's Narrator, who considers that the costs of their cohabitation (by this time, Albertine is no more and no less than his expensively kept woman) are more than compensated by the pleasure he derives from kissing, probing, and fondling her unresponsive body. This cost-benefit symmetry feeds into the literary metaphor, as I am going to explain, but covers only one side of it.

Old, ill, and so tired that he can hardly leave his bed, Bergotte, the novelist admired by Proust's Narrator, gets into the habit of meeting in his bedroom certain young women, with whom he trades large sums of money against slight sexual favors. At this advanced point in the novel, Proust's reader can easily gather that this passage ascribes to Bergotte the same "recourse to venality" which has thus far characterized the sexual encounters, all vicarious in nature, between the Narrator and young women from the lower classes.[7] Not that Bergotte is under the delusion of getting any sort of satisfaction through these mercenary transactions; yet they give him the energy to ponder the reasons why his dreams of sexual fulfillment cannot come true, and these reflections provide him with the materials for some new remunerative book.

This passage was written by Proust in the last six months of his life and added by hand to the third and last typescript version of *The Prisoner*.[8]

> Bergotte had not been out of the house for years. . . . He was particularly [generous] to women, girls rather, who were ashamed to take so much from him in return for so little. He excused his behavior to himself because he knew he could never produce so well as in an atmosphere where he felt he was in love. Love, no, pleasure well rooted in the flesh helps literary work because it cancels out other pleasures. . . . And even if this love brings disillusion, at least that too keeps the surface of the soul in motion, where otherwise it might become stagnant. Desire, therefore, can be useful to the man of letters . . . by restoring some movement to a spiritual machine which otherwise, beyond a certain age, tends to seize up. None of this makes us happy, but we can examine the reasons that keep us from being so, reasons which would have remained hidden from us if not for these sudden irruptions of disappointment. And dreams cannot be made real, we know that; still, perhaps, we would not form any without desire, and it is useful to have dreams so that we can see their collapse and learn from it. So it was that Bergotte said to himself, 'I spend more on girls than a multimillionaire, but the pleasures or disappointments they bring me allow me to write a book and make money.' On economic grounds this reasoning was absurd, but no doubt he took some pleasure in transmuting gold into caresses in this way, and caresses back into gold. (*Prisoner,* 165–66)[9]

Bergotte trades money in return for these young women's physical intimacy; these encounters trigger his reflections on the mysterious gap separating desire from satisfaction, and later on these reflections foster his creative inspiration. The young women's contribution to his new book is pivotal, however indirect. First, their presence in Bergotte's bedroom awakens his dormant desire, dulled by old age, and he indulges in "dreams" of sexual and emotional fulfillment. Second, these dreams "collapse" and fade into disillusionment, and this "collapse" in turn reawakens in him the well-known yet never fully absorbed lesson that "none of this makes us happy." Although this alternation of "pleasure and disappointment" costs a fortune beyond his means to Bergotte, it fuels the reflections that enable him to "write a book and make money."

The novel's Narrator, who has made frequent usage of the same "markers of social superiority" to obtain erotic pleasure,[10] and is moreover personally well acquainted with the partial kind of sexual satisfaction that Bergotte derives from it, judges the logic of the old man's reasoning "absurd from an economic standpoint." Nonetheless, he goes on to consider that "no doubt [Bergotte] took some pleasure in transmuting gold into caresses in this way, and caresses back into gold."

Clearly, Bergotte does not speak to himself in figural terms when he reasons thus: "I spend more on girls than a multi-millionaire, but the pleasures or disappointments they bring me allow me to write a book and make money ('*argent*')." Bergotte's transactions with these young women and the benefits he derives from them share the pecuniary nature of any ordinary sale and purchase of goods by means of money. It is noteworthy, though, that in the Narrator's rephrasing of Bergotte's words, the *argent* (French for "money") spent by the writer on young women and earned by the sales of his books becomes its universal symbolic equivalent on the marketplace: *or* (French for "gold"). According to the Narrator, Bergotte purchases and then sells "caresses" in return for "gold." This sentence makes a slight pun on *argent,* the customary French word for "money," whose literal meaning designates silver metal, and on *or,* money's symbolic equivalent, whose literal meaning designates gold metal, but whose figural usage by John Ruskin designates the artwork and the talent needed to craft it.[11] This pun on silver and gold subverts Bergotte's literalistic calculation of earnings and liabilities. In this passage we are being reminded of an important Ruskinian motif in Proust's novel, namely, the symbiosis between art and finance.

If the Narrator rejects as absurd the economic validity of Bergotte's double transaction of first exchanging money for sexual intimacy, and then a new book for money, it is, in my opinion, because he is not so much interested in Bergotte's lucrative gain as in the effects of inspiration on his creativity, which is an effect external to the logic of commodity exchange. The Narrator is a late bloomer as an artist, and, as a matter of fact, in the days of Bergotte's physical decline, he is not a writer yet. At this stage in his life, the Narrator has resigned himself to the condition of écrivain manqué, or failed writer, and he will not emancipate himself from this label before approaching forty, at the close of the novel, after the end of World War I. To him, trading money for sexual intimacy stops at the moment of gratification, as we saw in his fondling of his Sleeping Beauty, Albertine. Not so for Proust, to whom both love, even if hopelessly coveted, and sex, even if expensively purchased, provide fodder for his novel on Lost Time. There is a gap in awareness, here as in most of the novel, between the Narrator—unwittingly destined to devote the rest of his life to the craft of writing, hence to become a devotee of artistic inspiration—and his alter ego, the Author whose dedication to that very craft and sustained inspiration has brought the Narrator into existence. Only near the end of Proust's novel does the distinction between fictional character and historical author fade away.

In rejecting as absurd the economic validity of Bergotte's transactions, the Narrator rephrases Bergotte's words. Bergotte reasoned in terms of a new book destined to earn him money ("un livre qui me rapporte de l'argent"). The Narrator, talking like an alchemist, says instead that Bergotte transmuted gold into caresses and then caresses back into gold ("transmuter ainsi l'or en caresses et les caresses en or").[12] Like any ordinary young would-be artist, he is intrigued by the seemingly magic power of the inspiration that spurs Bergotte's artistic creativity, a prodigy that is still mysterious and elusive to him.[13] It is not accidental that Jean Santeuil, the fictional precursor of Proust's Narrator, uses the term *transmutation* to designate the imaginative conversion, as we saw, "of remembrance into a directly felt reality"—a conversion that has the power to make a cohesive whole of his past and present experiences.[14] Proust has thus assigned to the character of his Narrator, who is about ten years younger than he, some of the ideas on the interplay of aesthetics and economics which he learned from Ruskin in his own youth. I am referring particularly to Ruskin's argument, from *Sesame and Lilies,* that books are as precious as gold, and the patience and tenaciousness required in their composition are as strenuous as the exertions of gold miners.[15] In the Narrator's eyes, Bergotte's books are as many ideal ingots, but made of the sort of gold which is obtained by mysterious means reminiscent of alchemical tricks. But this book of mine shows that, as Proust writes this episode near the end of his life, he is less indifferent than his Narrator to the money earned by an author from the sale of his or her books.

We have finally pinpointed, in this passage from *The Prisoner,* the section from Proust's novel that is most evidently inspired by the favorable trade-off between the opportunity costs of the company he kept with Rochat and other such dreamboats and the revenue from his royalties.

More generally speaking, the Bergotte model, if I may call it so, of trading gold for caresses and vice versa, indicates that Proust was not unaware of the triangular interconnection linking to one another: the real-life opportunities that had fostered his creativity for several years; their costs in terms of time, money, and good health; and their long-term gains, both economic and aesthetic in nature.

With regard to the aesthetic side of the Bergotte model, let me cite words which Ruskin wrote in *The Political Economy of Art:* "The things that give intellectual or emotional enjoyment . . . continually supply new pleasures and new powers of giving pleasure to others. And these, therefore, are the only things which can rightly be thought of as giving 'wealth' or 'well being'."[16] To Ruskin, the sources of intellectual or emotional enjoyment, ranging from botanical gardens to works of art, are receptacles of wisdom and social virtue, and empower their creators to benefit their fellow human beings. This opinion is expressed with special fervor, one could say "in the manner of a secular sermon,"[17] in *Sesame and Lilies,* one of the two books by Ruskin that were translated into French by the young Proust.[18] Not surprisingly, this idea of Ruskin's informs Bergotte's last days, which are described in *The Guermantes Way.* "A dead author can at least enjoy fame without fatigue," considers the Narrator, adding that this is not the case with Bergotte, who is overwhelmed on his deathbed by the irrepressible vitality of the books that bring him glory: "His books, bouncing around the place like girls we love ['des filles qu'on aime'] but whose impetuous youth and fiery ['bruyants'] pleasures are exhausting to us ['vous fatiguent'], brought a daily succession of fresh admirers . . . to his bedside" (*Guermantes Way,* 322).[19] For obvious reasons I must reject Mark Treharne's English translation of "filles qu'on aime" with "daughters we love" in this passage: the girls figuratively bouncing around Bergotte's bedside are not his affectionate daughters, of which he had none that I know, but the promiscuous young women (*fillettes*) whose company he used to pay for.[20] Their exuberant energy enabled him to fill the last of his books with both the energy of youth and the wisdom of old age. Not only do these new books earn large sums of money for their author; more important, they turn him into an object of gratitude, insofar as they are "serviceable" to those who flock to his bedside, after having read them, as Ruskin recommends we should read, "with thanks and remembrance."[21] In the end, Bergotte's books crown deservedly his artistic career by earning him an afterlife in the memory of his readers.

Chapter 21

LOVE'S BOOKKEEPER

If the correlation between Proust's expensive habits and the creative opportunities they gave him was clear to the writer, it was bound to look rather blurred through a banker's gray lenses—especially after it entailed the vaporization of Proust's "war chest." Proust had tried to lighten the tone of his confession to Hauser about the hefty costs of his "torments of the heart" with a parenthetical remark: "Let's say that I was served in the guise of a pear" (COR XVII, 148, 151, 171). The irony of self-deprecation is evident, since in French domestic lexicon the term *poire* designates a simpleton or a sucker: when a pear is ripe, as sweet as fellow French diners liked to taste it in Proust's times, it is ready to fall. What I find less evident is the reason for Proust's foolhardiness. Had he really read Hauser's *Three Levers of the New World* as closely as he claimed? It would not seem that he had, or how could he miss the passage in which Hauser denounces "sensual love [as] artificial and sterile," opposing it to spiritual and reproductive love, and lamenting that novelists fill their pages with the former, confusing thereby a sensation with a sentiment?

Obviously, irony and self-deprecation would not suffice to absolve Proust in the eyes of Hauser. No sooner did their regime of epistolary intimacy make its debut than it went into bankruptcy: it was the end of their experimentation with mutual sincerity. As I said before, Hauser came to the conclusion that Proust's irresponsibility verged on the pathological. No paramour is worth 30,000 francs! The excision of this huge sum from Proust's balance sheet was even worse, in Hauser's eyes, than the money he had risked losing from his Liebig dividends for ten years running by neglecting to notify the Liebig Company of his new address in Paris. Proust would act wisely and counter his own mental instability by taking out a life annuity with some serious insurance company. Hauser continued:

> My dear Marcel,
>
> Can you picture the surprise of a medical doctor who, after struggling frantically for weeks and months to tear a patient suffering from typhoid fever from the grip of death, saw him on the first day of convalescence greedily enjoying a dish of sauerkraut? Well, this is the sort of impression I got from reading your last letter. I say, for more than four months I've been making superhuman efforts, at the risk of losing my mental sanity, to stretch your blanket enough to keep warm, if not your entire body, at least your most essential limbs, and no sooner do I turn my back than you amuse yourself at cutting away with a pair of scissors broad strips from the blanket and scattering them in the wind. If only you showed at least a hint of regret; but no, the smile on your lips is the tangible proof of your perfect recklessness. (COR XVII, 173)

As if the anger igniting his proposal of the life annuity was not enough to satisfy his disappointment, Hauser lingered on the advantages and timeliness of this proposal with the pedantry of a bureaucrat from Kafka's penal colony. Proust would derive substantial advantages from a life annuity insofar as, in his friend's view, the writer had a long life before him. Proust's illness, said Hauser, reminded him of the many ailments suffered by Voltaire, who, although old and frail, managed to escort most of his servants and acquaintances to their tombs. Nonetheless, it is likely that the medical doctor charged by the insurance company to evaluate Proust's state of health would find him very ill, suggesting therefore that the insurance company pay a high annuity on Proust's capital, at a rate of 8 percent, 10 percent, or even 12 percent. This way, Hauser concluded, "your capital would be sheltered from your heart's whims" (COR XVII, 173).

Three days later, Proust announced that he was "filled with consternation" by Hauser's letter. His friend was accusing him "of unweaving with one hand, incorrigible Penelope, what [he had been] skillfully weaving with the other hand." Proust took this occasion to elaborate a further reflection on the "nonmarital love," or, more precisely, the anticonformist love, subversive of bourgeois customs, that he talks about in his novel.

From the perspective of a theosophist such as Hauser, he began, love, *crudelis amor,* was not a passion that induced the lover to give up his life gladly, and even less so his wealth. Even in the worst amorous predicaments, a theosophist knew how to act like a reasonable man—or better still, like a bookkeeper. It was not without sarcasm that Proust chose this term to designate Hauser's stance toward the most noble of human sentiments. And yet, Proust went on, as Love's Bookkeeper, Hauser was right. It was he, Proust, who was wrong, when he challenged his friend's imperative that one's budget must always come first, by using Pascal's argument that "the heart has its own reason which reason does not know" (and, ironically enough, Hauser's bookkeeping would know even less). No, there is no merit whatsoever in surrendering to passion, Proust went on with revengeful and ironic verve, while there is immense merit in pulling back from the drives of one's own heart.

> My dear Lionel,
>
> . . . Whatever the outlook that is taken on from the yoke one is willing to endure [to achieve the goal of a balanced budget], this yoke is made magnificent by the urges of expansive self-expression it keeps in check, and which are grievously determined to submit to it. It doesn't matter if this yoke takes on the name of bookkeeping. When this is the case, we're then experiencing sublime bookkeeping, a form of bookkeeping worthy of Corneille. (COR XVII, 179)

Is this the last drop? Before discussing Hauser's reaction to this letter, it is worthwhile to underline the coherence of the position the writer assumed in it with respect to the relationship, posited in his novel, between personal identity, remembrance, and the experience of love. The contrast opposing Proust and Hauser is analogous in Proust's novel to the contrast opposing the Narrator and Henri Bergson, a French pioneer of neuropsychology and, incidentally, the husband of Louise Neuberger and therefore Proust's acquired cousin.[1]

In a 1901 lecture on dreams, Bergson declared that "we do not forget anything."[2] Proust's Narrator is equally persuaded that buried in the depth of the self there lies "an unknown region" where "all our inner riches, our past joys, our pains" are stored. When they are of no help in understanding our immediate sensations or our immediate needs, these memories are simply dormant, present in our memory but not to our memory. It is as if the memories we need at any specific moment push all the others into an opaque corral of temporary amnesia. To any set of memories prevailing over the others in certain circumstances, there corresponds a certain self, a *moi,* a certain personal identity. This mechanism of selective remembrance, described by Proust's Narrator, reminds me of the metaphor of the pyramid adopted by Bergson in his book *L'énergie spirituelle.* According to Bergson, the mass of memories stored in our memory is like the immense base of a pyramid; these memories try to climb up continuously "from the night of unconsciousness," to leave the rest behind and reach the tip of the pyramid, which corresponds to the level of conscious awareness. However, our "attention to life" gives precedence only to memories that can contribute to immediate action and immediate decisions.[3] In this connection between our memory of the past and our experience of the present lies a fundamental difference between Bergson and Proust's Narrator, however. This difference is principally owing to the fact that of our many possible identities, Proust's Narrator has a predilection for his "true self" ("vrai moi"), the "deep self" which Proust wrote about for the first time in *Contre Sainte-Beuve.*[4] While this self is linked to our deepest and most significant feelings, Bergson grants primacy to the self that is pragmatically tied to our immediate concerns. So there is an anti-Bergsonian thrust in Proust's suggestion that Hauser, being equally dominated by immediate interests, is Love's Bookkeeper.

To Bergson, the "harmony" between our past memory and our present experience is functional to the impending moment of our next choice, decision, or initiative.[5] To be fair to the French philosopher, this view of his is not the result of the way things ought to be, but rather of our pragmatic inclination to act according to utilitarian considerations. He phrases it thus in *Essai sur les données immédiates de la conscience:* "Our . . . social life has greater practical importance to us than our interior and individual existence."[6] In the view of Proust's Narrator, on the contrary, we must learn to rule over utilitarian considerations, so as to establish the true meaning and relevance of our present contingency; this can be achieved by means of an analogy between this present contingency and some impressions or sensations we went through in the past. Just like Hauser's balanced-budget imperative, the utilitarianism described by Bergson entails, to Proust, a renunciation of our most authentic identity. It amounts to a genuine self-betrayal.[7]

One such case of self-betrayal occurs in the episode of the trees of Hudimesnil from *In Search of Lost Time.* Riding in the carriage of his grandmother's good friend, Madame de Villeparisis, Proust's Narrator feels an inexplicable happiness at the sight of three trees. Try as he may, however, he cannot find a reason for his happiness. He wonders: are these trees, so strangely familiar, a memory from childhood, the remnants from a dream, a cryptic epiphany, or just an optical impression owing to eye fatigue. They seem to be asking of him that he "bring them back to the realm of the living"; he recognizes in their "naïve and passionate gesticulations . . . the impotent regret of a loved one who, having lost the power of speech [just as his grandmother would on her deathbed], knows that he will never be able to let us know what he wants." Having failed repeatedly to identify the source of his emotion, the Narrator gives up puzzling over it, and at that precise moment he is "as sad as though [he] had just lost a friend, felt something die in [himself], as though [he] had broken a promise to a dead man or failed to recognize a god" (*Young Girls in Flower,* 299).[8]

The Narrator of *In Search of Lost Time* retrieves memories of vital relevance to his most authentic identity, and leaves aside irrelevant memories, by neglecting those pressing and utilitarian interests whose primacy is acknowledged by Bergson. Most relevant, to him, are the "urges of expansive self-expression" mentioned in his letter to Hauser, while the needs pertaining to his daily existence or mere survival are of secondary importance. That is why my discussion of the monetary transactions occurring in Bergotte's bedroom treated the beneficial effects of such transactions as a metaphor of literary inspiration that is applicable to Proust himself. Proust's principal means of self-expression was his own art. You may see in the money he squandered on Henri Rochat either the price of sexual favors or the wasteful cost of an eccentric sort of gregariousness; regardless, the fact remains that the contribution of this squandered money to the Albertine saga in *The Prisoner*—hence to Proust's artistic self-expression—was priceless.

The crisis in Hauser's friendship with Proust was not irremediable, even if the reaction of Love's Bookkeeper to Proust's words would have been unworthy of Corneille. In a letter imbued with moralistic stoicism, Hauser threatened to make a more drastic break with Proust than he would ever be able to implement, given his temperament. Hauser did not belong, as we do, to Proust's posterity, nor had he had a chance to read *The Prisoner* and *The Fugitive* yet, since they would be unpublished for several years: Proust's complex vision of love is clearly illustrated in these books. How could Hauser possibly know or even suspect that, in Proust's universe, all affections—whether for paramours, friends, relatives, or kept lovers—drew the object of the writer's attachment into an emotional cobweb made thicker and more viscous by any attempt to escape? Although the banker's letter to Proust, dated October 25, 1918, speaks in an intentionally distancing voice, deliberately destructive of their relationship, by this time Hauser was reduced to a condition of mental captivity. A considerable portion of his inner life had become the toy of the whimsical child that Proust still was, whenever he felt inclined to play with someone else's emotions.

Hauser had written (lying even to himself): "At the risk of dispelling your illusions on that elastic notion people call friendship, which has been the source of many misunderstandings between us, I will tell you that all I did for you I would have done for anyone who found himself in similar circumstances, without expecting anything in return." Then he went on:

> As you know, since you read it in my book, according to theosophy man is the absolute master of his own actions, but not of their consequences. In light of this principle you are perfectly free to use your heart and your purse as you like, but if you act without thinking and invest unwisely both the heart and the purse, you'll have to face the consequences, and even if you are too proud to blame yourself, you will certainly regret having followed the lead that, such was your impression, came straight from your heart. . . . Your dissertations on the beauty of sacrifice are perfectly correct per se, yet I wouldn't encourage anybody to apply your principles, especially nowadays when the cost of living is so steep. Poets are the happiest of creatures for as long as they soar in their own dream world, but since they cannot possibly hover there constantly, they find themselves deservedly unhappy when they land on earth, something that must happen to them from time to time, at least at mealtimes. (COR XVII, 181)

By rescuing "the debris of Proust's financial shipwreck," Hauser had worked hard to ensure him higher revenues, since his friend had complained that what was left him was not enough to live on. Hauser had hoped he would be supported in his endeavor, but Proust had instead amused himself in shedding slice after slice of his own capital. "I think I can safely declare that you are a mediocre administrator. Obviously it's not your fault; if you were a bourgeois, in the derogatory meaning of the word, you wouldn't be a poet. The flaws that led you to your present financial situation are those that sprout out of your best qualities." Out of mere love for his fellow human beings, not to mention the affection he had felt for Proust's "admirable mother," Hauser was trying to find out by what practical intervention the remains of Proust's patrimony could be salvaged (Ibid.). This explains his proposal of the life annuity, a project which the two friends, after a few inconclusive discussions, did not carry out.

Proust reacted by declaring himself in perfect agreement with what Hauser had written about the affections and altruism "of the heart." It seemed to him that Hauser had not paid close enough attention to the words from his previous letter. When Proust mentioned the heart in reference to Pascal's aphorism, he did it to stress how determined he was not to seek comfort in Pascal's viewpoint. The fact was that "there is nothing as unrelated to the 'heart' as the selfish sentiment we call love." If the "reasons" of the heart were unrelated to rational thinking, as Pascal wrote, they were unrelated to the selfishness of love as well. As we saw earlier on, on the occasion of Hauser's first successful investment on Proust's behalf, the writer saw in the banker the paradigm of a truly noble heart, capable of greater devotion than a mother's toward her baby. Nonetheless, love was something entirely different: important to the philosopher, rich in vital precepts to those who analyze it, and atrocious to those who feel it, the lovers themselves—Proust could comfortably claim he knew a thing or two about this latter group of people. But he had never claimed that love could be identified with happiness.

At this point, the letter switched abruptly to the topic of Proust's apartment in Boulevard Haussmann: if Proust were to pay his rent in its entirety (he did not, as we know), it would cost him 6,500 francs a year. Hauser had accused him of being too vain to give up such luxurious quarters. Did Hauser truly believe that Proust squandered all that money out of mere vanity? How can vanity be a factor, when Proust never entertained at home? All the furniture in the dining room was piled up, one piece on top of another, under a thick layer of dust. In the twelve years he had spent at 102 Boulevard Haussmann, Proust had not eaten "a single meal" at home: when he was forced to stay in bed, that is to say, most of the time he spent at home, he fed himself with café au lait; when he got up, he ate his meals at the restaurant. But his apartment had a great merit: it gave him asthma attacks less frequently than other places did. Living in a different part of Paris or a different apartment building would worsen his state of health, and in his present condition he doubted he could handle the change.

And here, to harp one last time on the motif of cruel and pitiless love, Proust took leave of Hauser in the attitude of a subdued lover. Dawn had risen on Paris while he was writing these last words. "Like Scheherazade, I see morning rise, and act accordingly: 'She fell silent at daybreak'" (COR XVII, 182).

Chapter 22

MISSION ACCOMPLISHED

The armistice was signed in November 1918. Seven months later, Germany accepted the peace treaty conditions. Although these were not overly harsh to the defeated country—at least as far as their practical implementation was concerned—they were scarcely advantageous to France, which had suffered heavy losses in human and economic resources and was bracing itself for a slow, hard recovery (COR XVII, 187; XVIII, 135).

In spite of this state of affairs, everything in Proust's life converged harmoniously in 1919, the year he was crowned with literary fame. His literary success fed his worldly prestige, which attracted chic admirers; being favored by influential friends increased both his personal income and his narcissistic opportunities. Proust published three books in 1919: the second volume of *In Search of Lost Time,* entitled *In the Shadow of Young Girls in Flower;* the NRF edition of the first volume, *Swann's Way,* originally published by Grasset; and *Pastiches et mélanges,* which includes the collection of the pastiches he wrote at the time of the *affaire Lemoine,* the prefaces he wrote to his translations from Ruskin, and three articles published in *Le Figaro* from 1900 to 1907.

Proust earned 5,490 francs or $6,200 in royalties from Gallimard, a slender sum for now, but over time his royalties were clearly destined to grow exponentially. Literary journals as well as newspapers such as *Le Figaro* wooed him. In December 1919, he was awarded the Prix Goncourt, one of the most prestigious prizes to be bestowed by the French literary establishment. He became the unrivaled favorite of the aristocratic ladies from the Faubourg Saint-Germain, one of whom—Princess Murat—did not shy away from knocking at his apartment door in the heat of the night, only to be driven away by Céleste Albaret. The following year, no less than a queen would have her turn at being snubbed by the greatest Parisian writer (COR XIX, vii, 43).

The fieriest, and certainly one of the most qualified of Proust's admirers to appreciate his work, was Jacques Rivière, the NRF editor who contributed significantly over the next few years to the promotion and diffusion of his writings. In April, Rivière requested Proust's permission to publish an extract from his novel's still unpublished second volume in the new, postwar series of the NRF. He was planning to place it "at the head" of the other authors of the publishing house, in consideration of the rank that he expected Proust soon to occupy in French letters. When the writer objected that this publication might cause another delay in the appearance of his three books, Rivière countered that it was extremely important to inaugurate the new journal with these pages in particular, which were "exceedingly indicative of the new directions prevailing in literature" (COR XVIII, 69). Exchanges such as this one gave Proust a measure of the favor his new books were destined to receive.

The three books did eventually see the light. *Pastiches et mélanges* collected, together with the pastiches that had been published in *Le Figaro* at the time of the Lemoine affair, more recent ones that had not yet appeared in print. Proust refrained from including a new pastiche written in the voice of Saint-Simon because of tension with Paul Morand, an incident we will soon examine.

Robert de Montesquiou—the unchallenged arbiter of worldly and literary elegance in the French capital—behaved most exquisitely of all Proust's old friends, especially in the way he acknowledged being outclassed by Proust's new paradigms of artistic stylishness. Montesquiou was especially welcoming to the *pastiches,* which he defined "a miracle" in their genre; he appreciated his own flattering portrait in the ninth pastiche.[1] And he praised the essays collected in the *mélanges* section for "their quality in artistry and their quantity of insights"; but they were so rich in references and difficult to read, he quipped, that they reminded him of "a beehive full of alveoli dripping honey" (COR XVIII, 239). During the period in which Proust received this letter from Montesquiou, he wrote a reproachful one to Paul Morand: if literary fame had finally earned him the respect and attentions of Morand's lover, Hélène Soutzo, he would now have to adjust to the inconveniences of celebrity—in this case, to the frustration of seeing his own name exploited, through unpleasant innuendoes about his secret nightlife, to add luster to someone else's artwork. Morand had inserted an "Ode to Marcel Proust" in his new poetry collection, *Lampes à Arc,* in which he wondered "what dissipations" Proust indulged in at night, since they left him with "eyes so watery and worn out," and what was the forbidden nature of the nocturnal "dreads" that left him "so forbearing and goodhearted."[2]

Proust told Morand that were it not for their deep friendship (cemented, as we know, by the beauty of Hélène Soutzo), he would feel under the obligation to challenge him to a duel. Instead, he devised a longer-lasting retribution by giving up the original project he had announced in the first edition of *Pastiches et mélanges,* consisting of a new pastiche singing the praises of Soutzo and written in the voice of Saint-Simon.[3] Curiously enough, there remains no trace of the manuscript of this disowned pastiche, announced to the princess by Proust himself in a letter dated February 1, 1919. Did he perhaps destroy it altogether, furious at being publicly mocked by her lover? The hypothesis is not implausible.[4]

Proust's pastiches in the voice of Saint-Simon were not written under a lucky star, it seems. The first one, "Dans les *Mémoires* de Saint-Simon," mocked the Princess Murat's second-rate nobility (Marie, née de Rohan-Chabot, was the wife of Lucien Murat, a grandson of the Napoleonic king of Naples, whose title was of recent, imperial acquisition). This act of irreverence cost him the treasured friendship of Louis d'Albufera, who, as a cousin to the princess through his mother and the titular of an equally second-rank title, broke irrevocably with the writer after reading it.[5] Perhaps, this insult to his cousin gave Albufera a convenient excuse to retaliate against Proust, without giving vent to his irritation for the parallel, implicitly drawn in *In Search of Lost Time,* between the compromising establishments where both the character of Rachel and its model, Albufera's lover Louisa de Mornand, used to hang out in their youth.

Jacques Rivière was so enthusiastic about Proust's books that, with all due precautions and blandishments, he offered him a job as the NRF's literary critic. Proust described himself as "too unwell" to accept, but suggested the alternative of publishing a literary essay from time to time, in the guise of a letter addressed directly to Rivière. The editor was more than pleased with the idea; it amounted, after all, to an acceptance of his own proposal in a slightly modified form. This is how an extemporaneous and extremely fruitful collaboration between Proust and the NRF first began, resulting right away in the essay on Flaubert's style that we discussed earlier. Given the mock-epistolary form of this essay, it is noteworthy that, while praising Flaubert's style, Proust approvingly mentioned the widespread opinion that good writers are at their best in their correspondence rather than in their novels: the epistolary mode would allow writers to relax the constraints imposed by theme, characterization, plotting, and local color, so they could "let themselves go." Contrary to what one would expect, Proust writes, as much as Flaubert excelled in his famously rhythmic and uniform style—the "moving walkway" of his novels—he became monotonously dull in drafting his letters.[6] As we have seen, this was not one of Proust's problems: his stylistic and metaphoric effervescence is on display as much in his epistolary exchanges as in his fiction. During the last years of his life Proust considered forbidding the publication of his epistolary writings; however, this attitude was certainly not owing to stylistic considerations, but rather, I think, to content-related matters. The self-image he had created through his novel's pseudoautobiography needed to be shielded from the intrusion of the documentary evidence, not all of it commendable, that emerges from some of his letters.

The most obliging of all of Proust's admirers was by this time Walter Berry. As we saw, after tirelessly and vainly pulling strings to remedy the accidental sale of Proust's 100 Tramways de Mexico shares, Berry got deeply involved in the perennially frustrated attempt to cash his 30,000-franc Warburg check. Berry also acted as the messenger between Proust and Princess Soutzo. On one occasion the writer instructed Berry thus: "You will kindly explain to the princess that no sooner does my fever go down and I am rid of my sore throat—it could be as early as tomorrow—although I'm not very hopeful about it, I will go out and pay her a visit." From the persistent and awkward suitor he had been in the past, Proust was currently in a position to dictate precise conditions in anticipation of his public appearances. "I will drink a cup of steam-hot coffee in the hotel's gallery instead of the cold coffee I had the other day in the princess's salon, which forced me to put my fur coat back on, but a quarter of an hour too late"—which explains not only his sore throat but also whom he had to thank for it. Whoever wished to meet Proust would now have to respect the "rites" which Proust could "not transgress with impunity" (COR XVIII, 1).

Since Proust did not show up at a soirée given by Princess Murat, she went looking for him at home late one night. His incriminating pastiche à la Saint-Simon had not seen the light yet, of course. Proust instructed Céleste Albaret to tell her he was out: he was indeed at home, in bed as usual, but as a rule, female visitors, except Albaret, were *personae non gratae* in his bedroom.[7] Princess Murat told Albaret that she was far from surprised that Proust had not returned home yet, since everybody knew that the writer "[went] out a great deal" these days. Proust mentioned this episode to Geneviève Straus's husband, as an example of the chasm that was gradually opening up between his actual life as a disabled person and the increasingly fanciful conjectures people were making about his secret nightlife (COR XVIII, 63).

Analogously with his Narrator's secret and scandalous cohabitation with Albertine, it was at home that Proust abandoned himself to the pleasures that rumors claimed he was seeking in ill-famed brothels. Henri Rochat must have been an inexhaustible source of ecstatic torments in this phase of the writer's life. As I remarked earlier, a living arrangement of this sort with a woman, even one much older than Albertine or Rochat himself, would have been virtually impossible in the segregated world of the time, since the rest of this woman's life would have been unforgivingly marked by ostracism. For matters concerning his thorny affair with Rochat, Proust found a confidant in a young diplomat, Jacques Truelle. He told Truelle many of the problems he was experiencing with the young Swiss man, with an openness that suggests the young diplomat may have had a full grasp of the true nature of their relationship. Rochat wanted to go back home, to Switzerland (further developments show that this was mere wishful thinking on Proust's part), and needed a safe-conduct pass to travel. "Six months or perhaps a year ago," Proust had sought the same document through the services of a Madame Edwards, but the issuing of the document was delayed. Rochat had gone to wait for his safe-conduct pass on the French Riviera, and, having contracted syphilis and squandered all the money Proust had given him to go home, he had come back to Paris to convalesce in the writer's apartment. Meanwhile, the war-induced campaign against foreigners had made it impossible for him to go back to his previous job at the Ritz; hence, with cynical lightheartedness, he lived off Proust. If Truelle could take care of Rochat's safe-conduct pass, Proust could at long last get rid of his importunate guest (COR XVIII, 142).

One month later, Rochat was successfully dispatched to Switzerland. However, he left with the expectation of receiving an immediate job offer from his compatriots. Predictably enough, things did not go as smoothly as that, and a few weeks later he showed up again in Paris. At first he took a room in a hotel, but, shortly thereafter, penniless, he once again asked for Proust's hospitality. The word *no* seemed to disappear from the writer's vocabulary whenever he was in the presence of the young Swiss man. They lived together once again, and Proust confided to Truelle that the presence of Rochat in his apartment "poison[ed]" his existence. Sleep had become impossible. "I am no longer able to overcome my attacks. Although your friend Madame de Ludre gave me . . . plugs to seal my ears against noise, I am in a pitiful condition. I can't work, I can't do anything, I can't talk, I can't write" (COR XVIII, 195).

In 1919 Proust's financial initiatives increasingly escaped Lionel Hauser's control. As we noted, Proust embarked—or more precisely, had several friends embark on his behalf—on the epic attempt to cash the 30,000-franc check he had received from Warburg & Co. in 1914, which was still uncashed after five years. Hauser soon found himself cut out of this undertaking, even though he was the Paris agent of the German firm. He limited himself, in April, to defending the firm's solvency, about which Proust had expressed reservations. From Hauser's viewpoint, this defense of the good name of the firm that he represented in France amounted to upholding his own probity.

Five people were involved in the attempt to cash the Warburg check: Georges-Raphaël Lévy, but only for the brief interval needed to verify that the check was not honored even after Proust had endorsed it to his name; Walter Berry, who went so far as to consult the current minister of the interior, Jules Pams; Geneviève Straus, who made useless enquiries at the Paris Civil Court; and Céleste Albaret, whom Proust sent to query Auguste Besse, the sequestrator of the funds which the Comptoir d'Escompte held in France on behalf of the Warburg firm before the war (a week after Albaret's visit, Monsieur Besse spread the rumor that he was moving to Algeria "forever" and made himself impervious to further queries); and finally, Robert de Billy—last but, once more, not least, after his miraculous reduction of Proust's giant debt in additional collaterals on forwards contracts in 1912. In March 1920, Billy found a temporary solution by interceding on Proust's behalf at his own bank, the Mirabaud Bank, where the Warburg check was accepted as a guarantee against a 30,000-franc loan.[8]

Around the end of January 1919 Hauser learned from Proust that he had been evicted. Aunt Amélie and her daughter Adèle had sold the lower part of the apartment building on Boulevard Haussmann to the Varin-Barnier Bank, which intended to turn it into office space for a new branch. Proust could have continued living in his apartment, which was situated on an upper floor, but he feared the noise and dust from the works of renovation.[9] Proust reckoned that his rent arrears amounted to 25,000 francs. He had no idea where to find such a sum, and was considering putting his furniture, carpets, curtains, and armchairs up for sale. He asked Armand, Duke de Guiche (incidentally, the fourth principal model for the character of Saint-Loup in his novel), to handle the negotiations with the new owner of the apartment building (COR XVIII, 10, 77).

Aunt Amélie had sold the building without a word to Proust about it, and the writer was deeply hurt, according to Céleste Albaret. If he had known of his aunt's decision to sell, Albaret claimed, "he would have bought the building himself without hesitation," since "he could have afforded that amount without affecting his lifestyle."[10] In this regard Albaret is wrong. Amèlie Weil had bought Marcel and Robert Proust's half of the building at 102 Blvd Haussmann in 1907 for 193,000 francs, but this price was the result of a sleight of hand on her part; the year before, in the proceedings of Jeanne Weil's inheritance, the worth of the Proust brothers' half had been estimated at the more realistic figure of 284,100 francs; the entire property was worth 568,911 francs.[11] If we pattern the latter figure's appreciation on the inflation rate (which is a conservative way to evaluate the cost of real estate in time), we may infer that by 1919 the building on Boulevard Haussmann would have been worth at least 1,371,868 francs. Now, this figure coincides almost to the penny with Proust's personal worth in nominal terms (before debt) in 1919. (After debt, his worth was closer to 1,290,000 francs.)[12] So, even the cost of the *rez-de-chaussée* which his aunt had sold to the Varin-Barnier Bank would have been exorbitant to Proust, not to mention the cost of the whole building. Regardless, it would have been churlish on Amélie Weil's part to ask Proust if he was interested in buying a building whose value had quadrupled with respect to the meager price she had paid to him.

More than anything else, Proust was terrified at the prospect of moving out. He mobilized friends and acquaintances to find him new quarters in keeping with his many needs, an apartment where he would be able to breathe comfortably and write undisturbed by noise. It must be remembered that at this time Paris was a highly industrialized city, where air pollution was an endemic cause of lung disease; factories poured noxious smokes into the air with virtually no control on the part of the city authorities.[13] Proust's asthmatic condition was closer to a rule than an exception.

This consideration brings me to open a long-overdue parenthesis about Proust's legendary "fumigations," a steady object of scorn and derision on the part of readers, biographers, and graduate students through the years. It is high time to set things straight once and for all, as this issue has important ramifications, I think, vis-à-vis Proust's inimitable prose style. Proust's ritual fumigations were consistent with a widespread therapeutic practice of his times, which originated from the alternative medicine of Vedic tradition called Ayurveda, imported to the West by British colonialists. This practice consisted of the inhalation of fumes from the *datura stramonium,* the so-called Devil's snare, a plant of the nightshade family whose leaves are rich in tropane alkaloids, whose smoke has clinically tested bronchodilator effects as well as a broad variety of hallucinogenic effects, including mild sedation and even alternation or distortion of one's own memories. A variety of products derived from it, or closely analogous with it, ranging from Proust's favorite Legras powder to the Escouflaire powder, from Potter's Asthma Remedy imported from England to the Asthmador cigarettes imported from Germany, were sold in French pharmacies, not only in Proust's days but even in the recent past; it seems that at some time or other Proust tried most of them. Proust burned the Legras powder in a saucer near his bed upon waking up and before his breakfast. For fear of a coughing fit, he never used a match to light it; instead, he would light a small piece of paper from the candle that was always burning in the corridor near his bed (not in his room), and with it he would light the powder. So, there was nothing terribly eccentric about Proust's fumigations, except their constancy and intensity: Proust inhaled thick fumes from tropane alkaloids day in and day out for much longer than two decades, which amounts to saying that he was an addict. The first time Céleste Albaret walked into Proust's bedroom in 1914, she could hardly find her way around because of the density of the fumes. And since he likely wrote more often than not under their influence, one wonders to what extent their effects may have contributed to making his prose style as mysteriously, as neuronally irresistible as so many of us find it; one wonders as well if these addictive fumes contributed to Albaret's thousand happy returns to her master's bedroom at all hours of day and night—a quite intriguing matter to any Proust fan, yet not for me to probe, not in this book at least.[14]

Back to the there and then.

The writer moved temporarily to Rue Laurent-Pichat, in an apartment belonging to his friend, the famous actress Réjane, where a couple of his neighbors, he wrote, had sex, frequently, with the frenzy of two "whales in love" (COR XVIII, 178). In the fall, he moved to an apartment at 44 Rue Hamelin. After this final move to new lodgings, one that was long overdue in Hauser's eyes, the banker sent Proust his congratulations. He was persuaded that this change would benefit both his friend's health and his purse. Later on, he would be left speechless by the news that, at 16,000 francs a year, Proust's rent in Rue Hamelin was close to three times the amount he used to pay in Boulevard Haussmann (COR XVIII, 28); the apartment was furnished, and even if, with the landlady's consent, Proust had her furniture moved out, he had to pay an extra lease for it). But this turning point in the two friends' relationship came about after a few other skirmishes that we will examine first.

Another novelty regarding the new apartment was that Céleste Albaret could not use anymore the phone of the hospitable Café d'Anjou in the middle of the night. Resourceful as always, she struck up a friendship with the local baker, Monsieur Montagnon, whose premises were on the ground floor and who had a phone in his dining room. Since Montagnon was busy making bread most of the night, Albaret was allowed to reach his living quarters through the shop and use the phone whenever Proust asked her to call somebody.[15]

Proust learned from Antoine Bibesco, who was leaving for Rumania, that Rumanian banks paid 12 percent interest on deposits. He wrote of it to Hauser, wondering whether he should not consider moving his assets there. Hauser's indignant answer is better left unreported: just the thought that Proust could consider putting what was left of his personal fortune into the hands of Rumanian bankers gave him "goose flesh" (COR XVIII, 44, 45).

In July, after his first, temporary move to Rue Laurent-Pichat, Proust had written to Hauser to apologize for not sending him the two new books he had just published. The publisher had sent him only copies from the second and third edition. He had tried unsuccessfully to find first-edition copies in bookstores, but noted that "there must've been some sort of panic hoarding in order to sell my first editions later on at higher prices." If his friend was not insulted by a second or third edition, he would be glad to send him one of those. "I'm thinking of [Sainte-Beuve's] line, 'Oh, to see the light, live and then die in the same home'[16] and I regret that this couldn't be my fate." He then hinted, both awkwardly and cryptically, to a certain initiative undertaken by him and Walter Berry on Hauser's behalf, concluding thus: "But when I think of the worries you had . . . I tell myself that my own concerns are negligible. I had the pleasure (but I beg you, do not make any allusion to it in front of *anybody* I know) of being the *indirect* cause of the end of those worries of yours" (COR XVIII, 174 [emphasis in original]).

The war had been over for longer than seven months, and evidently Hauser failed to see the connection between certain worries troubling him back then and the role Proust and Walter Berry had played, without his knowledge, in resolving this matter by vouching for his trustworthiness (COR XVIII, 174 [note 5]). This misunderstanding unfolded in the sad pages of the epistolary novel I mentioned a while back. In the dark as regards Proust's reference to his past worries, in his answer Hauser did not even mention this issue, dwelling instead on the curious phenomenon of the "panic hoarding" of Proust's first editions, which was surreal in his opinion: "I see from your letter that the greed of speculators is boundless. It wasn't enough that they bought up our basic victuals, now they even corner goods that are indispensable to our 'snobbism,' if not to our spirit. This is what has led to the first edition of your two last works becoming the preferred merchandise of ignoble traffickers" (COR XVIII, 177). He clearly had more pressing things to worry about.

A few months later, Proust again mentioned Hauser's past concerns and, implicitly, the role he had played in their resolution. It was because of these concerns that he avoided bothering his friend with his own financial problems, and found himself resorting, from time to time, to the advice of Henri Gans, a young banker he had met a few years earlier in the house of the poet Anna de Noailles (COR XI, 34, 34 [note 2]). In relating a conversation he had just had with Gans, Proust made a truly awkward faux pas. Having recently moved to his new residence in Rue Hamelin, he complained to Gans that he had to pay 16,000 francs a year for the lease of an apartment that was not worth that sum. Gans pointed out to him that when the price of everything rose, the value of securities was also bound to increase, and one ought to take advantage of it. Gans had also given him a tip about certain securities whose value was likely to increase substantially in the near future. Proust wished to sell some of the securities he held at the London Bank to raise the capital he needed to invest in these promising securities (COR XVIII, 260).

The proverb attributing special virtues to the stone that kills two birds at one time may have rarely found a more literal application: the two cadavers piled on top of each other in this case, to pursue the analogy, were Hauser's comfort in seeing his friend smoothly transition to more affordable lodgings and his confidence in the newly found financial savviness of his money-squandering friend. His answer expressed a measure of his disappointment: "I firmly believed that . . . past experiences had taught you a harsh and memorable lesson. I see, alas, that I was wrong. This is why your letter has filled me with dismay." Proust's outstanding balance at the London Bank kept growing. The income that he had derived from the cleanup in his finances, made under Hauser's guidance, could very well have been more than sufficient for his budget, and could even have enabled him to gradually pay off his debt—but no! If Proust had moved out of his apartment when Hauser had suggested it, he would have certainly found an apartment for a lease of 3,000 or 4,000 francs that was comparable with the one for which currently he had to pay 16,000 francs a year. In his letter, Proust had defined his new apartment "a dump." Either he was wrong, or he had once again been "the victim of [his] own good faith." Hauser seemed to remember that Proust still had a disposable income of 25,000 thousand francs a year. If he paid 16,000 in rent and was still served by a footman and a housemaid, no matter how voraciously he fed himself "on air and illusions," once he paid their salaries and bought his own food, he would be left with "barely enough to buy a packet of menthol cigarettes." With the excuse of personal problems of Hauser's of which, "thank God," the banker knew nothing about, Proust had deliberately kept him in the dark about his disastrous choice of lodgings. Yet, Proust was ready to follow the lead of a Monsieur Gans, who suggested that he should give away his safe French government bonds to invest the proceeds haphazardly. "My arms are always open to help you out, but I refuse to use them to push you down into the abyss" (COR XVIII, 263). Hauser could not be aware that in Henri Gans, a subtle reader of Proust's novel, he was up against a man whom Proust held in high esteem. Even if Proust's biographers do not mention Gans too often, he stands out among Proust's friends for having enjoyed the privilege of being invited to dine in Proust's bedroom on several occasions, and not only on Boulevard Haussmann but also, which makes it positively unique, on rue Hamelin. (Dining with Proust, by the way, entailed sitting by his bedside and eating with the plate on one's lap. On most such occasions, the writer did not partake of the food.)[17]

Proust was more than willing—accustomed, by this time—to taking Hauser's dressing-downs. On this occasion, though, he felt his and Berry's discreet intervention on his friend's behalf should have earned him some gratitude. Never mind that he had maintained his own tact so zealously that Hauser, unbeknownst to Proust, still knew nothing of it, the writer could not stand Hauser's intimation that he was using some irrelevant setback of the banker's as a pretext for his own unwise actions. May I say: here Proust seems curiously unable to adjust the tone of his letter to the circumstances he is trying to address. Why not simply explain himself? Why not refresh Hauser's memory by spelling out the reason why he had to intervene on his behalf, and make thereby an open claim to the banker's gratitude, instead of taking for granted Hauser's knowledge of it?

You may wonder yourself what the nature of Hauser's wartime worries was, and why Proust and Berry's intervention on his behalf was required to solve them. More to the point, why have I not spelled out these worries for you yet? Am I guilty of the same excessive ambiguity of which I have just accused Proust? I confess I have been struggling with this quandary for the last few pages. If I have kept my silence about the bone of contention between Proust and Hauser, it is because a while back I promised you a sadly well-wrought epistolary novel. One of this novel's protagonists, Hauser, will be kept in suspense till the final revelation comes. I just do not think that you, who are now going to be this novel's reader, would want to be treated any other way, once the plot gets in full swing. Is not this the reason why we hate being told beforehand the plot of the new thriller we are eagerly planning to read? Right, I hear you: this is not a Le Carré novel after all. Just the same, I beg you to endure a little trepidation; with any luck, you will enjoy it.

So, instead of explaining himself, Proust adopted the lyrical mode as a weapon of self-defense. This was a devious sort of lyricism, though, contrasting the tactfulness of his own epistolary allusions to the initiatives taken by him and Walter Berry on Hauser's behalf with, of all things, the indiscretions Hauser had made himself responsible for in his letters to him. This was big news to Hauser, of course, to whom prudence was second nature.

This is the most poisonous missive that Hauser ever received from Proust. In it, Proust questions at first the tact shown by Hauser in dealing with the confidential matters that they corresponded about for years; then he teaches Hauser a lesson in business savoir-faire by boasting about his negotiations with the new owner of the building in Boulevard Haussmann; he then goes on to mention the substantial royalties that his novel (contrary to Hauser's poorly received book) will soon earn him; and finally—the true pièce de résistance—he reveals to Hauser that recent transactions made on his behalf by the Rothschild Bank have brought the writer's finances to a flourishing state, warranting the envy even of a smart banker like Hauser himself. It is a declaration of war on all the fronts that have seen the two friends cooperate with each other for the previous eleven years.

This answer from Proust was delayed for longer than three weeks—not because he was wounded by Hauser's words, he explained when he got down to writing this letter, but because of his illness. If he remembered correctly, in his last letter Hauser had accused him of turning any affection felt for him into pain and suffering. But was not this the natural course followed by human affection? The better we learn to disregard our own advantage, the more we take our friends' advantage to heart. Perhaps, in their recent exchanges, Proust had not expressed himself clearly enough regarding his own feelings toward Hauser (he is alluding to his own and Berry's still undisclosed intervention on Hauser's behalf), but he felt that the circumstances surrounding Hauser's wartime worries dictated "extreme discretion and great vagueness." Hauser might have found this need for tact exaggerated, since, after all, Proust was writing by his own hand and could have used less circumspection. Yet, for his part, Hauser was always dictating his letters to his secretary, and in spite of this, he talked freely in them of Proust's ruin, of his recklessness and irresponsibility, and so forth. Well, why should he not? In the banker's shoes, Proust would have done the same. He was a wholly unconceited person, Proust wrote, describing himself. Hence, Hauser could not be accused of committing an indiscretion when he used certain unflattering expressions in front of a third person, his secretary. (The crescendo of irony mingled with reluctant modesty is becoming noxious.) And even if Proust did not entirely approve of Hauser's disregard for his privacy, this would not change in the least Proust's scrupulous prudence in talking of the banker in front of strangers. He cited from Corneille's *Horace:* "Please understand that my duty is not dependent on his. He is free to infringe his, if he feels like it, but I must obey mine" (COR XVIII, 278, 278 [note 4]).

Here Proust shifted from devious lyricism to a sneakily matter-of-fact tone. Hauser had written to him that if he had consented to move at the time the banker had said he should, Proust would have found a comfortable apartment for 4,000 francs a year. Luckily enough, Proust had not followed his advice: he had instead stayed put on Boulevard Haussmann, waiting to be evicted, so that he had now earned a 20,000-franc discount on his rent arrears from the building's new owner, plus a 12,000-franc indemnity for moving expenses; and a further 6,000-franc indemnity from his aunt Amélie. By delaying a move that would have been inconvenient to his state of health, Proust had seen a total gain of 38,000 francs; not to mention the lucrative royalties that would soon accrue to him as a result of having completed the composition of his books, thanks to avoiding the distractions of an untimely move.

After this uncalled-for ostentation of good business instincts, Proust went on to explain his new investment plans. He did not care for Gans's risky tip, but further consultations with the young banker had persuaded him that he must trade his National Defense Bonds with a 5 percent annual yield against some first-rate bonds earning 6 percent, or else with some fixed-income bonds with a broader market, such as those of the City of Paris. Proust's tone was that of a dissatisfied client. "Therefore you will be so kind as to let me know what I own that is earning a yield of 5%, so I can sell part of it; better yet, you should let me know what portions of these bonds are not indispensable to securing my line of credit with the London Bank" (Ibid., 278).

The letter was not over yet, even if Proust's decision to undo Hauser's purchase of the National Defense Bonds on his behalf, which the banker rightly considered one of his most brilliant moves in his friend's favor, might read like a coup de grace. We must suppose that Proust was forgetting that, by the time the next National Loan was issued, he would be entitled to trade his National Defense Bonds against these new bonds at 29 percent discount, making a lucrative profit for himself and crowning Hauser's long-term financial planning with success. In any case, thus far his letter was still working up to the coup de grace—which now comes. On November 21 the Rothschild Bank had informed Proust that, using his owner's privileges, they had subscribed to 2.3 nominal Royal Dutch shares from the September 1918 issue, traded at 30,000 francs per share on his behalf. He now owned 6.9 such shares. This transaction had only cost him 43 percent of the subscription's value, which corresponded to the price of one single share (COR XVIII, 278, 278 [note 4])—which implied either that the bank had sold the rest of Proust's subscription privileges to pay for this purchase, or that the remaining 1.3 shares were paid for with revenues from last June's Royal Dutch coupon payments; or possibly both subscription privileges and coupon payments contributed to this result.

Proust's fatal letter finally came to an end. For good measure, he had not even used the lethal weapon of the reasons behind his and Berry's initiative on Hauser's behalf (which would come in handy the following year in a more vicious skirmish—part two, let's say, of their epistolary novel). But what about Hauser's friendship for him? And what about Hauser's role as his financial advisor?

Hauser felt the blow. He wrote that he was happy to learn that Proust's Royal Dutch shares kept giving birth to new baby shares of their own accord. He was not completely ignorant of the existence of these securities in Proust's portfolio, but had always thought of them, at best, as a well for times of drought. And he added in a theatrical tone, alluding to the forthcoming windfall from Proust's royalties: "Thanks to these emergency funds, and to other sources of revenue which I knew nothing about,far from being ruined, you are almost enjoying an enviable situation, given the hard times we are going through. In these circumstances, allow me to declare, my dear Marcel, that your case does not interest me anymore. . . . Until further orders, I consider my mission accomplished" (COR XVIII, 279). Having slammed the door in Proust's face ("your case does not interest me anymore") and having at the same time opened up a possible window of reconciliation ("I consider my mission accomplished until further orders"), Hauser tackled Proust's accusation of indiscretion. It was his turn to stage a small, yet effective, *coup de scène.*

In the last fifteen years, he had never written a letter in his own hand, except those he wrote "twice a week" to his parents. Normally, he dictated to his trusty secretary. Proust's remark about Hauser's secretary being privy to confidential information was, however, "as poorly logical as it [was] scarcely psychologically sound." After all, Hauser's accountant had been scrutinizing Proust's balance sheets for years, and, as a rule, he gave his conclusions to the secretary to write down. Therefore, this woman was left with no choice but to acquaint herself with Proust's financial situation—not to mention Hauser's accountant, "who knew everything." "This addresses the logical side of the equation. As for the psychological side, you'll be surprised to learn," wrote Hauser, "that it was only after they thought you were ruined that my employees developed genuine admiration for you. Undoubtedly they saw in you someone in the league of Balzac, Alexandre Dumas père, or Verlaine, to mention a few great writers." Now that the same employees had learned that the situation had turned fully around in favor of Proust's patrimony, Hauser was afraid that "[the developments] that you perhaps expected to support your rehabilitation in their eyes will end up seriously undermining their admiration for you" (Ibid.).

Between these two friends, a few shrewdly placed words were worse than a hail of blows, and they inflicted more damage. If Hauser could have imagined the price that Proust paid for his creative inspiration day in and day out, or if he could have put himself in the writer's shoes for twenty-four hours, he would have grasped that his friend Proust had never wished for himself the dubious prestige of such harrowing conditions. But in order to trade places with the artist and pay in imagination the same dues that Proust owed to his demanding muse, Hauser would first have to give credit to the innumerable symptoms the writer complained about. This was something Hauser could not do; he was too literalistic a fellow, too down-to-earth, not to take Proust's symptoms for the whims of a hypochondriac. The two friends were caught in a loop of endless mutual retaliations. To the occasional observer, unaware of the yoke that tied them both to the royal coach of their infrangible friendship, it might have seemed as if they were engaged in a sadistic version of the Aunt Sally game.

One month after telling Hauser that his Royal Dutch shares had increased to 6.9 units, Proust informed Geneviève Straus that he was the owner of 11 Royal Dutch shares. In March 1920 he wrote to the same woman that his Royal Dutch shares had risen to 12 and were currently traded at 35,000 francs apiece (COR XVIII, 323; XIX, 64). Both jumps, the one in the share's unitary price from 30,000 to 35,000 francs, and the double increase in the block held in his Rothschild portfolio, from 6.9 to 11 and then from 11 to 12, might be taken as rhetorical hyperboles, but this is unlikely. As a matter of fact, in 1919 Royal Dutch shares were traded at an average unitary price of 8,500 Dutch guilders, that is, 42,500 francs each. Proust probably based both misquotes in his letters on the prices at which he had bought Royal Dutch shares in the past. More important, that same year the Dutch company's capitalization grew by 106 percent and its share price by 67 percent. This was reflected the following year in a dividend growth of 33 percent in guilders or, at current exchange rates, of 78 percent in French francs. Under such favorable conditions, Proust's subscription privileges may truly have brought about a miracle. As a matter of fact, these privileges would lead to a second miracle two years later, in 1921, when the average price per share would go down to 4,095 guilders, that is, about 17,000 francs, but his block of such shares would take to multiplying like the loaves and fish of the gospel.

A few more figures help us keep track of Proust's balance sheet in 1919. We can posit that, out of his newly acquired Royal Dutch shares, those he paid for with coupon earnings and/or sold-off subscription privileges brought an increment of 153,000 francs to the value of his Rothschild portfolio.[18] Thanks to this fruitful operation, as well as to the general increase in stocks' prices after the end of the war, Proust's net wealth grew to 1,176,000 francs in 1919. His yearly income was about 84,000 francs, inclusive of the 5,490 francs in royalties earned from Gallimard and the 38,000 francs he received from the new and old owner of the Boulevard Haussmann apartment building. It was an astounding increase with respect to the previous year.

Chapter 23

WORDS LIKE A HAIL OF BLOWS

Proust's instructions to Princess Soutzo:

> I don't want you to think of me as someone 'who doesn't want to meet royalty,' who'd be as ridiculous as someone who desperately wanted to meet them. Granted that I do not feel the same pleasure in meeting anyone else as you (it was to set this principle on a firm footing that last year I didn't attend your party in honor of Her Majesty the Queen of Rumania),[1] I'm not so stupid that I'm uninterested or indifferent to getting to know a woman [that is, the Queen of Rumania] who not only is very beautiful but also involved in many [important] events. To preserve my respect of good manners, you will be so kind as to arrange things this way. You will tell Her Majesty the Queen of Rumania that you found me so ill that you didn't tell me anything of her reception, for fear I would attend it against my better judgment. But [you will add that] this coming Sunday you will let me know that I'm welcome to pay Her a visit after dinner, and you will tell me this only late at night, so I won't feel under the obligation to leave my bed. This way, since I will appear to be completely in the dark, I won't give the Queen the impression of being bad-mannered or pretentious, like someone who likes to be invited twice. (COR XIX, 149)

It was now June 1920, and the power relations in Proust's social life had been turned upside down. Proust was the fashionable writer in Paris, the reclusive artist about whom endless rumors circulated, hinting at a tireless nightlife filled with "uninterrupted delights." This is what Robert de Montesquiou heard and tended to believe, for instance. In September of 1920, the count was still imploring his friend Proust to pay him a visit; but in November, suspicious of being deliberately snubbed, he resorted to the threat (rather inoffensive for a writer as widely read as Proust) that he would not read Proust's new works: "If you are not sending me your books, well, then in spite of my eagerness to read them, I won't; I tell myself that if you do not send them to me, it is because you prefer that I do not read them, and I add: *fiat voluntas tua*" (COR XIX, 233, 344). Behind this reproach lies the rather well-grounded fear regarding the moment of truth—which Proust preferred to postpone—when Montesquiou would have the evidence in sight that he was the main model for the homosexual character in the novel, Baron de Charlus. Proust eventually tried to placate his friend by confiding to him that he "had thought for a minute of the late Baron Doäzan" as a model for Charlus, but mainly by insisting that in his novel there were no "keys" for the identification of real and fictional characters: "In the entire work (I am not talking about the individual volumes but of the whole set) there are at most two or three keys, and even those don't open the lock for longer than an instant" (COR XX, 98).

Proust was worshipped by the literary critics. Not by all of them, it is true; he had several detractors. The polemics surrounding the award of the Prix Goncourt had been virulent, and it was still rumored that there had been some sort of foul play. For the first Prix Goncourt awarded after the war, everybody had expected that the prize would go to the war novel *Les crois de bois* by Roland Dorgelés, which had been awarded instead the Prix Femina–*Vie Heureuse.* With agile sarcasm, the influential cross-dresser, novelist, and critic Rachilde, chair of the Prix Femina committee, wrote that the decision of the Prix Goncourt committee was a "mystification" that would eventually damage Proust's reputation. The Femina should have gone to Proust, she argued, whose previous book, *Swann's Way,* she had defined "soporific," and the more prestigious Goncourt to Dorgelés's virile novel. Yet, her fellow judges, among whom were duchesses, princesses, and poets, had shown little sympathy for Proust's protagonist, that strange fellow surrounded by docile girls *en fleurs* whom he liked better to gaze at than to pursue, and, like as many "birds of paradise," had gone en masse instead for Dorgelés's "coq gaulois," their coveted Gallic rooster, or cock.[2] A memorable turn of phrase, this one—which goes to prove that the celebrated Rachilde was remarkably more mordant as a lightweight reviewer than a fiction writer.

The antagonism of such detractors saddened Proust, and, even worse, compelled him to contact them either by letter, as he did on January 10, 1920, with Rachilde, or in person, in the half-clumsy and half-shameless attempt, so typical of his self-centeredness, to help them understand his novel.[3] Since history has harshly vilified these critics, in this book I will not give them the time and attention that the undeserving target of their attacks bestowed on them.

Proust's admirers were too numerous to include on a single list. Émile Blanche wrote in the *Revue de Paris* of May 1, 1920: "Marcel Proust walks like the new owner into a long uninhabited house and opens wide all the windows looking out onto the view of a vast land which it is now time to explore. Marcel Proust's style, inimitable after all, may establish a new canon, like color and form in Cézanne." And Jacques Rivière told Proust that André Breton, "the Dada in chief," numbered among Rivière's proofreaders, and that he had "an intense admiration for [Proust], based on the poetic treasures he discovered in [his] work" (COR XIX, 156).

A few months later, the final proofs of *The Guermantes Way* were in Proust's hands. While he was writing to Gallimard that the typographic errors were so frequent and made his sentences so unintelligible that he had considered committing suicide, Proust was reminded of the influential leader of Dadaism. The flippancy of his onomastic imprecision regarding Breton is an obvious refutation of his suicidal state of mind: "Monsieur . . . (the charming Dada who read my proofs and whose name escapes me due to an instant of amnesia) Breton thinks he has read [my proofs]. Jacques Rivière does too. Neither one realized that every time I talk of the novels by Bergotte, the proofs read 'the novels by Bergson'!" And he closed this letter with a touch of fatalism: "Well, if these well-read readers didn't see it, let's count on the blindness of the others" (COR XIX, 213).

Proust was in a hurry to have the rest of his novel published, but he was afraid that he would lose the sympathy of many critics when the theme of "sodomy" openly emerged as one of the leading motifs of *In Search of Lost Time*. In the November 14, 1920, issue of *Le Temps*, Paul Souday mentioned the "feminine touch" in the prose of Marcel Proust. The writer scolded him:

> Dear Sir,
>
> At the time when I brace myself to publish Sodom and Gomorrah, after which, since I will be talking of Sodom, nobody will dare to take my defense anymore, you pave the way

> to all my future slanderers (with no ill intention, I'm sure of it) by defining me as "feminine." Feminine is one short step from effeminate! (COR XIX, 312)

Proust complained that those who acted as seconds in his duels could testify that he did not have the feebleness of effeminate individuals (COR XIX, 312). (On the occasion of his duel with the novelist Jean Lorrain, a homosexual poet who alluded to Proust's affair with Lucien Daudet in a newspaper article, Edmund White reports that one of Proust's seconds was a "celebrated he-man duelist, Gustave de Borda." But this was twenty-four years earlier, in 1896.)[4] A few days later, he wrote again to Paul Souday: "If you find me feminine, it's your right to say so." But Souday's remark did not go unnoticed and similar opinions had begun to peep out of the pages of *Le Figaro*. "They haven't asked me to return the Knight's Cross [of the Legion of Honor] yet (but it's only a matter of time)" (COR XIX, 324).

On January 1, 1920, Proust sent his New Year wishes to Lionel Hauser. He was sorry that Hauser had "resigned" from the post of financial consultant which Proust had offered him in 1908. There was a passage in Hauser's last letter, however, that "amused" Proust, in which Hauser accused him of "a recurrent lack in psychological insight." If Hauser was right, it was regrettable that no one had taken care to alert Henry James about this lack of his, seeing that the late American writer had spent the last year of his life annotating *Swann's Way* (COR XIX, 3). This was not the best way to reopen the epistolary conversation with his friend Hauser, who, in fact, did not even bother to return Proust's greetings.

Proust waited three months and then tried again. It seemed, he wrote, that Hauser was applying Alfred de Vigny's aphorism: "Only Silence is great, all the rest is weakness." Toward the rest of the world, Proust implemented the same principle, but slightly modified: My silence is constant, but caused by my own limitations. This was why he did not reply to the "one thousand letters of congratulations" he had received of late. Before he could write a single letter, he had to dose himself with drugs. He had not meant to write this letter to Hauser, in fact, who seemed to be the only person who did not care to hear from him, but a fatality forced him to do so. Proust had meant to take advantage of the higher value of the British pound by selling his Liebig securities. The previous night, he had consulted André Neuberger, Léon Neuberger's son, to this purpose. Neuberger had replied that he should not sell his Liebig "unless that superior human being, Lionel Hauser, [was] of a different opinion." At the same time, and still with the caveat that Proust ought first to hear the opinion of "the great-hearted man who is Lionel Hauser," Neuberger advised him to sell his gold mine securities. Proust had no intention whatsoever of bothering Hauser, who evidently did not like to be bothered by him. Rather than doing that, he would rather let the gold mines produce gold at their own leisurely pace, Liebig factories condense the fortifying substances of beef at their own fanciful whim, and Brazilian and Chinese bonds add a touch of exoticism to his portfolio. However, he had just been hit by a new emergency: that morning, he had received a voluminous package of correspondence from Hamburg containing a sheaf of cryptic paperwork from Warburg & Co. He was enclosing it in the hope that Hauser could help him make sense of it. This letter amounts to moral blackmail, because clearly Hauser could not avoid dealing with this client of the German firm he represented in Paris (COR XIX, 69).

This letter marked the beginning of a new, long-distance boxing match between the two friends, even nastier, as I said, than the one fought by the two friends a few months earlier: Part 2, page 1 of their epistolary novel.

Hauser wrote to Proust that if he had not returned the writer's season's greetings, it was because they did not deserve returning, since Proust had added to them unconvincing considerations of a psychological order. He preferred to leave aside all those matters, however, and instead answer Proust's latest letter. The Warburg paperwork, like all the statements that Proust had received every semester from Hamburg since the end of the war, was a plain report on his Warburg portfolio. Since Proust had involved himself in the complications of the uncashed Warburg check, Hauser felt dizzy just at the thought of the number and caliber of the financial advisors with whom he had surrounded himself. This should help Proust understand why his gratitude for their cousin André Neuberger's words of appreciation, explained Hauser, could not induce him to accept Proust's offer.

At this point in his letter, Hauser contradicted his opening statement and gave Proust the response that his season's greetings "did not deserve":

> On the other hand, you'd be perfectly wrong in taking my decision [not to be your financial advisor anymore] as a resignation, as you wrote on the first of January. It's more correct to say—and this is the way I interpret it—that I completed my mission. Hence nothing has changed between the two of us and I still am

> the friend I've always been for you. If in spite of this categorical statement on my part, you should still feel the need to complain over and over again about your misfortune—a misfortune that is the product of your imagination—then this is a private matter to be settled between you and your Muse, one that I choose to stay well out of. (COR XIX, 70)

What Hauser offered was a word to the wise; yet he ought to have known that Proust was a stranger to common sense, and he should therefore not have expected the writer to abide by his clearly formulated stance.

Proust charged again, in fact, and this time with a blow that, however cryptic—or perhaps owing to its unusual conciseness—caught Hauser unaware and marked a turning point in their correspondence. For the next five weeks or so, Hauser would be turned, once again, into the captive-protagonist of their extended epistolary novel; the other protagonist, Proust, would act also as the puppeteer who pulled the threads leading to the suspenseful ending. Proust starts his letter with another ambiguous allusion to the still undefined initiative undertaken by him and Walter Berry on Hauser's behalf: "Rather than indulging in my disillusionments, I remind myself, being less forgetful than you are, that on a past occasion I contracted a debt of gratitude with you, which is still intact. This one won't cancel out that one" (COR XIX, 73). What debt of gratitude was Proust talking about? And whose was it? Hauser must have been taken aback by his friend's puzzling tone. He rose to the bait, answering Proust blindly, on impulse, point by point.

It must be noted that while Hauser was very familiar with Proust in his role as stock-exchange speculator (an irredeemably imprudent one) and prolific correspondent (an occasionally pedantic but always brilliant one), he did not know him too well in his persona as the *auteur* Marcel Proust, even if he had certainly read his works. Not even Proust himself, I submit, knew this persona of his well enough: namely, the artist who was gradually assuming the habits and the mannerisms of the greatest living French writer. Neither of the friends, in a word, was mentally equipped to foresee the sweeping plot that would presently absorb their correspondence. As it turns out, this plot is somewhat analogous to the far-reaching design that, at the inception of his masterpiece, had induced Proust to draft both the first and the last volume, long before having drafted or even fully conceived the several volumes that came in between. While some critics accused him of passively following the spontaneous flow of memory, Proust was weaving a weft of plots destined to flow together into a pattern of exemplary rigor. What makes the closure of *In Search of Lost Time* so masterly is that it offers an unexpected solution to the dilemma of Lost Time, with which the Narrator struggles for many years: through the conception of the artwork as a privileged receptacle for the treasured memories of his most authentic identity, the Narrator redeems his past, eludes time's rule over his own existence, and, in doing so, exorcizes his own fear of death. In his correspondence with Hauser, Proust would presently adopt, unwittingly I think, an equally sweeping compositional principle.

For the time being, he limited himself to throwing in the seed of an obscure allusion: "this one" will not cancel out "that one," he told Hauser. *This one* and *that one,* Hauser must have been wondering: to what was Proust referring? Two possible interpretations lent themselves to this letter's uninformed addressee. Either Proust was saying "my disillusionment with you won't extinguish my debt to you," that is, I will honor the debt of gratitude I owe you in spite of my disappointment in you; or "my debt to you won't lessen my disillusionment with you," that is, the debt of gratitude I owe you will not diminish my disappointment in you. The tenor of each version obviously diverges from the other. But above all, what debt is Proust talking about? Even if Hauser could justifiably expect Proust to feel indebted for all the occasions he had rescued him from financial troubles, the fact remained that, in the light of the recent miscommunications between the two friends, the banker could not identify with certainty the nature of either the "disillusionment" or the "debt" mentioned in Proust's letter. Proust would make him wait more than a month for a clarification, although, during this period, the two friends engaged in an enervating scuffle. As with the closure of *In Search of Lost Time,* which was destined to tame the most dissatisfied critics by a surprising move that had the whole novel come smoothly into its own, Proust kept a secret move up his sleeve that would help him prevail over Hauser. But in this case, contrary to Proust's long-distance duel with his unappreciative critics, the mortification or silencing of his rival would be tantamount to a defeat for the writer himself; Proust seemed oblivious to this evident fact, that one of the most intense friendships in his life was flailing and needed to be rescued rather than put to the test once again. Let us follow closely the progress of this epistolary novel sui generis.

It was Hauser's turn to write. He had felt reluctant to answer Proust's last letter. Then he had concluded that if Proust was so aggressive toward him, after seeing Hauser's affection for him proven in a thousand different ways, it meant that the writer believed sincerely in the legitimacy of his grievances. To Hauser, they were pure fantasies.

> My dear Marcel,
>
> . . . What I find most surprising in your letter is the passage where you declare that rather than lingering on your disillusionment you prefer to remember, *being less forgetful than I (?)*, that in the past you contracted a debt of gratitude toward me which remains unchanged for you. . . . Have you ever thought about the meaning of the word "disillusionment"? I don't think so, because if you had you wouldn't have felt this emotion toward me. A disillusionment is simply the loss of an illusion. Can you please tell me what disillusionment I caused you and precisely in what respect you have been disillusioned? (COR XIX, 75, emphasis in original)

Hauser went on to recall how some years previously, Proust—who was dear to him because of their shared childhood memories—had asked him to put some order in his finances, which he did without reserve. Moreover, Hauser had never asked for gratitude and never took Proust's "flaming compliments" or his promises of eternal thankfulness too seriously. These days, Proust was more famous than he had ever been: he was wooed, flattered, pampered, celebrated, and he received letters in the thousands from his admirers, who included first-rate men of finance. Given these circumstances, Hauser thought he had the right, without having invectives hurled at him by Proust, to let people who were better qualified than he oversee his friend's interests. Proust ought to acknowledge, the letter continued, that Hauser had loved and held him in the esteem he deserved from the outset, without waiting for the official consecration of his talent, or joining in the praise arriving from certain society fellows who refused to think with their own heads. This entitled Hauser to treat Proust as the spoiled child he was, always ready to sulk with anyone who did not give in to his whims. Hauser was afraid that the glory had gone to his friend's head. If Hauser were in his shoes, he would itemize the effects of glory under the rubric of "gains and losses," and instead of confusing his best friends with those who told him the most pleasant things, he would look for truth where truth resided, even if its discovery had the effect of mortifying his self-esteem. "To me you are the same as you always were,"

Hauser concluded, "and my friendship for you is the same as always. You are free to believe it or not, to see me as the executioner and you the innocent victim, but that would be just literature, my dear Marcel, and I refuse categorically to follow you there" (Ibid.).

Proust wrote back to Hauser later the same day, alluding once again to the unspecified "bothersome matters" with which he had burdened himself in 1915 on the banker's behalf. Although he still abstained from explaining the nature of these matters to his friend, Proust added insult to injury by saying that their "burden" was anyway lighter to him than messing with Hauser's self-righteousness:

> My dear Lionel,
>
> You are trying to deceive yourself. But you are too smart to do so. I think of you as a very good man (I dare admit I think the same of myself), but your goodness is lined with a layer of self-righteousness that at times keeps it from making itself manifest and at times turns it into its very opposite. This is something I became aware of at the beginning of the war, and in 1915 I chose to burden myself with several bothersome matters rather than going deep into that dangerous area of your heart where I don't want to experience anything but goodness. Later on, alas, I received harsher confirmations of my insight, and had I been an evangelist, I would've challenged your self-righteousness and explained to you where you erred and why your spontaneous good feelings toward me were repressed. But even if I could persuade you that it was pride that made you act unfairly toward me in the past, what would we gain from it? . . . My dear Lionel, if your letter hadn't shown me to what extent your feelings for me are strangled by vanity, saddening me deeply, there are two things in it that would make me smile. (COR XIX, 77)

The first of these amusing things, the letter explained, was that Hauser thought Proust was annoyed with his latest letter because it showed that they did not share the same views on the management of Proust's patrimony. Yet Hauser had not written a single word about it in that letter, nor had he criticized or blamed Proust's financial ideas. The second amusing thing was that Hauser thought the Prix Goncourt earned Proust many new relationships. "I wish you could see me, you'd know then that I never see anybody." At the most, Proust meant to pay a visit to Walter Berry soon, in the hope that Berry might be willing to handle his Warburg & Co. interests (a remark seemingly designed to taunt Hauser for his indifference). Moreover, Proust had not seen Berry in ages, and the American was a gentleman whom Proust appreciated enormously. Proust was being congratulated for his literary prize by people he had known for twenty-five years; the prospect of replying to all their letters drove him mad because of how fatiguing it was, but it certainly did not go to his head. A prize conceived as an encouragement to a novice writer was not particularly glorious when one was awarded it at forty-eight, he added. He was pleased with it nonetheless, "precisely because [he was] not a conceited man." And he concluded, "I am sorry that memories that should've made us closer have kept you away from me, but as far as I am concerned . . . they increase my affection for you" (COR XIX, 77).

With a return to the motif of time squandered that was so dear to the banker, on April 8 Hauser wrote that he could not help regretting that both of them—Proust who was so ill that he could hardly write, and Hauser himself, who was so busy with his job—wasted so much precious time telling each other uselessly unpleasant things. This correspondence of theirs was superfluous. A victim of his own prejudices, Proust only found what he wanted to find in their exchanges of correspondence and accused Hauser of saying things he had never meant to say. Proust had argued, for instance, that in his next-to-last letter Hauser had not made any criticism of the way his friend managed his assets. On the contrary, Hauser had told him he was wrong in surrounding himself with too many financial advisors. Furthermore, Hauser had never referred to the new relationships that the Prix Goncourt had brought into Proust's life, but had only remarked that, after being awarded the prize, Proust was "wooed, flattered, pampered, celebrated, etc." Then he went on: "After putting up with me for a number of years, you suddenly tell me that my goodness is lined with a thick layer of self-righteousness, that it's pride that made me unfair to you, and, what's worse, that in 1915 you chose to handle certain bothersome matters by yourself rather than getting deep into the self-righteous part of my heart, inside of which you don't want to find anything but goodness." Hauser was ready to acknowledge his own defects. At times it was difficult to establish where one's defects ended and one's virtues began, especially because so-called civilized humankind was the captive of "habits, prejudices, and traditions lazily adopted from previous generations." He continued relentlessly: "You adore polite and well-mannered people, I detest them; their politeness is a mask one must get through in order to find out what it hides." As a matter of personal consistency, Hauser tried to be neither polite nor well-mannered. "I've neglected the salons where people spend their time chatting to pay frequent visits to places where people work instead." Other people had accused him of self-righteousness before Proust, but these people had not made any effort to understand him. Hauser had been under the impression that Proust would make that effort.

> I don't dare suggest any more that you lack in psychological insight because you would invoke again, to silence me, the testimony of your friend Henry James. But before deciding how to answer your accusations, I'd like to know the reasons why you're revealing to me the flaw that you detected in me so long ago but kept carefully to yourself until now. If you called my attention to my flaws because you think they are real enough and sincerely wish that I should get rid of them, I'd be infinitely grateful if you stated your accusations more precisely. This issue interests me no less than it does you, and I promise I will tackle my case with the detachment I would apply to someone else's. I only beg you to supply me with the necessary information, since I can't find it in your indictment. Is it indeed the result of your own personal impression or the effect of a third party's testimony, substantiated by other reports or facts which you couldn't verify? And the bearers of this testimony, would they be willing to be held accountable for their opinions, or did they share their confidences asking you the greatest discretion? I'm a little uncomfortable in assigning you so many tasks, but I'm sure you see that the fault is not all mine. On the other hand, you'll need to provide me with the information I ask only if you sincerely wish to verify the correctness of your accusations; in case you simply prefer to stick with the opinion you have formed about me, though, it'd be a pity if you were to waste any of your time to please me. (COR XIX, 83)

As typical of our efficient banker, Hauser's letter was first introduced and then closed with the recommendation that Proust should not waste any time.

What is evident here is that Proust did not mind neglecting "one thousand letters" from his admirers, nor did he leave off gulping down drugs and caffeine in preposterous doses or wasting large amounts of his usable time, as long as it all enabled him to keep up with this exchange of raving letters with Hauser. The same day he received Hauser's letter, punctuated with injunctions of transparency—inviting him to provide detailed information about his accusations and to relate frankly and precisely any opinions expressed by others regarding Hauser's perceived temperament—Proust replied in a brisk tone: "How can you possibly think that I 'put up' with you! The fact that I realized that a certain flaw of yours coexisted with many remarkable virtues didn't diminish my affection for you, it only compounded it with a shred of melancholy." Hauser was wrong in regard to Proust's recent reference to Henry James. He had never even met the American writer. But after James's death, Proust learned that James held his work in a high opinion, while Proust had no idea that a single line of his had ever crossed his sight. Then Proust mentioned, barely in passing, the topic of Hauser's alleged self-righteousness, but not before having corrected his friend on a detail pertaining to the notorious 30,000-franc Warburg check. At the end of the previous month, Hauser had defended the Warburg firm's solvency, arguing that, at the time of the check's issue, this firm certainly had sufficient funds at the Comptoir d'Escompte in France. Proust objected (awkwardly mixing up the Comptoir d'Escompte with the Crédit Industriel in the process) that the French bank responsible for honoring his check had always declared that there were insufficient funds, and the sequestrator of Warburg's French funds had taken the same position. (As we know, the sequestrator was Auguste Besse, and the fact that he made himself scarce after meeting Proust's housemaid throws Proust's version of the matter into doubt.)

At this point, it might seem that Proust had to finally face Hauser's demands for transparency. Yet he found another way out: "As to the moral debate that has informed our recent correspondence, allow me to not address it today. The very shortcoming that I detected in your temperament would keep you from taking advantage of my criticisms ('criticism' is an inaccurate term, incidentally), and would only further increase your dislike of me, or by all means make the thought of me disagreeable to you." He signed his letter after these words of leave-taking, but then changed his mind and added a postscript. In it, he steered scrupulously away from the issue of Hauser's self-righteousness, to dwell instead on another of their disagreements.

> Dear Lionel,
>
> . . . You tell me that you patronize the salons where people work rather than chat. I confess that I cannot declare myself either in favor or against this view of yours for the simple reason that I have no opinions whatsoever about the salons where people chat because I do not go there. As to the salons where people work, I'm persuaded that one cannot frequent them for the simple reason that they cannot exist. The life of the salon is incompatible with work. . . . Regarding instead politeness and rudeness, it is quite true that when the former is a travesty and the latter an expression of personal honesty, the latter is a thousand times preferable. But there are cases when politeness may have a good cause and rudeness a bad one. . . . It goes without saying that I'm not talking of you now. But even you must have met unpleasant or downright violent men whose motives were not honorable. It's too easy to assume that sincerity and rudeness go hand in hand. The most slandering and abusive newspapers are often the least honest. . . . But I'm digressing from our case! (COR XIX, 84)

Hauser waited a week before answering. On April 15 he wrote that he had been hoping Proust's last letter would provide the clarifications he had requested, but nothing of the sort had happened. Proust's reply to some of his remarks indicated that his friend had not even tried to grasp what Hauser was talking about. Worse than that, Proust had excused himself from tackling their "moral debate" with the pretext that it was Hauser's flaw at the heart of this debate that would prevent the banker from taking advantage of Proust's criticisms. In sum, after making his accusations, Proust was refusing to corroborate them, because the accused party would be impeded from deriving any advantage from his words by the very flaw he was accused of having. "What's my role in all of this? First you accuse me of self-righteousness, but when I ask to be judged, you decide to grant me amnesty, undoubtedly not to be forced to withdraw your accusations in case I succeeded, in spite of my pride, to prove that your accusations lack substantiating evidence." Proust was free to keep silent, of course, but this way of shrugging off the problem was inelegant and, what is more, did not change the terms of the problem. As to the rest of Proust's letter, Hauser wondered "to what extent the fact of whether you were or were not personally acquainted with Henry James might change the relevance of my remarks on your lack of psychological insight." Or perhaps Proust had never looked too closely into the meaning of the term *psychology*:

> My dear Marcel,
>
> . . . Do you think that one individual can claim to have full knowledge of the soul of humankind as a whole? . . . It's very nice to succeed in analyzing the mentality of people in one's social circle, and on this I agree completely with the opinion that the late Henry James had about you. You have admirably described and analyzed the mentality of the people you know best. But you go too far when you seek to apply your psychological views to people who evolve in environments you know nothing about. . . . If you ever decide to write a book on Bolshevik society, I suggest that you spend some time with these gentlemen and weigh more carefully their criticisms on the accuracy of your assessment than those of people who know nothing about Bolshevism except what they glean from conservative French newspapers. (COR XIX, 95)

At this point, Hauser touched on the hoary topic of the Warburg check, referring to Proust's remark that the Crédit Industriel had always denied that there were sufficient funds available. Proust must have certainly meant to refer to the Comptoir d'Escompte. There is a hint of sarcasm in Hauser's parenthetical observation: a bank's proper name makes a significant difference to a banker, and rightly so. In this regard, Hauser could only repeat what he had already said, namely, that a statement of this sort from the bank that issued the check in France did not automatically entail that Warburg & Co. did not possess a 30,000-franc credit at the moment of issuance. If the check had been promptly cashed at the Comptoir d'Escompte, it would certainly have been honored, but at the declaration of war, French banks "started requisitioning the enemy's funds in France to make up for the frozen funds they had in Germany." When Proust tried to cash his check, the reserve funds that Warburg & Co. held at the Comptoir d'Escompte had been requisitioned. This was just a hypothesis, Hauser explained, but until proven wrong, he considered it to be accurate. It is indeed the most plausible explanation.

> After ending your letter, you open it up again to tell me that you've never heard of salons where people work instead of chatting. Neither have I. That's why I was careful to talk of "places where people work." Once again I must deplore the superficial way you read my letters. . . . And you close your post scriptum with a long dissertation on politeness and rudeness that tells me that you have no recollection of a book which, at one time, you seemed to have read with vivid interest: I'm referring to *The Three Levers of the New World.* If you bother to take a look at page 70, you will find a chapter devoted to politeness that in precise detail counters all your criticisms on the subject. Having said this, my dear Marcel, allow me to return to my occupations. (COR XIX, 95)

In chapter 14 of his *Three Levers of the New World,* Hauser writes with disapproval of people who are gentlemen only by name, polite but lacking in nobility of character, and remind him of bottles of champagne full of vinegar. After this reference to his own book, Hauser reminded Proust of his own eternally serious "occupations," which could be pursued with no risk of wasting time.

I presume it was out of respect for Hauser's steadfast industriousness that Proust devoted the first part of his next letter to financial matters. He started out by admitting he was so in the dark as to the world of bankers that he was not sure whether he would do Hauser a favor by transferring his portfolio from the London Bank to Hauser et Cie. If Hauser saw even a tiny personal advantage in this operation, Proust would do it with joy. To him, the switch would entail some inconvenience, it was true, because he would lose his line of credit at 5.5 percent interest, but it would be a minor problem, since he took advantage of it only rarely. In the event he found himself in urgent need of cash, he could just sell some securities. And if it turned out that these securities earned him more than 5.5 percent, well, it would neither ruin him nor make him rich. This proposal is not bizarre per se, but it seems conceived by someone who was wholly unaware that its instrumental or manipulative goal—the equivalent of a bribe—would be repulsive to a person of Hauser's integrity. Proust ought to have known better. Having completed this unfortunate introduction, Proust engaged in the "moral debate."

> My dear Lionel,
>
> . . . I find you excessively irritable and it seems to me that you apply a double standard to this issue, according to whether it concerns me or you. After granting you all possible merits and virtues, I took the liberty of accusing you of self-righteousness and also of pride, which are not the worst of vices, and you immediately persecute me cruelly with your request for explanations. In return, you find it all too natural to tell me: "I never gave the least weight to your declarations of gratitude." Fortunately I didn't pay any attention to these words, otherwise, were I as irritable as you, since this affirmation amounts to accusing me of insincerity, I'd be justified in demanding even more clarifications than the ones warranted by my mildly offensive accusation of self-righteousness. (COR XIX, 98)

In spite of his doctor's severe prohibition against too much writing in order to avoid strain, Proust meant to give a substantial reply to a passage in Hauser's last letter, in which, referring to Henry James, the banker had made some off-the-point remarks on psychology. "In common speech one often hears references to 'the psychology of the priest, of the Norman, of the Jacobin.' But the psychology I talk of in my novel is of another kind, not founded on observation but on intuition, and it's focused on deep mental layers where the differences between the psychologies of the priest, of the Norman etc. are insignificant." Proust must be thinking here of a passage from *In the Shadow of Young Girls in Flower,* in which the Narrator argues that the observation of personal habits and attitudes is useless, because one can simply infer them from psychological laws. Proust continued:

> If I didn't find it ridiculous to divulge the praise I receive, I'd send you an article entitled "Marcel Proust and the Classical Tradition," by Jacques Rivière (whom *L'Humanité* is going into raptures over after the publication of his study on Bolshevism.)[5] Anyway, even if we stick with the meaning that you attribute to my usage of the term "psychology," I'll tell you that the great psychologists of the kind you refer to have rarely bothered to survey diverse social milieus, for the simple reason that society is modeled on their works and not vice versa. This is why

> Balzac, whose books are considered great frescos of human society, never left his room to paint it, but the next generation, infatuated with his books, got abruptly peopled with [his characters in flesh and blood,] who were like Rastignac and Rubempré, people he had invented but who came to life [only after he wrote about them]. (COR XIX, 98)

I cannot help reading the phrase about Balzac's never leaving of his room as an allusion to Proust's quasi-permanent confinement in bed, as if the latter were immodestly counting himself among the "great psychologists" of his time. We do, however, know that Proust surveyed tirelessly and scrupulously his own favorite social milieu, but kept secret his idiosyncratic approach to on-site fact-finding.

This letter has two capital implications. First, Proust's remark on the artist's power to influence the psychology of his contemporaries unveils the ambitious agenda that, in Proust's eyes, justified the sacrifice of friendship, as well as of love, wealth, and personal health, to his artwork. Hauser was a casualty of this ambition. Second, Proust's distinction between observation and intuition in psychological matters is quite important, as it aligns him with certain views of his acquired cousin, Henri Bergson, who professed the reciprocal dependence of empirical observation and personal insight. Thus far, we have paid some attention to the divergent views opposing Proust and Bergson in matters pertinent to memory work. But the analogy they share, in their common belief that mind and body operate in tight interaction with each other, is not less remarkable. The following passage from Bergson's *Matière et mémoire,* which describes the process whereby the concrete immediacy of a perception acquires its proper meaning through the contribution of a mental catalogue of interpretive keys, marks one of the aspects of closest proximity between Proust's and Bergson's respective views of memory work.

> Memory does not consist at all of a regression from the present to the past, but on the contrary of a progress from the past to the present. At first we place ourselves in the past. We begin from a "virtual" condition, then we proceed by degrees, through a series of different planes of conscience, to the stage where [this virtual condition] materializes itself in an actual perception, that is to say, to the point where we experience it as a

> present and active condition. . . . At the moment when a remembrance actualizes itself . . . by acting on us, it is not anymore a remembrance, it has become again a perception.[6]

From the perspective of memory work, the difference separating Bergson from Proust is as crucial as the analogy that links them to each other. Bergson's theory of memory work hinges on the "adjustment" obtained between the remembrance deposited in one's memory and one's present impression, the "precision" of this adjustment depending on one's successful effort in paying "attention to life," or, if you will, on one's spontaneous "impetus" (élan) toward the future.[7] Proust's theory of involuntary memory, on the contrary, hinges, as we saw, on the "transmutation" of one's present impression[8] into the recognition of analogous qualia from the past,[9] and the "miracle of this analogy" depends on one's ability to make a cohesive whole of distinct moments in time (*Finding Time Again,* 180).

It is hard to imagine how Proust, who was always depleted in energy or close to a physical breakdown, who required increasing amounts of stimulants to work and sedatives to rest, could find the strength to write another message to Hauser on the same day of the previous letter. But he did. He wanted to remind his friend that he had never learned the name of the accountant who had taken such good care of his balance sheets. Proust had originally planned to present him with an autographed copy of the *Young Girls in Flower,* but would he please him more with a 300-franc tip?

Hauser answered that after the beginning of the war, Hauser et Cie was not equipped to handle conventional bank operations, especially the management of a client portfolio. Hauser limited himself to notifying his clients about loans, bonds, and other interesting securities, but after the clients had underwritten or subscribed to the options of their choice, he asked them to pick up their stocks and bonds and deposit them at their regular bank. Then he went on to discuss the "moral debate." Proust was wrong if he thought that Hauser did not take his gratitude seriously or would like to see it expressed in more tangible ways. However, Hauser did not attach any importance to words that were not confirmed by facts; he found it simpler to just take note of facts and disregard the words that preceded or followed them. In this regard, he appreciated Proust's efforts to persuade his friends to write reviews of his book, seeing it as an amicable thing to do, and he did not hold Proust responsible for their unfriendly attitude toward him.

Hauser's argument has swiftly plunged into the spiral of obtuseness that was becoming the preferred register adopted by the two friends in their confrontations on the "moral debate." Hauser must have realized this rather promptly, though, judging from the fact that he switched abruptly to another topic, namely, that of the young collaborator about whose name Proust had inquired. He dealt with the matter in a tone of levity. Roger Levy—such was the accountant's name—was prey to cruel indecision owing to the dilemma forced on him by the generosity of Monsieur Proust. Should the young man opt for a book signed by the great Marcel Proust, or, in a more utilitarian spirit, accept his generous tip? Levy would appreciate receiving the money; but, in contrast, he would be proud to own a signed copy of the book. He had been wondering, "with the speculative wit that is typical of the children of Israel, if there [was] true incompatibility between the two alternatives." In sum, why did Proust not send young Levy both the book and the tip? The amused tone in this passage is possibly the harbinger of an improvement in the way the two friends regarded each other. And as if to bring this point home, Hauser took on the efficient, pragmatic stance that best suited him. Since Proust had written him that he had lost track of his account at the London Bank, Hauser meant to make a personal inquiry about it, although he was afraid that the bank might not consider him authorized to be privy to Proust's information (COR XIX, 102).

Proust's answer, no less than Hauser's letter, swayed between the practical solidarity of two friends doing business together and the resentful recrimination of two friends in conflict. He had not recently modified his London Bank account in the least, so he would send Hauser his last statement together with the whole bank dossier; these documents should suffice to give him the whole picture, without bothering with a personal visit to the bank. But before saying this, he revealed to Hauser, almost as an aside, the true cause of their recent, furious exchange of correspondence: "I find you unfair concerning words and actions. If I limit myself to a sad reminiscence, at the time when you were the victim of the most unjust calumnies, my friend Walter Berry and I took some concrete initiatives that weren't wholly ineffective. One couldn't regard them as mere words" (COR XIX, 106).

The plot of the epistolary novel—with Proust and Hauser as the two protagonists—has been woven long enough. The master weaver, who was acting (or in this case, writing) in response to the urges of his temper rather than under the direction of a well-wrought plan, was Proust himself. Even in this minor biographical episode, the writer shines as an unequalled master in the far-reaching design and multilayered narrative plot that, as our story unfolds, are bestowing on him a worldwide literary reputation. His fellow protagonist, who was both the interlocutor and, like us, the spectator of this ongoing two-man drama, has been kept in suspense for several weeks, spurred on by the writer's unusual reticence. Up to this stage, Hauser was still in the dark as to the nature of the "disillusionment" that had ensnared him in this rapid-fire exchange of letters. The moment has come for Proust to draw the two long legs of his compasses together, to gather the scattered threads of the conflict with his friend (this amateurish, self-styled expert of psychology!) and, why not?, teach him a lesson on the multifarious ways one can both explore and exploit the hidden recesses of the human psyche.

One month or so earlier, as you will remember from the prologue to part 2 of our epistolary novel, Proust had hinted at a sort of mutual debt that had been the cause of his disillusionment with Hauser. He now comes into the open with the reference to the "unjust calumnies" that Hauser had been the target of in the past, and the initiatives undertaken by him and Berry to protect him. At long last, the crux of the conflict is out in the open. Hauser was guilty of showing only indifference and ingratitude for Proust and Berry's generous help to him: this was the nature of the disillusionment that could have lessened Proust's sense of gratitude toward Hauser, had the writer been lacking in personal integrity. All of a sudden, Proust's frequent allusions to his actions in Hauser's favor (actions rather than mere words), which were too cryptic not to seem inaccurate, and too unsubstantial not to appear conceited, become glaringly obvious to the banker. At the time when, as the British agent of a German firm, Hauser was afraid that the French government might accuse him of being a spy, Proust and Berry had intervened in his defense. Proust has finally put his cards on the table!

Hauser answered Proust's letter the next day, on April 27, 1920.

> You make our situation more complex by informing me of certain initiatives of yours and adding, correctly in my opinion, that one shouldn't classify them as mere words. . . . It would never occur to me to define an initiative that consists of an act by the term "words," and as far as the initiatives you're referring

> to are concerned, it would have been even harder for me to classify them as words insofar as only today are you revealing their existence to me. Therefore it is not of them that we have been debating thus far. (COR XIX, 108)

Having said this, Hauser went on to illustrate his own pragmatic notion of gratitude. There is something insincere, sordid even, not to mention anticlimactic, in his hasty decision to disregard the long-postponed revelation of his debt of gratitude toward Proust and Berry. A punch in the face, he explained, has the same efficacy, regardless of whether it is announced with words of threat or comes out of the blue. What matters is the pain caused by the punch, not the words that accompany it. The same principle applies to acts of gratitude. One must learn to distinguish these acts from verbal expressions of gratitude, or, in other words, to separate promises from action. In sum, one must ignore verbal pledges and "take note of actions as if they were vulgar blows." This was Hauser's philosophy of gratitude (COR XIX, 108).

If what truly mattered to Hauser was this dreadful idea of recording actions as if they were punches in the face, giving no importance to the intentions behind them, one can only conclude that Proust's last metaphorical punch must have knocked the common sense out of him—that very common sense of which he was so rightly proud. It is somewhat curious that Hauser's viewpoint was anticipated by Proust in the book that earned him the Prix Goncourt a few months earlier, in which he credits the impact of words with more than expressive power, giving them the executive power, if you will, of tribunal verdicts. In his first meeting with the former ambassador Norpois, the Narrator of *Young Girls in Flower* remarks that "each time Monsieur de Norpois used certain expressions, [however] trite . . . and which he spoke with emphasis, one could sense that, by virtue of having been uttered by him, they became an act" (*Young Girls in Flower,* 31).[10]

The same day of Hauser's answer, Proust brought their boxing match to an end with the sober words of the crowned champion. "You will acknowledge that on my part it was kinder to act as I did, with no ostentation whatsoever. . . . Besides, I thought that Monsieur Berry had informed you of what we did, to some extent at least." Proust's delusion that he was the constant focus of his friends' conversation had made him wrongly assume that Berry would have informed Hauser of the initiative he and Proust had taken in his favor earlier on. The consequences of this narcissistic prejudice are not negligible in this case. Proust went on: "[I'm noticing] a curious attitude on your part. At a time when doctors believe that a few gentle words, even if they are not followed by acts, may have a therapeutic effect, you argue that acts should not be complemented with words or should at the most be accompanied by stinging words" (COR XIX, 110).

Thus ends the epistolary novel.

Chapter 24

FINANCIAL COMEBACK

Almost eight months of silence followed Hauser's knockout. It was Proust who took the initiative in December 1920 by sending Hauser a copy of *The Guermantes Way* and apologizing that it was only a third edition. He added: "I'm sorry to see that, regardless of whether I'm healthy or ill, I do not exist for you anymore" (COR XIX, 361). This gave Hauser an opportunity to shield his wounded self-esteem, show himself inflexible in his pedagogical-esoteric vocation, and suggest at the same time that he would be willing to bury the hatchet—or to hang up his boxing gloves, to stick with my long-extended metaphor—and return to the ordinary regime of tender friendship with Proust. Neglecting to mention that he had recently published a thirty-one-page monograph titled *The True Solution to the Working-Class Problem* (*La vraie solution du problem ouvrier*), Hauser added to his response the good news that Proust would soon be in control of his Warburg portfolio again, which had increased in value by a 5 percent yield, compounded every year since the beginning of the war. And he added:

> My dear Marcel,
>
> . . . I don't understand what led you to assume that you don't exist for me anymore. Is it owing perhaps to the fact that I didn't join in the ovations by which a delirious crowd welcomes the appearance of your new masterpieces or your induction to the Order of the Legion of Honor? This would be quite unfair to me. . . . I didn't wait for your consecration by the crowds or by the Government before giving your intelligence, your powers of observation, and the captivating charm

> of your prose the esteem they deserve. Each of your letters (I'm referring of course to the purely impersonal ones you wrote me whenever you surrendered to the inspiration of your Muse) was a pure masterpiece that conveyed the essence of all of your published books and potentially the contents of the still unwritten ones. I had the privilege of drinking straight from the source of that pure and crystal-clear water of yours, which later on, having flowed downhill, has been analyzed by knowledgeable savants and deemed worthy of being consumed by the masses. (COR XIX, 364)

The enthusiasm of those among Proust's old friends who had chosen to wait for the moment of his double triumph before expressing their approval brought a smile to Hauser's lips.

> Having dealt with occultism for a long time, I enjoy looking at the occult side or if you prefer, the hidden side of things, actions, and words, and if I had your kind of talent, after introducing your readers to the disquieting mysteries of Sodom and Gomorrah in the book whose publication they are waiting for with ill-concealed eagerness, I would offer them a new book entitled, "The Subconscious of a Society Man" in which I would prove that, notwithstanding the constraints of society's implacable laws, which in given circumstances force a society man to automatically perform certain things and automatically say certain words, he still has access to a subconscious which—as long as society won't decide otherwise—is his own secret garden. (COR XIX, 364)

After this mildly cutting remark about Proust's opportunistic admirers and frequent visitors, Hauser thanked him warmly for the present of his new book. He preferred to take the reproach that came with it, of having neglected Proust for too long, "as a declaration of love." What he regretted was that Proust had tried too hard to find him a first edition, when in the past he had gone to great lengths to explain his indifference to these sorts of details.

> If I were a touchy person I should be offended by it, but luckily for you, I am not. . . . Reading your book holds an additional

> interest for me because the countryside location where it unfolds has become very dear to me since my family and I spent our last holidays and go often on Sunday to a tiny place near Chelles, that is, a few kilometers from Guermantes, and therefore very close to Villeparisis, Villevaudé, Monjay, and other splendid little spots that must awaken so many of your childhood memories. (COR XIX, 364)

As Philip Kolb remarks in his annotation to this letter, "Chelles (Seine-et-Marne) is actually nine kilometers away from Lagny, in whose environs is the castle of Guermantes. But Proust just evokes this name [in his novel], since it seems he wasn't acquainted with this area." (Ibid. [note 3]).

The month before this letter, Proust had drafted a letter for the London Bank, declaring that he wanted to pay off his debt by selling his bonds from the French National Loan, and invest what would be left from this sale in the new French Loan earning a 6 percent yearly yield. He was also planning to sell his Suez Canal Bonds. By the middle of January 1921, however, it seems this letter had not been mailed yet (COR XX, 19 [note 3]). Hauser would take charge of these transactions later on.

In 1920, Proust's royalties became a significant part of his annual revenue, fulfilling the sweetest dream of any writer.[1] His total income came to 75,000 francs, of which 10,000 came from Gallimard and 5,000 from the Prix Goncourt, awarded in December 1919 but paid a few weeks later. At long last, his Warburg portfolio was unfrozen, having grown in the meantime to a total of 77,000 francs. His portfolios were virtually unchanged, nominally speaking, with the sorry caveat that a 21 percent inflation rate was wolfing down everything, lowering Proust's real income from 84,000 francs in 1919 to 75,000 francs. The French currency meanwhile had lost 44 percent of its relative worth with respect to the U.S. dollar (after losing 58 percent the year before). His nominal income in present-day U.S. dollars thus shrank more than proportionally, going from $95,000 in 1919 to $47,000 in 1920.

By the end of 1921, Proust and Hauser were fully reconciled. The next year, the last of the writer's life, he would be too distracted by his literary and commercial success, and the subsequent, hectic exchange of letters with old and new correspondents, to find any time for Hauser.

By the end of 1921, Proust had become an exceedingly well known man and, on top of that, better off than he had ever been: his nominal income was 99,000 francs, which, thanks to a negative inflation rate of minus 8.61 percent, corresponded to real income of 109,000 francs. This was 45 percent higher than the year before, and 73 percent higher than in 1908, at the beginning of his collaboration with Hauser. (Adjusting income and wealth for the previous year's inflation does not tell the whole story, of course. From 1905 to 1920, the French index of consumer prices underwent a cumulative increment of 176.87 percent, which undercut remarkably the real value of personal revenues, but in the same period the index of stock prices swelled up to 141.33 percent [at the April 1920 peak of market volatility],[2] which hugely amplified the wealth of shareholders such as Proust—two opposite trends which I factored in by various corrections, as explained in "Proust and His Banker: Numerical Documentation.") In 1921, the French currency recovered part of its relative value vis-à-vis the U.S. dollar (while the index of consumer prices shrank 23.84 percent), hence Proust's income in dollars increased 128 percent, from $47,000 in 1920 to $107,000 in 1921.

His two guardian angels, Rothschild and Hauser, worked briskly and efficiently on his behalf. Thanks to André Neuberger's resourceful management of Proust's Royal Dutch shares at the Rothschild Bank, his stash went from 11 to 17. Although their unitary price had meanwhile gone down to 4,095 Dutch guilders, that is, about 17,000 francs,[3] it is legitimate to assume that this increased Proust's Rothschild portfolio by 59,000 francs. Proust wrote of this progress to Hauser. If his friend could manage to buy him two more such shares while handling the restructuring of his portfolio with the London Bank, Proust expected his owner's subscription privileges would entitle him to acquire 13 additional shares from the next issue at a small cost—thereby reaching a total of 32 shares (COR, XX, 180).

Judging from the contents of Proust's portfolio at his death, listed in the "État des Valeurs en Depot chez Messieurs de Rothschild frères sous le dossier de Monsieur Marcel Proust à la date 31 Décembre 1922," this plan was never implemented, as it appears that Robert Proust, Marcel's sole heir, inherited exactly 17.3 *actions* Royal Dutch from his brother (see illus. 6 and 7).

First purchased in 1908 as an awkward speculative investment to benefit his friend Reynaldo Hahn—my starting point in illustrating Proust's instinctive talent for the exploitation of "opportunity costs"—the Royal Dutch shares in the writer's portfolio contributed significantly to the postwar reconstruction of his personal wealth.

Over the year, Proust closed his account at the London Bank—since the negotiations subsequent to the accidental sale of his Tramways de

Mexico had failed to bring satisfactory results—and opened a new account at Cox & Co. Having paid off his debt with the London Bank (ibid., 278), he transferred about 200,000 francs to this new Cox account. The rest of his financial situation seems to have remained unchanged. Given the skyrocketing inflation rate of the recent past, it is likely that his 30,000-franc loan from the Mirabaud Bank (guaranteed by the equivalent value of his Warburg check) had vanished into his household expenses even before the end of 1920. It also looks as if Proust persuaded his landlady to modify the lease contract of his apartment in Rue Hamelin, from furnished to unfurnished, thereby lowering the rent to about 9,500 francs a year.

Etat des valeurs en Dépôt
chez Messieurs de Rothschild frères à Paris
sous le dossier de Monsieur Marcel Proust
à la date du 31 Décembre 1922

500	Capital	Brésilien 4% 1910
17 800	Actions	Royal Dutch de 1000 fl
25	"	Malacca Rubber
15	"	Rand Mines
6	"	Cie des Eaux pour l'Etranger
24	"	Cie Gale des Eaux nom
32	"	Cie Gale des Eaux jouisce nom
2	"	Gelsenkirchner Bergwerks de 600 m
2	"	Assces La Sécurité nom.
1	"	Assces Maritimes L'Equinoxe nom
3	"	Assces Comptoir Maritime nom
2	"	Assces Maritimes La Prévoyante nom
3	"	L'Atlantide nom
10	Obligations	Russe Consolidé 4% 1e Sie
35	"	Russe Consolidé 4% 2e Sie
2	"	Crédit Foncier d'Egypte 3% à lots
18	"	Chinois 4% Or 1895
2	Lots de	Panama
2	Lots de la	Presse 1905
1	Obligation	Communale 3% 1912
60	Capital	Brésilien funding 5% 1914
72		Rente Française 4% 1918
2800	Obligations	Verbandes Gross Berlin 4%
4	Actions	Raffineries Sucreries Say

Paris le 31 Décembre 1922

Marcel Proust's Rothschild portfolio at his death, December 31, 1922.
Archives Nationales du Monde du Travail, Fond Rothschild, cote 132 AQ T58
(with the permission of The Trustees of The Rothschild Archive Trust Limited).

But this time, a third guardian angel had walked unexpectedly onto the scene: it was Proust himself, whose royalties, at long last, earned him lucrative compensation for the fabulous and seemingly absurd opportunity costs he had shouldered all these years. If only had he had another ten years to live, so as to enjoy the fruits of so much work, so much talent, and so much waste! In 1921, Proust earned more than 40,000 francs from royalties alone. He would earn even more the following year—although it would fall to his heirs, and especially, I think, to Gaston Gallimard's NRF, to benefit from the long-term exponential growth in his royalties.

Fig. 3 highlights the Lilliputian size of Proust's patrimony in real terms in 1915, compared with 1911 on the far left of the chart and 1921 on the far right (with all the intermediate years in between).

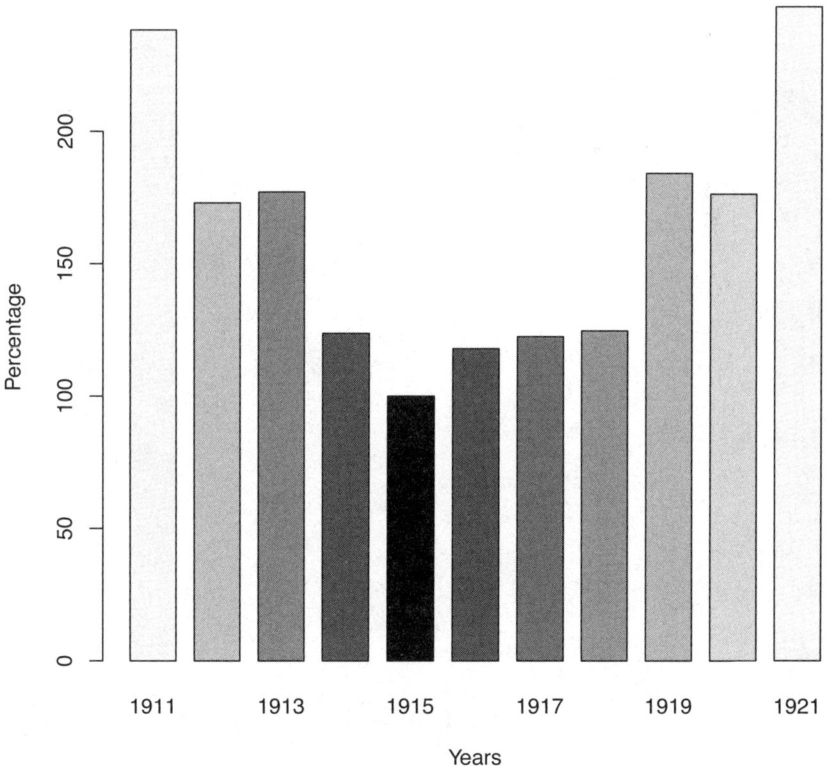

Proust's net worth (1911–1921) relative to 1915.
Source: Gian Balsamo, "Proust and His Banker: Numerical Documentation," Item 2.

The symmetry between the 1911 and 1921 bars in fig. 3 makes it clear that Proust's financial debacle from 1911 to 1915—respectively, the year that marked his ruinous debut on the forwards-contract market and the year he dodged bankruptcy by a hairbreadth— was punctually overturned by his financial successes after World War I. Give or take a few thousand francs, the same huge chasm divides Proust's patrimony in 1915 from his personal wealth in 1911 and in 1921. In other words, Proust's comeback after World War I fully made up for his financial losses before the war.

Chapter 25

A RELATIVITY THEORY OF SEX

Although he was not exactly a best-selling author, Proust was the favorite of literary critics. In the *Revue Hebdomadaire* of April 5, 1921, André Malraux wrote a polemical article against the critics who accused Proust of neglecting all religious concerns: "The accusation of a lack of morality is illegitimate with regard to Proust's novel: the search for one's soul is the ground of moral life, and Proust sheds a terrible light on our darkest depths. His art has the indifference of the sun: everything in it is torn away from the shadows, even that which nobody dared mention before him" (COR XX, 56, 56 [note 4]).

In an article entitled "*Billet à Angèle,*" André Gide wrote: "Should I confess it? Every time I plunge back into the place of delight that is Proust's novel, for several days afterwards I cannot pick up my pen, being disinclined to accept that there can be a different way of writing than his, feeling disinclined to see nothing but *poverty* in what has been called my style's 'purity'" (COR XX, 106). Gide wrote these words after reading *The Guermantes Way.* Shortly later he read *Sodom and Gomorrah* and, annoyed by the pitiless treatment of Charlus's homosexuality, wrote Proust that he was glad he had written his comments praising the novel before reading this last installment. What he wished to tell him about his treatment of homosexuality, he added, would lend itself better to a face-to-face conversation than to an article. Here, however, was the concise version of what he would say if he had to put his impressions down in writing: "By taking an impartial point of view, the vantage point of the true naturalist, Monsieur Proust paints a portrait of 'vice' that is more stigmatizing than any invective. He brands with infamy what he talks about, and is thereby of better service to the customs of respectable people than the most aggressive treatise on morals" (COR XX, 127).

This accusatory letter was followed shortly later by the conversation we discussed earlier, whose contents were included in Gide's journal. In it, Proust regretted the irresolution that had induced him to hide "all the graciousness, tenderness, and charm from his homosexual memories" in the shadow of his girls in flower, so that, regarding the homosexual people of *Sodom and Gomorrah,* he could only deal with "grotesqueness and abjection."[1] Ten years later, on the occasion of the publication of a new book of poems by Anna de Noailles, Gide recalled the exaggerated compliments that Proust used to address to this poet, and came to the conclusion that Proust's words tended to be like a warm breath that, indifferent to truth, stirred up his listener's self-esteem.[2] One wonders whether Gide, enlightened by this insight, did not question, retrospectively, the sincerity of the words which Proust had addressed to him in 1921. Already in a letter dated October 1, 1927, Gide had defined Proust a "great master of dissimulation."[3] But in this case Gide was accusing Proust of the same "artistic hypocrisy" ("hypocrisie artiste") whereby Oscar Wilde filled his pages with admissions that only some initiates could decrypt. Did it not occur to him that, in real life, the same sort of hypocrisy could fulfill the opposite need, and let the initiate see or hear whatever he was predisposed to see and hear? So, as in the case of Gide's rejection of Proust's manuscript in 1912, in the case of his contribution to the image of Proust as an artist utterly committed to the homosexual cause, one is left to wonder, or to wander, rather, on the edge of the cliff of aesthetic and introspective denial.

In the light of these considerations, I am tempted to translate Proust's regret of having disguised all homosexual virtues in his novel behind the façade of pretty girls into the following proposition: in the days of her pubescent erotic games with the Narrator at the Champs Élysées, the character of Gilberte—however inspired by the variety of girls, such as Jeanne Pouquet, who, as adult women, would each claim credit as the principal model—was also derived from the transposition of the "graciousness, tenderness, and charm" of Proust's reminiscences from the years spent side by side with his favorite male schoolmates at the Lycée Condorcet. In this regard, we have at our disposal a proliferation of letters burning with repressed lust, written by the young Proust to Jacques Bizet, Robert Dreyfus, Daniel Halévy, Gaston de Caillavet, and others (COR XXI, *Appendice*).[4] Gilberte was a hermaphrodite, in sum, a Janus-like object of desire, and the Narrator, her paramour, lusted now after one of her sexual sides, now after the other.

In this regard, the literary critic Marie-Françoise Vieuille has insightfully opposed Proust's "androgynous imagination" to Gide's "homosexual militancy."[5] (J. E. Rivers devoted a whole chapter of *Proust and the Art of Love* to arguing a somewhat analogous position.) I find highly convincing Vieuille's hypothesis that the sexuality of Proust's Narrator hinges on some imaginative sort of hermaphroditism. For one thing, it justifies the assemblage of originals from both genders as inspiring the characterization of Albertine Simonet, which we discussed earlier. For another, it justifies the importance assigned by Proust to the faculty of imagination in sex-related matters.

In his remarkably original analysis of the social-class dialectic informing the narrative texture of Proust's entire novel, Edward J. Hughes describes the novel's Narrator as an enterprising heterosexual whose libido is inseparable from the symbols of his social advantages, regardless of whether he is attracted to noblewomen or to servants and laborers. Thus, these marks of social belonging brand his attraction for Albertine, whose upper-class origin does not hold her back from "kiss[ing] him with dog-like enthusiasm," so that "in moments of physical intimacy . . . her cheeks become rougher like those of working-class women from the suburbs." Hughes also points out that, in his novel, Proust undertakes a "transposition . . . from homosexual to heterosexual encounter."[6] To Hughes, in sum, the difference in sexual preferences between Proust and his Narrator is unproblematic, since the homosexual engagements of the former mirror the heterosexual engagements of the latter, both in physical situation and in social connotation. Along analogous lines, Joshua Landy argues that Albertine's bisexuality or homosexuality is an impenetrable barrier to the heterosexual Narrator, thereby "representing . . . the breadth of the gulf that separates her consciousness from his."[7]

The hypothesis of androgynous imagination takes this discussion off its hinges. In Albertine's complex sexuality, I submit, Proust's Narrator finds an irresistible erotic trigger to his own desire. In the world of the Narrator's sexual imagination, there are three Albertines, and a different androgynous fantasy corresponds to each.

The first Albertine is found on or by the beach of Balbec. Her beauty "glittering" by the blue shimmering sea, Albertine is "the fairest rose" in the bouquet of the handsome girls and women surrounding her (*Prisoner*, 59). She is coveted by several of these women and perhaps "enjoyed" by some, which not only makes her supremely desirable in the eyes of the Narrator, but turns also all these other women, and especially Albertine's supposed favorite, Andrée, into "objects of horror," hated and feared competitors for Albertine's sexual favors. Male competitors are altogether absent from the scene, so much so that the Narrator seems to attribute a lesbian nature to his own desire. He must keep Albertine from sharing with these surrounding "Temptations" the sexual favors, admittedly rather slight at the time, which she shares with him.

The second Albertine is secluded within the Narrator's apartment. Once she becomes the Narrator's domestic captive in Paris, living *more uxorio* with him, and torn away from her bouquet of flowers, Albertine is "reduced to her dull self." Since she can "no longer succumb to their temptation," her lesbian suitors on the beach of Balbec become sexually tempting to the Narrator, who wishes he could enact with them the role of Albertine's surrogate (*Prisoner,* 155–56).[8]

The third Albertine is exiled to the hereafter. The Narrator's surrogate role is pushed one step farther after her demise, when, for a time, her memory permeates his sexual fantasies and enhances their intensity. Seeing in Albertine's favorite friend Andrée the incarnation of Albertine's desire, for instance, for the first time the Narrator finds her "beautiful" and desirable—only promptly to realize that Andrée's features bear a striking resemblance to his own younger and beardless face in the days of Balbec, in the days, that is, leading to his imaginative transformation, at first unintentional, into Albertine's sexual stand-in (*Fugitive,* 511, 514).[9] This is the clearest of several occasions in the novel when the Janus-like ambivalence of the beloved meets the lover's hermaphroditic yearnings.

In this context, two considerations must be kept in mind. The first is that to Proust's Narrator, the condition that makes a person "desirable" is that this person be "a creature . . . of imagination" ("un être d'imagination"), someone about whom it is possible to fantasize (*Fugitive,* 420)[10]: someone, in other words, whose presence in his arms is complemented by a degree of absence or evasiveness, sufficient to make her into an imaginary object of longing. No pleasurable sex, no object of desire is worth attaining without this complicity of imagination; as you may recall, inaccessibility is the first predicate of the love object in Proust's love flowchart (followed by jealousy, denial, and forgetfulness). The androgynous imagination hypothesized by Vieuille entails that the Narrator's sexual life is fueled by his ability to picture to himself a sort of divalent sexual partner, who is here in his physical sphere, at hand's reach, if you will, at the same time that he or she is out there, unreachable, a fantasy in the mental sphere of imagination—so that the Narrator can long for him or her in one of the hermaphroditic ways implied by the citations above from *The Prisoner.*

The second consideration regards Proust's very personal notion of the way imagination functions in the service of sex. The problem with imagination is that one can only imagine something that is absent, that is, an object of either memory or fantasy, as Aristotle, with whom Proust agreed, argued long ago.[11] When the object of desire is before your eyes, instead, its image in your mind coincides with this visual; you cannot truly imagine it to the extent that you are looking at it. Yet, in Proust's view, to desire is to imagine; in order to imagine and therefore to desire the person in front of you, you must find a way to treat her or him both like a presence and like a remembrance. This is what I call Proust's Relativity Theory of Sex, as I am going to explain.

A further obstacle to the application of imagination to a sexual encounter is that, in Proust's view, you cannot even imagine an object of memory in an erotically satisfactory way, as long as your remembrance of it is willful, deliberate, or planned—as long as your recollection lacks, in other words, the genuine and spontaneous enchantment of desire; in such a case, your effort to remember makes your desire intellectual rather than erotic. Proust's solution taps the resources of involuntary memory, which we discussed earlier. With the collaboration of an unpremeditated and unrehearsed act of remembrance, your imagination can draw a mental bridge between any present sexual encounter and any past one whose significance ricochets off it—turning them both, thereby, into a wholesome and cohesive whole.

Let me explain the Relativity predicate in this theory of sex. I must start from a simplified model of the world we live in. Try to imagine yourself as a grain of sand in an hourglass. You are gradually sliding down toward the neck leading to your future. Your desire manifests itself as a light beam traveling forward in time, faster than you move down toward the bulb's neck. This hourglass is a model of the space-time continuum of Albert Einstein's theory of Special Relativity. From your position in the upper bulb, your desire reaches the bulb's neck, crosses it into the future, and hits a sand grain in the lower bulb. Given your relative position, your light beam can hit a variety of the sand grains in the lower bulb, by all means not all of them. Now allow me to turn our hourglass upside down, so that you belong now in the future. There is a variety of sand grains in the upper bulb, by all means not all of them, that can hit you with the light beam of their desire, just as you did when you belonged up there. When any of these light beams does hit you, the stimulus of its desire reaches you from the past. Your present situation, your now, consists of either being touched by the desire which a sand grain shot at you from the past, or touching with your desire a sand grain in the future—or both things at once, of course.

In this model of Relativity, the first tenet is that your future is always in the process of happening, as long as one of your light beams has not reached any target yet: if you do not mind mixing metaphors and scientific theories, picture yourself as a butterfly flapping your wings in Paris and causing, years later, the Summer of Love in California. The second tenet is a bit less ordinary, in that it stipulates that your past is always in the process of happening as well; it keeps going on, as long as some grain of sand's light beam is still traveling toward you. Think of a long-delayed love letter reaching you from a remote land. And the third tenet is that your past and your future ricochet off each other, both feeding your now in an interrelated way, since it is all a complex matter of the relative positions linking you to a variety of sand grains. Its specific application to sex-related matters aside, this is the magic and, by now, the commonsense of Einstein's Relativity.

When you think of it, it is not surprising that early critics saw an analogy between Einstein's Relativity and the concept of time in Proust's novel. Slightly more intriguing is that the first essay on this subject, "Proust et Einstein" by Camille Vettard, appeared in the correspondence section of the August 1922 issue of the NRF on the enthusiastic recommendation of Proust himself (followed by Vettard's article "Proust and Time" in the January 1923 issue).[12]

But let us not forget, what we are concerned with here is Proust's usage of imagination in the service of sex. More precisely, I am in the process of sketching the Proustian way that fantasy concurs to position you with respect to your sexual encounters, the term *fantasy* standing here for a token that gathers together the distinctive and interrelated effects of sexual taste, orientation, preference, inclination, gratification, fulfillment, and attraction.

So, we may now rephrase Relativity's three tenets in the vocabulary of sexual encounters: 1) each new sexual encounter emerges out of your future, cutting off other possible encounters (to the exclusion, of course, of the impossible ones, such as, say, you meeting a young Brigitte Bardot or a young Alain Delon by a swimming pool in Saint Tropez); 2) as this new encounter becomes your now (pushing into the past some current, antagonistic encounter), it exhumes memories of some previous encounter; or in the complementary case, this new encounter is triggered by some fantasy-driven exhumation from memory); 3) last, previous and present encounter ricochet off each other, feed off each other, acquiring thereby a new, cohesive significance—so that your sexual life is "freed from the order of time," as Proust himself would phrase it (*Finding Time Again,* 179–81).[13]

To Proust, as we saw, any willful, deliberate, or planned remembrance is not beneficial to sexual fulfillment. Hence, it is the task of involuntary memory, triggered by present circumstances, to scan the repertory of your past encounters, till it finds the one that matches or binds with the present one. This scanning of past memories is only seemingly random; in reality, it is patterned by sexual fantasy, because, even if your memory does not know what it is that it is trying to remember, it knows perfectly well what it is that *you* are *not* trying to remember; this explains the sense of cogency, the *coup de foudre,* that you feel when your memory complements your present encounter by bringing back to you, from the past, the true object of the quest, the true object of your desire. In sum, just as Einstein's Relativity would entail, your past history keeps happening.

Your past history keeps happening in another and broader way as well, of course, which is the one adumbrated in my previous discussion on the reversal of evolutionary time as a relevant thread in Proust's novel. Earlier on, when I broached Proust's Darwinian agenda, I refrained from going into the androgynous, hermaphroditic, and Darwinian imagery disseminated throughout Proust's novel, but there is a plethora of it indeed; reliable textual evidence about it was put forward by E. J. Rivers as early as 1980, and by many other critics as well.[14] For instance, the novel itself, in *Swann's Way,* begins with the androgynous (and parthenogenetic) image of the young Narrator on the verge of a nocturnal emission, while in his dream his thigh engenders and merges with that of a woman (*Swann's Way,* 4); and it ends, in *Finding Time Again,* on the Darwinian image of men and women as "monstrous beings" (*Finding Time Again,* 258), that is, portentous creatures stretched, as Rivers suggested, throughout the entire "evolutionary . . . history of the race."[15] But to drive my point home, it suffices that we tackle only the most relevant and most explicit allusion to Proust's evolutionary concerns.

Sodome and Gomorrah begins with a dance of seduction between Monsieur de Charlus and the character named Jupien, and this dance, duplicated in the nearby scene of a bumblebee's pollination of an orchid, is modeled on what Proust learned from Maurice Maeterlinck, symbolist writer and 1911 Nobel Prize winner, regarding the ingeniousness of the orchid in luring to itself the insect that will be its pollen carrier. Maeterlinck described this phenomenon in *L'intelligence des fleurs* (1907). Proust's second source was Amedée Coutance's preface to the French translation of Darwin's *The Different Forms of Flowers on Plants of the Same Species* (1878).[16] In Proust, argues Rivers, the sort of homosexual union enacted by Charlus and Jupien "reverses the flow of time by recovering the hermaphroditism of the first plants and animals."[17] For precision's sake, one should remark that reciprocal pollination differs from narrowly defined hermaphroditism, but in his long introduction to the dominant theme of *Sodom and Gomorrah,* Proust goes to great length to describe their evolutionary interrelation. The seduction and subsequent intercourse between Charlus and Jupien goes on for a long while, implying rather than describing its sexual tenor by the detail that at the apex of their sexual intercourse, Charlus chatters no end while no word comes out of Jupien's lips, otherwise occupied. Given the significant age gap between the two men (Charlus is already in his fifties), Proust enhances the Darwinian thrust of the passage by comparing Jupien's exclusive attraction for older men to the short-styled *Primula veris*'s imperviousness to pollen which is not coming from a long-styled flower of the same kind (*Sodom and Gomorrah,* 6–7, 29–30).[18] Incidentally, this explains why, no longer than one year before the publication of *Swann's Way,* the character of Charlus was still supposed to be called Monsieur de Fleurus.[19]

All of this insistent imagery and allusion throws Proust's two characters into a condition elusive of narrowly existential experience. They are players on a sexual stage that pertained to their own genetic endowment long before having sprouted out of their personal memory and personal history. Their dance of seduction bespeaks their (and our) inescapable participation in the history and embodied memory of the species. They belong, in sum, in the dimension of evolutionary time, which in Proust's novel is astutely buried underneath the reader-friendly layer of existential time. It is the thematic thrust of evolutionary time that justifies Proust's discreet yet radical critique of optimal sexual roles; this critique, compounded of an existential dissatisfaction, is hinged, in my opinion, on the paradox that in the balance of optimal reproductive fitness, we are but misfits, precariously balanced between the past limitations the species has just overcome and the future adaptations upon which the species will embark after our demise. It is in this condition of recalcitrant adjustment to evolutionary adaptation—one could talk, in Proust, of misadjusted adaptation—that we ought to look for the secret of "that something troublesome," that "quelque chose de pénible" which Proust's Narrator, as he experienced it side by side with Albertine, felt he "could not talk about in [his] narration."[20] Be it as it may, I will leave this topic aside for now, as it is clearly the subject for another book, and move back to the interplay of sex and imagination.

By a reciprocal encroachment of present and past sexual experiences, as we saw, you can enjoy a divalent sexual partner, who is here by your side, but also, at once, there in the imaginative world of fantasy and remembrance. The sexual gratification that Proust's Narrator obtains from Albertine is proportional to the intensifying effects of his imagination. More to the point, even when in bed with her, the Narrator desires Albertine's sexual intimacy by imagining it; he can imagine it because her intimacy is the repetition of the sexual favors that were desired and possibly enjoyed, or so at least did he imagine, by some of her female suitors in Balbec. His desire converges with the desire for Albertine felt by her female friends on the beach in the summer; in Balbec, this past experience fostered his jealousy—jealousy being the second predicate of any affair in Proust's love flowchart. When recalled by him, this past experience ignites his lust (*Finding Time Again,* 181).

The imaginative enhancement of an erotic experience by the recollection of an analogous one from the past is typical of the sexual world of Proust's novel. Among its several representations, one that stands out, with which we crossed paths once before, is found in the "almost sacred" nourishment that Albertine's tongue leaves oftentimes in the Narrator's mouth before she retires for the night; the sensuous power of this ritualistic kiss ricochets off the memory of the goodnight kiss which the Narrator, as a child, used to receive from his mother, who, on exiting his bedroom, left behind an Eucharist-like sense of "real presence" (*Swann's Way,* 13; *Prisoner,* 4).[21] During their cohabitation, time and time again, Albertine is empowered to resuscitate the Narrator's "real self" (from its debilitating "need to be redeemed," as John Updike would put it), with her tongue's offering of this same, maternal "heavenly food" (*Finding Time Again,* 181).[22]

It seems to me that the hypothesis that Albertine's complex sexuality is complicit with the Narrator's androgynous imagination is the most logical explanation for the Narrator's jealousy of Albertine, which compels him to prolong his cohabitation with her, regardless of its increasing squalor, long after he has come genuinely to dislike her. Just like Swann, who married a woman who "was not [his] type" in order to extinguish his unbearable jealousy through the contractual possession of her physical being (*Swann's Way,* 396),[23] Proust's Narrator hates the idea that the woman he would vehemently like to break up with (so that he could at long last travel to Venice or flirt with other young women) may be sharing with another woman the same intimacies that she shares with him; moreover, even when Albertine has completely lost the charms of "the glittering actress of the beach," the Narrator cannot let her escape his Parisian apartment because, at this juncture, her return to Balbec would deprive him of his imaginative role as her sexual surrogate (*Prisoner,* 156).[24]

But what about Proust's own sexuality? Marie-Françoise Vieuille warns us that while androgynous imagination shapes the erotic world of the Narrator of *In Search of Lost Time,* Proust's biography points to a more ordinary, homosexual penchant. I could not disagree more. To my knowledge, since Proust's correspondence is cryptic about it, if not purposefully misleading, the biographical information at our disposal consists mainly of the questionable gossip that Proust's contemporaries left us on the writer's sexual habits. As I have argued earlier, as well as at length elsewhere, the story told in Proust's novel coincides with the autobiography or pseudobiography that he elected to leave behind as his own, just as the fiction of Dante's poem the *Divine Comedy* is Dante's self-elected autobiography.[25] In the *Divine Comedy,* Dante violates the conventional scheme according to which his autobiographic persona in the poem ought to approximate his historically documentable identity; instead, he makes his historically documentable identity a mere allegory of the authentic individual brought to life by his verses. The same principle must be applied to *In Search of Lost Time:* near the closure of Proust's novel, the distinction between fictional character and historical author loses its force: they coincide with each other at the point of intersection of fiction and reality, of allegory and personal history, when the Narrator, equipped at long last with the means and determination to write the novel which we have almost finished reading, becomes the authentic personification of the man who wrote it.[26]

In this light, let me ask one more time: What do we know of Proust's sexual habits and preferences? Close to nothing, I submit—except that the sexual life of his novel's Narrator is meant as the authentic implementation of the sexuality enacted in Proust's documentable life. This explains, by the way, the new and controversial way I read his letters to such beauties as Hélène Soutzo, Marie Scheikévitch, and others, and, side by side with his secret homosexual life, interpret their romantic implications. The Narrator's sexual habits and morals are closer to Proust's "true life," to "reality as [he] experienced it" (*Finding Time Again,* 189),[27] than any rumor—least of all, than the tall tales of sexual and bestial perversions spread about him by Jean Cocteau, Marcel Jouhandeau, Albert le Cuziat, and Maurice Sachs, whose factual reliability has been convincingly discredited by Roger Duchêne.[28]

André Gide's disappointed response to the treatment of homosexual characters in *Sodom and Gomorrah* was compensated by Jacques Rivière's enthusiasm. Since the editor was one of Proust's proofreaders, he was familiar with both *The Guermantes Way* and the first volume of *Sodom and Gomorrah;* after editing both, he wrote Proust a letter full of emotion: "Too often have I found myself listening to distorted notions of what love is, not to feel a delightful relief in listening to someone who can talk of love in your healthy and well-balanced way" (COR XX, 107).

"Healthy and well-balanced": regardless of his deep affection and devotion for Proust, I expect that Lionel Hauser would have found something to object to in this characterization. I have kept Hauser in the background long enough to provide this book with an indispensable piece of scaffolding. Throughout the last fourteen years, with remarkable tenacity, Proust had been pursuing the mirage of the perfect love, wasting enormous sums of money in its quest and trying to keep his patrimony from shrinking proportionately by means of acrobatic speculations. Throughout the last fourteen years, in turn, Hauser, Love's Bookkeeper, had been doing his best to restrain Proust from acrobatic speculations in order to keep his patrimony from shrinking. To opposite extents, they were both victims of what I called earlier Proust's pansensualism. Now I have finally explained my take on the major features of this pansensualism. Whether or not these features might contribute to our new discussions of sexual identity, it is not for this book to debate. (I think they do.) But they play an essential role in this book's plot.

It is time for Hauser to come back on stage.

Chapter 26

SUICIDAL OBSTINACY

About the middle of January 1921, Proust sent Céleste Albaret to Lionel Hauser's offices with the excuse that it was time to take some initiative regarding the London Bank. Albaret was very well received, and Proust rejoiced, assuming that Hauser was favorably disposed toward him. He wrote Hauser right away. Considering that Proust's entire oeuvre is devoted to the cult of memory, one might almost take it as a professional bias (if not a self-destructive urge) that from the very first lines, his letter started digging up their past exchanges.

He went back to Hauser's notion that words are useless compared with facts and concrete actions, and therefore leave no tangible traces, while acts have the long-lasting effects of a punch in the face. As we will see shortly, Hauser was no less stubborn than Proust when it came to exhuming the past. Hence, their friendship could be taken as emblematic of their own time: this is a moment when the simultaneous publication of the writings of Proust and of Bergson converts many of their contemporaries to the practice of constantly intertwining present experience and past reminiscence. There is no comparable precedent in the history of civilization for such a brusque turning point in the appreciation of the practical advantages to be derived from personal memory; what begins in France at this time soon spreads to the whole of Europe.

Not that Proust and Hauser only derived advantages from their constant archeology of mutual resentment. Proust wrote to Hauser: "[I expect] you'll tell me that words of gratitude don't matter much to you and will cite the Roman proverb: *verba volant.*" Proust is referring to the Latin saying "Speech flies away, while written words remain." He continues: "But I think that Hervieu's opposite view is truer, that words last longer.

Besides, between the two of us it was never just a matter of words." (Paul Hervieu was the author of a comedy titled *Spoken Words Remain* [*Les paroles restent*]; COR XX, 19, 19 [note 5]).

By the month of March, Hauser had again taken on his old role as Proust's financial advisor. He found mention of a block of bonds in an old statement from Proust's Warburg portfolio. It was a block of Japanese Treasury notes, whose coupons from the previous February and August had not been cashed yet. These notes could be traded on the London Stock Exchange, where the currency exchange was favorable to the French franc. Hauser inquired whether Proust would be interested in selling them (COR XX, 58).

This letter was immensely pleasing to Proust, who answered it the same day. Hauser had written that he hoped his friend's state of health was infinitely better than the general political situation. Proust misunderstood the sense of this sentence and made an ironic comment. After spending weeks on the brink of death, he found Hauser's expression humorous, and quoted it in an unfaithful version: "in the hope that your health is always excellent." In contrast to Hauser's words, the writer alluded to a verse by Alphonse de Lamartine about the "boredom" which we feel when we are expected to die more than once—a regret no less bothersome to others than to ourselves.[1] But then he apologized for these gloomy thoughts, and in doing so pushed the irony level up a notch. "Since chance has it that your letter is reaching me at a moment when my brain is lucid and my hand can hold the pen. . . . I make haste to answer you in a cheerful spirit" (COR XX, 61).

It is evident that two of Proust's old wounds were not wholly healed: the first caused by Hauser's accusation that he, the author of *In Search of Lost Time,* was inclined to squander too much of his time; and the second caused by Hauser's reproach that the writer counted too much on words and not enough on acts. If he "[made] haste" to write to Hauser, Proust said, it was because he feared that, were he to postpone his letter, his friend would accuse him of "not moving into action fast enough." As Proust's letter went on, it read more and more like a one-on-one search for Lost Time—and, more particularly, like a recrimination about past errors and their inherent regrets. Even Hauser's query as to Proust's intentions with respect to the Japanese Treasury notes (whose acquisition, incidentally, was one of the first investments that Hauser had suggested to Proust, in 1912) triggered an important memory in Proust. The Japanese Treasury notes were not in his portfolio anymore, he explained; they had been sold to take care of his household expenses, and the agent handling them was the very Henri Gans who, in 1919, had been on the verge of usurping Hauser's role in the management of Proust's fortune. He reckoned that Hauser could fully understand by now the reason why, at the time, Proust had taken care not to involve him in any of his own dealings with the German bank, Warburg & Co., for fear of causing Hauser further political complications. "You see, having been involved more than anybody else ... with the imbecilic problems that they were trying to pin on you, I would have scrupulously refrained from running even one millionth part of the risk of thoughtlessly launching them again, even if only to a tiny extent." I do not think that Proust ever wrote a sentence as overflowing with pointless qualifiers as this one; if bad style is symptomatic of a bad conscience, this is a case in point. In any case, without missing a beat, and "in a cheerful spirit," Proust moved on to talk of the London Bank. As we know, sometime previously he had drafted a letter destined to the London Bank, instructing them to sell his bonds from the French National Loan (a decision in which Hauser may have suspected Gans having a hand). In sum, Proust would have liked to put the whole matter of the London Bank in Hauser's hands. Would it perhaps be convenient to pay off his debt with this institution and close the account? Whatever Hauser decided, "it [was] all the same" to Proust. In a postscript, the writer had words of praise for Philippe Hauser, Lionel's father, who years before, without any consultation, "almost like a medium," had diagnosed Proust's health problems better than many of the doctors who had meanwhile visited him (Ibid.).

Hauser did not keep Proust waiting for an answer. By this time, between the lines of their respective letters, these two old friends managed to read meanings that would elude anybody else. Reassured by their new regime of mutual benevolence, neither friend seemed able to resist the temptation of engaging in a supposedly detached review of their tenacious and obtuse recriminations.

My dear Marcel,

If I ever found myself doubting, even for an instant, of the existence of an immanent justice on earth, your letter would suffice to prove its existence to me. You start out by accusing me of having traded my heart for a stone as black as Indian ink and then conclude with the acknowledgment, which you don't seem to doubt in the least, that I've probably been a much better

> friend for you, I surmise, than those whom you'll keep sheltering in your heart till the day you have to drive them out because of the disillusionment [they caused you]. (COR XX, 65)

He goes on: "You declare . . . that I wrote: 'In the hope that your health is always excellent,' while I wrote, 'In the hope that your state of health is infinitely better than the general political situation.' Now, one must be entirely disinterested in general politics to misinterpret my wishes as you did. . . . Your health may be infinitely better than Europe's, even if it remains extremely precarious" (Ibid.). Yet, Hauser knew all too well by this time that no rhetorical stratagem of his would return his friend to good health. He knew equally well that if Proust's good health was the terrible price (or the "monstrous condition," as Proust himself would define it in a 1922 letter to Gallimard) that enabled him to complete *In Search of Lost Time* (COR XXI, 258), then his friend's health had been lost long, long ago. Lost, perhaps, but not squandered: although this is a distinction that Hauser might have been unable, or unwilling by all means, to grasp.

Maybe this is the reason why Hauser gave in, stopped recriminating, and tried to give some gentle advice to his friend. He started with some easy moralizing. Although Proust was approaching his fiftieth birthday, he was still the spoilt child whom Hauser had met almost forty years earlier. He had never stooped to adapting himself to his fellow human beings, expecting everybody else to adapt to him instead. Because of this, he had grown up feeling misunderstood by his own world. Then his literary talent and personal charm had provided him with a convenient subterfuge for affirming himself in a circle composed of the elite of the literary world, "not to mention the high society where [he had] become an idol." In sum, Proust had lived under the illusion that he could evade the world of down-to-earth people by creating a world in his own image. It was his parents' loss, Hauser argued (with a distinct disregard for the chronology of facts), that had brought Proust back to earth. "When I met you again after long years of separation, you were already suffering from the terrible choking crises that kept getting worse and worse as years went by" (COR XX, 65). Proust interpreted those symptoms as asthma, yet asthma was not an illness in Hauser's view, but rather the result of some organ functioning badly. (Personally, I confess I do not fully grasp this distinction between illness and organic malfunction, which must originate from some of the banker's theosophical persuasions.) Hauser had tried hard to help Proust find a practical remedy for his bad health, persuaded as he was that almost any illness, when caught at an early stage, could be cured, as long as one detected its true origin. He had no doubt that the treatments adopted by Proust were "contrary to nature's laws and to simple common sense." Two elements that were indispensable to good health were the sun and clean air. Yet Proust had always fled from the sun, and instead of breathing oxygen, he persisted in breathing the air from airtight rooms, made foul moreover by the fumes of the various medicinal plants he inhaled to subdue his choking. It was a way to avoid pain by making his condition worse. "This is why I had consulted my father about you, and I am far from surprised in learning from your letter that his diagnosis was correct." Before switching to Proust's financial affairs, Hauser closed this generous but fatally ineffective tirade with one last reproach, at once amiable and disconsolate: "You are cruelly unfair when you suggest that I resent you for not dying fast enough. What I resent bitterly is the obstinacy by which you commit suicide" (Ibid.).

As far as the London Bank was concerned, it was currently managed by rather mixed personnel, partly foreign, harboring in some cases Bolshevik sympathies. "It would be a mistake to let feelings prevail over decisions," as the executives who had rendered good services to Proust in the past were not with this firm anymore. Shortly after this letter, Hauser extinguished Proust's debt with the London Bank and, as I said before, moved the rest of his portfolio to a new account at Cox & Co.

About this time, Proust wrote to his editor Jacques Rivière that he had just finished a new essay, written in the same epistolary form that he had used for his article on Flaubert, and equally addressed to Rivière. It turned out to be his well-known article in defense of Baudelaire, which contains this memorable and significative passage: "In a thirty-year interval, someone like Baudelaire or, even better, like Dostoyevsky, creates, between an epileptic crisis and the next, a work of which the language of a thousand artists in good health could not match a single paragraph."[2] This standpoint is remindful of the concise decadent manifesto, as I called it, which Proust wrote in response to Hauser's *Three Levers of the New World,* in which he declared physical illness a condition of intellectual originality.

Proust had wished to forewarn Rivière about the completion of this essay on Baudelaire because it was an "enormous" text that would take up many pages in the next issue of the NRF. Long gone were the days when Proust had to submit his writings in the vain hope that some journal or newspaper would accept them. This letter to Rivière is not written in Proust's hand; we do not know who was holding the pen. Proust apologized for not penning it himself, but he was suffering from choking crises that "last[ed] all night and all day long and [left him] dazed with tiredness" (COR XX, 100).

On May 10, Proust asked Gaston Gallimard why he failed to show up at the Ritz, especially when he knew that the writer would make a special effort to get up and meet him there, after spending thirty-five days in bed. Proust's health was getting increasingly worse and he wanted to put all his manuscripts in the hands of the publisher (COR XX, 137). But Gallimard was evasive, slow in answering Proust's letters, late in paying his royalties, and at times so rude as to avoid him on purpose.[3] Proust resorted to the third-person singular for his accusations: "When he is at the editorial offices, he instructs his secretary to tell me he is not there," which reminded Proust of the gray days when he had submitted the first volume of *In Search of Lost Time* to the NRF and kept calling on them "with fruitless naïveté three times a day." Those days were far gone, as I said, and Proust's publisher was being given due warning. So much the worse for Gallimard, if instead of finding the time to give advice to his author, "he slip[ped] between his fingers like an eel," and their meetings, when they managed to see each other, were unpromising and unproductive. Astoundingly, Proust published an extract from the second volume of *Sodom and Gomorrah,* entitled *Jealousy,* with another publishing house named Fayard. This book was presented as a self-contained novel in the series *Oeuvres libres,* and Proust received a first installment of 10,000 francs for it.[4] He then challenged Gallimard: "You think that an extract published in the *Oeuvres libres* will negatively affect the imminent appearance of my next book.[5] But since the title is different, it's possible that things will go the opposite way with the general public. As to the public of the NRF, which is my public, they will easily understand that it's the continuation of my last book." In any case, wrote the author, Gallimard had no need to worry: he had told Monsieur Duvernois, who represented Fayard, that they would never get another line from him. "My decision . . . is final. I won't publish anything more in the *Oeuvres Libres* (and I would've never done it in the first place if you had just asked me the night you came to see me)" (COR XX, 273).

Less than one year later, Proust broke his word and started new negotiations with Duvernois, after Gallimard broke his own word several times regarding publication dates, royalty payments, and marketing. Toward the end of October 1922, one month before his death, Proust signed a contract for the publication of an extract from *The Prisoner* in Fayard's *Oeuvres libres,* under the title *Useless Precaution* (*Précaution inutile*), which he called an "idiotic" title. This book would see the light in February 1923 as number 20 of *Oeuvres libres* (COR XXI, 373, 373 [note 7]).

At the end of the year, Proust's good friend Robert de Montesquiou died. His well-founded suspicion of being the model for the Baron de Charlus had brought this gentleman to quarrel with the writer at first, but later on he had granted Proust a broad-minded reconciliation. In April, Proust had attempted to dispel the conspiracy of silence around his friend's writings by warmly requesting Jacques Boulenger—editor of the journal *L'Opinion* and admirer of the writer—to take Montesquiou on as a collaborator. "I think that the best art critic of our time is Robert de Montesquiou and . . . nobody asks him for a single article" (COR XX, 97). After Montesquiou's death, Proust wrote a memorable eulogy in a letter to the Duchess de Guiche, who was very close to the baron. "The small success of my books and the frightening neglect of his [are] one of the great injustices in these times of ours. . . . But injustices have a short life. At least in spirit and in truth, [Montesquiou] will have a second life" (COR XX, 342). The first time I read this letter in its original French I sensed a strident note in that "at least," as though Proust's words of condolence were not all that one was meant to read in them, or the addressee was not just the declared one. Only much later did I learn from Céleste Albaret's memoir that Proust thought Montesquiou "perfectly capable of pretending he [was] dead . . . to see whether he [was] famous and people still remember[ed] him."[6] So, just in case, Proust wrote his condolences in a spirit of precaution.

It is astonishing that Proust was able to find the energy to promote his friend's work, write articles destined to exercise a durable influence on literary criticism, and publish his novel in alternative versions and editions while his health was going irreversibly downhill and his strength was vanishing day by day. "What a strange idea you have of my life," he had written in April to Montesquiou, who had alluded in his letter to the writer's intense socializing at the Ritz and to his fabulous royalties. "I earn close to nothing from my books. And even if I did, would it make any difference? What pleasure can someone like me feel, when I can't even pronounce words correctly anymore." He had recently ventured to walk into a restaurant, but had to repeat his order ten times before they could understand what he wanted to eat (COR XX, 98).

A few days earlier he had complained about the decline in his state of health with Madame Bugnet, the wife of a promising poet. He had been taken with a rheumatic fever that deprived him of the use of his limbs. "Thanks to aspirin, sparteine, morphine, and a hundred other drugs," he was managing right that moment to change his position in bed, so he was taking advantage of it by writing to her. His recommendation was that if her husband truly wanted to excel in poetry, she should dissuade him from undertaking a literary career. As strange as this advice was, it recalls the opinion of Franz Kafka, who also loathed the idea of turning literature into a profession. Charles Bugnet, the addressee's husband, "writes things that are too splendid to deserve the trivialization of professional exploitation. The narrower the cage of his different job, the more abundantly will poetry drip out of him, and he will have the added certainty that the drops he collects are absolutely precious" (COR XX, 82). In his answer to a letter from Charles Bugnet himself, Proust alluded to the same verse by Lamartine which, as noted earlier, is found in a recent letter of his to Hauser, regretting that he had to apologize for the delay in his reply with the usual excuse of his illnesses. "It's not the first time that life leaves me for a while and then comes back. Lamartine is right when he talks of the pain we get from *having to die more than once down here*" (COR XX, 73, emphasis in original).

Proust's correspondence with the seventy-two-years old Geneviève Straus, who, as we know, is immortalized in the witticisms of Oriane de Guermantes, seemed devitalized by the nervous exhaustion which distressed her as much as her famous friend. Madame Straus, whose initial neurasthenia dated back almost two decades, gave Proust dubious medical advice. She had fought her addiction to Veronal, a barbiturate, "by swallowing large doses of various other poisons"; then she had tried not to take anything anymore and found herself on the verge of suicide; she had finally substituted Veronal with Dial Ciba, a barbiturate derivative. "And I don't change anymore!" Alas, she took too much of it! If Proust felt intoxicated with Veronal, he should switch to Dial Ciba and give it a boost with a Didial sleeping pill, "but not every day" (COR XX, 87). It is quite a squalid world, don't you think?—the one which the old Geneviève Straus shared with Proust at this time. Where have the verve and fluency of her literary alter ego gone?

Fernand Gregh, who had fraternized with Proust in 1892 and 1893, when they both contributed to a short-lived journal, *Le Banquet,* has preserved for us some of Madame Straus's most famous witticisms, her *célèbres mots* as he calls them.[7] It seems to me that she had a special flair for compound witticisms. Here are two examples. In her early thirties, during a performance of the *Hérodiade* by Jules Massenet, the composer Charles Gounod told her that he found that music "quite octogonal" ("bien octogone"), a witticism in its own right, to which she whispered back, "You stole the words from my mouth" ("J'allais vous le dire").[8] And in 1908, on the occasion of a celebrated woman writer, Marcelle Tinayre's refusal to accept the coveted medal of the Légion d'honneur, on the witty pretext that she would be expected to put the medal's ribbon, red like a wine stain, on display on her chest, Madame Straus remarked, with an obvious allusion to the radically low-cut necklines of evening dresses at the time: "Women's breast is not made for honors" ("La poitrine des femmes n'est pas faite pour l'honneur").[9] Are depression and drug addiction in old age the price one has to pay in order to enjoy such memorable sort of esprit?

I wrote in the early part of this book that Proust's novel is mercilessly driven toward the physical, social, and, in some cases, mental decay of its characters. I neglected to warn you that the literary comfort brought us by this lesson from the lives of imaginary others would not be enjoyed by Proust's real-life models, several of whom fell victims, as exemplified by Madame Straus's final days, to a sort of demobilization of the soul. (Geneviève Straus died on December 22, 1926, having somehow survived for four years the double blow, in November 1922, of the almost simultaneous loss of her suicide son Jacques and her friend Marcel.) Alfred Agostinelli is the shiny exception to the rule, but he died young, loved by the gods. As to Lionel Hauser, he was immune from that rule because he was, as you know, the lonely exception to that other complementary rule, which tasks Proust with cannibalizing the unsavory core of his friends' and acquaintances' inner lives.

In the dog days of summer, tragically ill, Proust managed an almost ironic tone in a letter to Jacques Boulenger. "I hope you are not too badly affected by the heat, since they tell me it is quite hot out there and normal people suffer from it. As I write you from my bed under seven woolen blankets, one fur, three hot-water bottles, and the fire [burning in the fireplace], I complain of the excessive heat only on your behalf" (COR XX, 236). (Incidentally, there was no fire burning in the fireplace, since, as Céleste Albaret explains, the fireplace of the apartment of Rue Hamelin was defective and was therefore never used, not even on the coldest winter days.[10] In spite of his regrettable health conditions, Proust would not give up his penchant for fictional autobiography.)

This book has kept silent thus far about an important, if indirect, player in the epistolary idyll between Proust and Hauser, and this player takes center stage, however briefly, in these dog days of the summer of 1921. I am referring to Hauser's wife, Jeanne, kept backstage in our story by the absence of any significant mention of her name and even, with few exceptions, of her existence in the fifteen-year-long dialogue between our two protagonists. On August 6, an international conference convened by a group of British theosophists and meeting in Calais, France, founded the New Education Fellowship (Ligue international pour l'Education nouvelle or LIEN, as was called in France), a movement aimed at propagating pedagogical principles centered on the vital spiritual force innate in every child—a militant platform for the diffusion of the science of education in European countries. Jeanne Hauser adhered to the movement and by 1925 was nominated French representative and treasurer. Although she was not a professional educator like most of the leaders and militants in the new movement, she was destined to play a significant role as organizer and administrator. Adolphe Ferrière, one of LIEN's executives, defined her as "a mother extremely dedicated to the work of the *Ligue,"* and someone ready to sacrifice the advantages of her own theosophical group to the interests of humankind.[11] The same year, her husband Lionel Hauser was nominated adjoint-treasurer of the Compagnons de l'Université Nouvelle, the university branch of the New Education Fellowship in France. The joint activism of the couple lasted several years.[12] The initiatives of LIEN declined in the late 1930s, owing to the tragic political situation in Europe.[13]

This is mere guesswork on my part, but judging from what we have learned thus far about Lionel Hauser's temperament and lifestyle, I reckon that this couple held the same open account in both of their hearts, to use one of his favorite expressions, and not only did they keep a steadily positive balance in it, but also get paid the warm returns of domestic bliss. Meanwhile, not for much longer, Proust's heart was kept under ice.

Chapter 27

ARS LONGA, VITA BREVIS

It took Proust almost one month to reply to Hauser's last letter. His answer reads as if it were written by someone who was not so much indifferent to Hauser's rebuke for his suicidal obstinacy as unaware or oblivious of it. It gives us a sense of the writer's resigned or powerless attitude to what laid before him. Proust explained that he had left his bed only once since Hauser wrote to him; he did it with the intention of dining with Hauser himself, but it turned out that the banker had left Paris for the Easter holidays. The strain of getting up had compounded Proust's usual fever with a rheumatic one. "My excellent doctor treats my body with morphine, aspirin, adrenaline, euvalpine, sparteine, in a word, all the drugs you can—or can't, I hope—imagine. Thus far the result is slight, save for the great brutalization that justifies the sordid banality of this letter" (COR XX, 80).

In July, Hauser received the autographed copy of the second volume of *The Guermantes Way,* and his letter to Proust described his family members' "demonstrations of mirth" after the delivery of the book. He found it hard to believe that Proust's bad health could go on in this fashion. The banker tried to forgo the preachy tones of his past letters and adopted instead the courteous (or rather, acquiescent?) tone of a kind friend. "I still hope that the day will come, when you least expect it, that will return you to the good health which has deserted you for a while" (COR XX, 231). Ten months later, having received the second volume of *Sodom and Gomorrah,* Hauser wrote that not only was he impressed by Proust's spiritual fecundity, he was also "happy to think that [Proust was] able to compose a 700-page volume, which [was], moreover, just a fraction of the whole novel"—from which he inferred that "[his] state of health must be at least satisfactory" (COR XXI, 130). It was mere wishful thinking. Only a fellow artist could grasp the perverse logic of the lethal syndrome that fueled Proust's titanically creative energy.

Proust had been complaining of speech disorders for some time. Not only was he forced to communicate in writing with Céleste Albaret because of his coughing fits; even when he got a respite from coughing, it also turned out that he could not pronounce words distinctly anymore. A neurologist, Dr. Babinski, tested him with some tongue twisters, which the writer was unable to articulate; it did not occur to Babinski, it seems, to prescribe lower or less frequent doses of the Legras powder, the fuel of Proust's daily "fumigations," as extracts from the Datura's leaves are known to cause speech impairment. Hauser's words of comfort, to the effect that his personal secretary, tested by him, could not pronounce the same tongue twisters either, were no consolation to Proust. "If only I were able to finish all my books," Proust burst out in his self-commiserating reply. He then cited, in Latin, Hippocrates' first aphorism: "Ars longa, vita brevis" ("A long art, a short life"; COR XX, 252).

The fourth-century-B.C.E Greek physician did not intend his aphorism exactly the way Proust applied it to his own short life, although both men had in mind the time-taking practice of their respective vocations. To Hippocrates, this aphorism meant that the long-lasting benefits obtained by a skillful physician were the results from hard-earned expertise, timely seized opportunities, and shrewd decision making; in other words, enduring results would take up most of a physician's time. To Proust, it meant instead that the composition of his time-transcending artwork had imposed on him a self-destructive lifestyle: the "monstrous condition" that would cut short his life span (COR XXI, 258).

Hippocrates' aphorism could be adopted as a maxim for the closure of the last volume of *In Search of Lost Time*. In his much-celebrated article on Flaubert, Proust had complained that this proverbial master of literary style lacked the fundamental requisite, a gift for metaphors.[1] He was talking, as always, in a semiautobiographical key, hinting at his most important stylistic skill, a talent, that is, for coming out with the right metaphor at the right time.

In Search of Lost Time ends with an unforgettable metaphor of life's duration:

> [It is] as if all men are perched on top of living stilts which never stop growing, sometimes becoming taller than church

> steeples, until eventually they make walking difficult and dangerous, and down from which, all of a sudden, they fall. . . . I began to be afraid that the stilts on which I myself was standing had already reached that height, and it did not seem to me that I would for very long have the strength to keep this past attached to me which already stretched so far down. Therefore, if enough time was left to me to complete my work, my first concern would be to describe the people in it, even at the risk of making them seem colossal and monstrous ["monstrueux"] creatures, as occupying a place far larger than the very limited one reserved for them in space, a place in fact almost infinitely extended, since they are in simultaneous contact, like giants immersed in the years, with such distant periods of their lives, between which so many days have taken up their place—in Time. (*Finding Time Again,* 357–58)[2]

In his fine translation of this passage from *Finding Time Again,* Ian Patterson renders "monstrueux" with "unnatural," but I see no reason for muffling down Proust's intended meaning, also in consideration of Proust's epistolary usage of the same term, noted above, to define his way of life. I have restored the original term, *monstrous.*

Who knows whether Hauser ever read *In Search of Lost Time* to the end, including the three volumes (*The Prisoner, The Fugitive,* and *Finding Time Again*) that were published posthumously by Proust's brother Robert, in collaboration with Gallimard, respectively in 1923, 1925, and 1927? I want to believe he did. And who knows if Hauser, who at one moment thought he would please Proust by telling him that he would be reading his book in the village of Chelles, "right near Guermantes," ever did manage to grasp—and accept—the virtues of Proust's moral sextant (COR XIX, 364). Never in his life had Proust set foot "right near Guermantes," or in the "other splendid little spots" where many of his childhood memories survived—or so believed Hauser and the other literalist readers of *In Search of Lost Time* (COR XIX, 364 [note 3]; COR XXI, 130, 130 [note 4]). Proust's allegedly autobiographical details in his novel are a fabrication from start to finish, meant to tell a more cogent truth than the one found in verifiable facts and historical evidence. They do not correspond to "the plane of [their author's] individual life," but rather to "the mode of existence that represents his true life" (*Young Girls in Flower,* 133).[3] Proust had no more use for the banker's literalistic common sense than for his horror of the products of squandered time. All the writer cared for was the invention of metaphors exquisitely balanced between experience and remembrance, between the present and the past, between permanence and impermanence—metaphors meant to assuage his readers' fear of death by showing them that their temporal existence is not just temporary, and that their individuality transcends the boundary of time.

In the same letter, Proust pointed out that Walter Berry was the last friend with whom he had managed to meet; it must have been no later than five months previously. Did Hauser still see their common American friend from time to time? (COR XX, 252) "As to your friend Berry," Hauser answered Proust, "I haven't seen him in years, which is explained by the fact that I have nothing to tell him and I detest going see people for the mere pleasure of wasting their time" (COR XX, 268). Once again and one last time, the motif of time squandered makes its appearance.

The story of Proust and his banker ends here, as Hauser hammers down one more nail into the coffin of his fatal incomprehension. The time of Proust's life and writings has not yet run out, though. As a matter of fact, the 1922 volume of his correspondence is one of the largest in the collection edited by Philip Kolb. This is undoubtedly owing to the fact that either the lure of posterity or the spur of personal vanity prompts most people to preserve the letters from famous or important figures; and Proust was more famous and important than ever in 1922. However, I like to think that Proust's intense correspondence in the last year of his life is owing to the titanic, logically unexplainable energy—his "mystical vigor," as Julia Kristeva calls it[4]—which he invested in his writing endeavors every day of his adult life. In Paris, the year 1922 is the year of the acclaimed publication of James Joyce's *Ulysses* and the much talked about performance of Luigi Pirandello's *Six Characters in Search of an Author*—two literary stars over whom Proust shines a more extraordinary light. He was well known, celebrated, influential, and used to the homage of high-ranking people from all walks of life; there were too many subjects he felt driven to give his opinion on and pontificate about. His strength was at its limits, and yet he kept on writing as much as he did before, and even more, if that is humanly possible.

Too many things have been told by his biographers about his last year of life, and especially about his last days and last hours, as if in a feeble effort to provide a rational explanation, or in some cases a romantic justification, of the "monstrous condition" that Proust accepted as his way of life (COR XXI, 258)—the terrible price his visionary muse demanded of his body. It is a price he kept paying till the moment when, like one of his "monstrous creatures," he lacked the strength to keep himself joined with a past "which already stretched so far down" away from him (*Finding Time Again*, 357–58).[5]

We will not be pursuing Proust's last days along with these biographers. We will only waste another few minutes in the company of the metaphor of time squandered that runs throughout so much of Lionel Hauser's affectionate dialogue with Marcel Proust. This metaphor was born out of Hauser's generous yet uncomprehending efforts to appreciate his friend's lifestyle and artistic ambition. But the banker was commonsensical by vocation and, I dare say, literalistic by trade. He would have liked his metaphor of time squandered to have had the efficacy of a hail of blows; and indeed, whenever he used it, he was in a fist-fighting mood. For him, time came in scarce quantities, like currency, gold, mineral oil, all rare commodities, and therefore had to be frugally saved. The most astute among us could invest it profitably and maximize its profit yield. First and foremost, though, time was not to be squandered, which is what his spendthrift friend, Proust, kept doing over and over again.

Indeed, Proust did not spare either time or money in the creation of his novel. In return for this economy of waste, he earns the artistic gold which in youth he learned about from John Ruskin. Ruskin's artistic gold is a metaphor of worth, but of a rather special kind to Proust, insofar as it allows him to solve the enigma of the role played out by love, desire, sex, gratitude, friendship, and grief in his life.

When it comes to the superior worth of art compared to ordinary wealth, by the end of his life Proust is obviously indebted to Ruskin. A well-wrought artwork becomes synonymous, to him, with survival in the hereafter of collective memory; its value must therefore be primarily measured in the metrics of generosity, altruism, and abnegation, and only secondarily in the metrics of money hoarding. This is probably the reason why one of the most Ruskinian sentences of Proust's entire novel is devoted to Bergotte's natural death and artistic "resurrection": "They buried him, but all night before his funeral, in the lighted bookshop windows, his books, set out in threes, kept watch like angels with outspread wings and seemed, for him who was no more, the symbol of his resurrection" (*Fugitive*, 170).[6]

Maître René Barillot was the Parisian notary who handled all matters pertaining to Marcel Proust's inheritance. The writer's sole heir was his younger brother Robert, who from December 1922 through the summer of 1923 withdrew all of Marcel's financial assets from the vault of Messieurs de Rothschild frères in Paris (see illus. 7). In time, Robert Proust's own heir, Suzy Proust-Mante, together with her daughter Marie-Claude Mante-Mauriac and Marie-Claude's three children, must have earned a hundredfold times as much from their forebear's royalties.

RENÉ BARILLOT
Notaire
50, Rue La Boétie
TÉLÉPH. ELYSÉES 17-64

REÇU
-1 FEV. 23

Paris, le 31 Janvier 1923

Messieurs,

J'ai l'honneur de vous adresser sous ce pli un intitulé de l'inventaire dressé après le décès de Monsieur Marcel PROUST et une procuration qui m'a été donnée par Monsieur Robert PROUST, son héritier, à l'effet de toucher le montant du compte courant et d'effectuer le retrait des titres que vous avez en dépôt.

Je vous prie de transférer au nom de Monsieur Robert PROUST le montant du compte courant et d'effectuer le dépôt à son nom, des valeurs.

Je me tiens à votre disposition pour vous fournir toutes pièces et vous donner toutes signatures que vous jugerez utiles de me demander.

Agréez, Messieurs, mes salutations distinguées.

Messieurs de ROTHSCHILD, 21, rue Laffitte

Maître René Barillot's letter to the Rothschild brothers, January 31, 1923.
Archives Nationales du Monde du Travail, Fond Rothschild, cote 132 AQ T58
(with the permission of The Trustees of The Rothschild Archive Trust Limited).

However, one does not have to be a relative of Proust, or of Bergotte, for that matter, to belong to the writer's spiritual progeny. At their death, both the real writer and the fictional one from *In Search of Lost Time* leave behind a solid fortune. Their inheritance is obviously to be measured in the assets generated by their own creative capital—assets I have labeled creative equity. In Proust's case, this equity consists of a manuscript a few thousand pages long and of its long-term yield. Yet Proust's genuine inheritance is to be measured in terms of the wealth or artistic gold he shares with you and me, his readers. His true afterlife is more durable and more precious than ingots, but also less sparkling. It is no fancier, in point of fact, than the sort of afterlife which his Narrator wants to see secured for the brotherhood of writers who work with the generosity of a reader's best friend and the industriousness of a selfless bee.

As I see it, there is an afterlife secured permanently for Marcel Proust. The pages of his novel are feathers on angel wings. And the wisdom of their words is the gravestone whose inscription, handed down from one generation to the next, "marks [his] tomb, and protects it from rumors and, for a time, from oblivion" (*Finding Time Again,* 342).[7]

Proust's afterlife, it is us.

NOTES

INTRODUCTION

1. Duchêne, *L'impossible Marcel Proust,* 110, 115, 151. Alphonse Darlu was hired as Proust's private tutor in 1894 and 1895, to help the future writer prepare for the exam in philosophy that on March 27, 1985, earned him the *licence ès lettres et philosophie* from the Sorbonne. See Kristeva, *Le temps sensible,* 449. Proust mentioned Darlu in the dedication to *Les plaisirs et les jours,* entitled *"À mon ami Willie Heath":* "le grand philosophe dont la parole inspire, plus sûre de durer qu'un écrit, a, en moi comme en tant d'autres, engendré la pensée" (8). However, as Tadié points out, Proust changed his mind on Darlu's teachings when he discovered John Ruskin's aesthetic ideas, and especially Ruskin's "mistrust of theories" (353). This is probably why in his *Carnet 1 (1908)* Proust defined Darlu's influence on him as "bad" ("mauvaise"; 100). See also Large, "Proust on Nietzsche: The Question of Friendship," 618.

2. Parenthetical references are to Marcel Proust, *Correspondance* 1892–1922, ed. Philip Kolb, 21 vols. (Paris: Plon, 1970–1993). Hereafter abbreviated as COR.

3. All of the above is confirmed, at least from 1914 onward, by Céleste Albaret, who writes that when she became Proust's *femme de chambre,* the writer's outings were solely designed "to verify a fact or an idea or to see again one of the models for one of his characters," and Proust never got together with Hauser, only wrote to him. Albaret, *Monsieur Proust,* 67, 212.

4. Proust, *Contre Sainte-Beuve,* 224. This analogous concept of *moi profond,* contrasted with the *moi superficiel,* is found in Henri Bergson, *Essai sur les données immédiates de la conscience,* 93.

5. Balsamo, "The Fiction of Marcel Proust's Autobiography," 577–84.

6. Proust, À l'ombre des jeunes filles en fleurs I, 445. Parenthetical references are to James Grieve, trans., *In the Shadow of Young Girls in Flower* by Marcel Proust (New York: Penguin, 2005).

7. See Balsamo, "Proust and His Banker: Numerical Documentation," Item 1.

8. Proust, À l'ombre des jeunes filles en fleurs I, 446.

9. Proust's translations of Ruskin were published respectively in 1904 and 1906.

10. Ruskin's influence on the young Marcel Proust is evidenced not only in Proust's decision to be the first systematic translator of Ruskin's books in France, but also by the long list of essays (not to mention the book reviews) that he dedicated to the British art critic, especially in the first decade of 1900, the most notable being: "En mémoire des églises assassinées," "La mort des cathedrals," "Journées de lecture," "La bénédiction du sanglier" (this is an unpublished pastiche written à la manière de Ruskin), "Pèlerinages ruskinien en France," and "Un professeur de beauté."

11. Ruskin, *Sesame and Lilies,* 34–35.

12. Ruskin's notion of "artistical gold" refers to the class of the "art-intellect" as a whole, which ought to be nurtured by society through proper training and education. Ruskin, *The Political Economy of Art,* 37–38, 153.

13. See Shell, *The Economy of Literature,* 131–32.

14. Proust, *Le Carnet de 1908,* 69. Joshua Landy has stressed the autobiographical tenor of this phrase from the *carnet* in *Philosophy as Fiction,* 22.

15. *Le Figaro,* July 26, 1914; COR XIII, 156, 156 [note 15].

16. Adjusting patrimony for inflation does not tell the whole story, of course. I discuss this later in the book, in a passage which I insert here too for the reader's ease. From 1905 to 1921, the French index of consumer prices underwent a cumulative increment of 153.03 percent, which undercut remarkably the real value of revenue and personal assets. However, more than 94 percent of this increment was owing to the war and postwar years, and it affected in the same devastating way most private fortunes, not just Proust's.

17. Kristeva, *Le temps sensible,* 232.

18. White, *Marcel Proust,* 51.

19. Robichez, *Précis de littérature française du xxe siècle,* 178.

20. Proust, *Le temps retrouvé,* 547.

21. Proust, À l'ombre des jeunes filles en fleurs I, 606.

22. Proust, *Le temps retrouvé,* 528. Parenthetical references are to Ian Patterson, *Finding Time Again* by Marcel Proust (New York: Penguin, 2003).

23. Proust, *Sodome et Gomorrhe* II.i, 147. Parenthetical references are to John Sturrock, trans. *Sodom and Gomorrah* by Marcel Proust (New York: Penguin, 2005).

24. Ricoeur, "Time Traversed," 363.

CHAPTER 1: THE SENTIMENTAL FINANCIER

1. It will not do any harm to repeat here that in this book all dollar amounts are based on this currency's 2008 purchasing power.

2. Duchêne, *L'impossible Marcel Proust,* 465.

3. Kolb, "*Marcel Proust speculateur,*" 179.

4. Duchêne, *L'impossible Marcel Proust,* 8.

5. See Duchêne, "Un inédit proustien: le testament de 'L'Oncle Adolphe,'" 673–77.

6. COR VIII, 115 [note 17]; Duchêne, "Un inédit proustien: le testament de 'L'Oncle Adolphe,'" 680. Adèle Weil, the aunt of Proust's mother Jeanne, is not to be confused with Jeanne's mother Adèle, née Berncastle.

7. Revah, *Un maranne d'aujourd'hui,* 14–15.

8. Tadié, *Marcel Proust,* 518.

9. Gamble, *Proust as Interpreter of Ruskin,* 144–53. For the text of Henri Bergson's formidable presentation of Proust's translation *La Bible d'Amiens* to L'Académie des Sciences Morales et Politiques, see COR IV, 73 [note 2].

CHAPTER 2: OLD MISTRESSES FROM THE STOCK EXCHANGE

1. See Proust's letter to Raphaël-Georges Lévy, in which the writer declares that he inherited these stocks from his "parents." A comparative analysis of the portfolios left behind by Adrien and Jeanne Proust, as preserved in the dossier of Marcel Proust's inheritance at the Rothschild Foundation, indicates that in this diction, the French

parents must be taken to mean "relatives" (that is, Louis Weil) rather than "mother and father." Pyra Wise, who included this letter in "Trois lettres et une dédicace inédites de Marcel Proust conservées à la Pierpont Morgan Library," dates it tentatively from the beginning of 1908; http://www.item.ens.fr/index.php?id=76053, note 36; accessed February 27, 2015.

2. Proust, *Pastiches et mélanges,* 7 [note *]; 682; 694 [notes 1 and 3].

3. See Vidal, *The History and Methods of the Paris Bourse,* 26.

4. Proust, *Le* côté de Guermantes II.ii, 807. Parenthetical references are to Mark Treharne, trans., *The Guermantes Way* by Marcel Proust (New York: Penguin, 2005).

5. Ibid., 852; COR VIII, xxiii; COR VIII, 162 [note 2].

6. Rey, "La guerre dans *Le temps retrouvé.*"

7. Proust, *À l'ombre des jeunes filles en fleurs,* 23 [note 1].

8. Prestwich, *The Translation of Memories,* 8–9, 40.

9. See COR XXI, 384, 385; Tadié, *Marcel Proust,* 777.

CHAPTER 3: A FRIEND'S HEART

1. Walter Benjamin, "The Image of Proust," 215.

2. Gregh, *L'age d'or,* 168–69.

3. Duchêne, *L'impossible Marcel Proust,* 119, 783 (note 4 from notes for pages 110–16).

4. Twenty-one years earlier, in the salon of Gaston de Caillavet's mother, Léontine, Proust had become acquainted with his literary idol, Anatole France. Léontine de Caillavet, née Lippman, was Anatole France's lover at this time. Duchêne remarks that she "came from the same Jewish bourgeoisie of Proust's mother Jeanne." See Duchêne, *L'impossible Marcel Proust,* 162–64.

5. Duplay, "Proust avant Proust," 4.

CHAPTER 4: ENTER ALBERT NAHMIAS

1. Proust, *Albertine disparue* I, 77; *Young Girls in Flower,* 40–41; *À l'ombre des jeunes filles en fleurs* I, 459–60. Parenthetical references are to Peter Collier, trans., *The Fugitive* by Marcel Proust, in *The Prisoner* and *The Fugitive* (New York: Penguin, 2003).

2. Proust, *Le Temps retrouvé,* 609.

3. Proust's Narrator finds an ideal love of sorts in the person of an underage girl, Mademoiselle de Saint-Loup, but this is another story. I tell it in Balsamo, "The Fiction of Marcel Proust's Autobiography," 573–606.

4. See Frank, *The Widening Gyre,* 23; Man, *Allegories of Reading,* 16; Martin-Chauffier, "Proust et le double 'je' de quatre personnes," 56; Rousset, *Forme et signification,* 144; Shattuck, *Marcel Proust,* 38; Terdiman, *The Dialectics of Isolation,* 173. In contradiction to my thesis, Joshua Landy argues that the literary work titled À la recherche du temps perdu should be understood at once as a novel by Proust, its author, and as a "memoir" by Marcel, its narrator—a memoir preparatory to the "autobiographical fiction" that Marcel "has in mind" but not written yet at the end of the novel (*Philosophy as Fiction,* 38–47; see also Landy, "Proust, His Narrator, and the Importance of the Distinction," 115, and "'*Les moi en moi,*'"120). Regarding my own thesis, see Balsamo, "The Fiction of Marcel Proust's Autobiography," 578.

5. See Quennouëlle-Corre, "The Paris Bourse and the International Capital Flows Before 1914," 5–17, where this whole set of operators and its historical evolution are described.

6. Pyra Wise, "Marcel Prouset et Albert Nahmias: quelques lettres inédites." *Bulletin d'information proustienne,* no. 37 (2007): 21–26.

CHAPTER 5: SUCKERS AND BELIEVERS

1. See COR XI, 5, 15.
2. COR XVI [note 3]; Carter, *Marcel Proust,* 111; Balsamo, "Proust and the Lessons of War," 204–6.
3. See also COR XI, XI [note 2]; 15, 15 [note 6]); COR XII, 54 [note 2].
4. Proust, *Du côté de chez Swann,* 285. Parenthetical references are to Lydia Davis, trans., *Swann's Way* by Marcel Proust (New York: Penguin, 2004).

CHAPTER 6: BLIND EYES

1. Duchêne, *L'impossible Marcel Proust,* 652–56.
2. COR XIII, 12 and 12 bis; Proust and Gallimard, *Correspondance,* iv.
3. Duchêne, *L'impossible Marcel Proust,* 653.
4. Duchêne, *L'impossible Marcel Proust,* 653, 820 note 3; Tadié, *Marcel Proust,* 576 note†; Albaret, *Monsieur Proust,* 284.
5. COR XIII, 12 and 12 bis.
6. White, *Marcel Proust,* 117.
7. White, *Marcel Proust,* 96–97, 117.
8. Carter, *Marcel Proust,* 553.
9. COR XII, 66 [note 3].
10. *Le Figaro,* May 1, 1913.

CHAPTER 7: ENTER ALFRED AGOSTINELLI

1. See Tadié, *Marcel Proust,* 556.
2. Proust, *Pastiches et mélanges,* 66–67; *Le Figaro,* November 19, 1907.
3. Proust, *Pastiches et mélanges,* 66–67.
4. Ibid., 66 [note *]; Tadié, *Marcel Proust,* 488–99.
5. See Tadié, *Marcel Proust,* 609–10.
6. The securities to be traded by Hauser were two Royal Dutch shares held in his Warburg portfolio. We learn from this letter that Proust involved Hauser in his speculations on Royal Dutch shares, although to a small extent. Having bought two of them with Hauser's help, he left the banker in the dark as to the block of shares he eventually stashed in his Rothschild portfolio.
7. Proust, *Pastiches et mélanges,* 66 [note *]; Tadié, *Marcel Proust,* 488–99, 556; Carter, *Marcel Proust,* 556.
8. Gide, *Journal,* vol. 2, 297 (July 22, 1931).
9. Gide, *Journal,* vol. 1, 1124–27 (May 14 and 15, 1921).
10. See Landy, *Philosophy as Fiction,* 20.
11. Rivers, *Proust and the Art of Love,* 243.
12. Ibid., chapter 5: "Monsters of Time."
13. COR XIII, 12 and 12 bis; Proust and Gallimard, *Correspondance,* iv.
14. Proust, *Du côté de chez Swann,* 51–52. Lydia Davis translates *vertèbres* with "bones."
15. Brooke, "Proust and Joyce," 17; Rivers, *Proust and the Art of Love,* 55.
16. COR IX, 115.

17. Painter, *Marcel Proust,* vol. 2, 208; Carter, *Marcel Proust,* 137, 295–96, 338, 362–63, 370–71, 676 ; Duchêne, *L'impossible Marcel Proust,* 213, 219 ; Tadié, *Marcel Proust,* 333, 849 note 299. I am leaving Marie Finaly out of Painter's list of relevant models for the character of Albertine (38–39). Duchêne argues that Proust's courtship of Marie Finaly, or Mary, as she was called by Fernand Gregh in *L'age d'or* (166), was a mere act of politeness to her family, whose guest he was in the summer of 1892 (*L'impossible Marcel Proust,* 221). Just as throughout this book I take caution never to overstate Proust's financial success, so I do not overstate Proust's attraction to women, even if in her *Monsieur Proust* Céleste Albaret identifies in Marie Finaly a relevant flame in the writer's youth (175–76).

18. Albaret, *Monsieur Proust,* 45.

19. Tadié, *Marcel Proust,* 349.

20. I discuss the signifiers of sexual parade, made the more pervasive by the unbreachable prohibition of consummation, in "Son, Knight, and Lover: Perceval's Dilemma at the Castle of Beaurepaire."

21. COR IX, 115.

22. Even if the original source for the legendary "girl of Cabourg," as Rivers calls her (*Proust and the Art of Love,* 49), is the slightest discredited biography of George D. Painter (*Marcel Proust,* 77), the accumulation of anecdotal evidence is overwhelmingly in favor of the veracity of this story. See COR IX, 60, 115; Proust, À un ami, 151, 168; Lauris, "Préface," 30; Bibesco, "The Heartlessness of Marcel Proust," 424; Rivers, *Proust and the Art of Love,* 49.

23. Albaret, *Monsieur Proust,* 25, 40–41.

24. Ibid., 48.

25. Ibid., 117.

26. Proust, *Du côté de chez Swann,* 13; *La prisonnière,* 520.

27. Proust, *La prisonnière,* 686. Parenthetical references are to Carol Clark, trans., *The Prisoner* by Marcel Proust, in *The Prisoner* and *The Fugitive* (New York: Penguin, 2003). In her translation of *The Prisoner,* Clark renders the passage pertinent to the phrase *quelque chose de pénible* as: "In the case of Albertine, living permanently with her was *a source of pain in another way* which I cannot describe in this story" (163, my emphasis).

28. Proust, *La prisonnière,* 677.

CHAPTER 8: A WING'S WILD BLOW

1. Ellmann, *Oscar Wilde,* 510–16; COR XIII, 156.

2. Tadié, *Marcel Proust,* 589–90; Duchêne, *L'impossible Marcel Proust,* 684; COR XIII, 124 [note 8].

3. In Antibes, Agostinelli had enrolled in the flying school of Joseph Garbero. See COR XV, 1 [notes 7 and 8].

4. Mallarmé, *Collected Poems and Other Verse,* 67.

5. Duchêne, *L'impossible Marcel Proust,* 684.

CHAPTER 9: ENTER ALBERTINE SIMONET

1. See Rivers, *Proust and the Art of Love,* 245–46; Gaubert, "Proust et le jeu de l'alphabet," cited in Rivers, 245–46.

2. Proust, *Albertine disparue* I, 50–51; COR XIII, 124.

3. Proust, *Albertine disparue* I, 37–39.
4. Albaret, Monsieur Proust, 191.
5. Proust, Albertine disparue I, 60.
6. To my knowledge, Edmund White is the only biographer claiming that Proust "was able to cancel [the order for the airplane] after the chauffeur's sudden death." White, *Marcel Proust,* 93.
7. See Duchêne, *L'impossible Marcel Proust,* 632.
8. Proust, À l'ombre des jeunes filles en fleurs II, 230.
9. See Tadié, *Marcel Proust,* 680.
10. Ibid., 561, footnote†.

CHAPTER 10: WARTIME FINANCE

1. *Le Figaro,* July 22, 1914. See COR XIII, 154 [note 6].
2. *Le Figaro,* July 26, 1914. See COR XIII, 156, 156 [note 15].
3. In spite of the intervention on Proust's behalf of the eminent economist Raphaël-Georges Lévy and of the legal attorney recommended by Lévy himself, Gustave Brunet, the Comptoir d'Escompte refused to honor the check, claiming that, by issuing it, the Warburg Bank had become indebted with them of 30,000 francs, and if now the Comptoir paid this sum to Proust, the Warburg Bank's debt would rise to 60,000 francs. See also Hauser's ingenious defense of the Warburg Bank in COR XIX, 95.
4. The London Stock Exchange only reopened on November 18. See *Le Figaro,* November 15, November 17, November 18, and November 21, 1914. See COR XIII, 168 [note 4].
5. COR XIV, 102, 102 [note 11].

CHAPTER 11: THE COBBLER AND THE BANKER

1. Tadié, *Marcel Proust,* 549–50.
2. Proust, *Albertine disparue* I, 105–6.
3. Bibesco, "The Heartlessness of Marcel Proust," 423.
4. Proust, *Albertine disparue* I, 111.
5. Ibid., 77.
6. Lévy's sister was the wife of a cousin of Proust's mother. See COR VIII, 109 [note 11].

CHAPTER 12: A RUINED MAN

1. Chevalier, "Notice" (sur *Albertine disparue*), 1007–8, 1023, 1030.
2. Proust, *Albertine disparue* III, 218–19.
3. See Item 6 (Quantitative Methodology) in Balsamo, "Proust and His Banker: Numerical Documentation."
4. Albaret, *Monsieur Proust,* 216.
5. La Fontaine, Livre VII, 12. See COR XIV, 145 [note 3].
6. See à propos Balsamo, "Proust and the Lessons of War," 207–17.
7. Proust is referring to the third part of his novel's last book, *Finding Time Again,* where he gives a graphic description of the baron's masochism.
8. Proust, *Carnet 4,* 397 and 396 note19, in Proust, *Carnets,* 333–416; see Gregh, *L'age d'or,* 160.
9. Albaret, *Monsieur Proust,* 244–45; Bergstein, *In Looking Back One Learns to See,* 2.

CHAPTER 13: OPIUM AND DYNAMITE

1. Proust, *Les plaisirs et le jours*, "Fragments de comédie italienne," VII: "Snobs," 43–45, which consists of an article published at the age of twenty by Proust in the journal *Le Banquet*, no. 3 (May 1892).

2. Albaret, *Monsieur Proust,* 211–12.

3. See Archives Nationales du Monde du Travail, Fond Rothschild, cote 132 AQ T58, Dossier "Dr. Adrien Proust, succession (1904)," and "Mme Proust, succession (1905–1906)."

4. Zanden, *Appendices. Figures and Explanations, Collective Bibliography, and Index*: Tables 2.4.1 and 2.4.2.

5. When Céleste Albaret accompanied Proust on his last vacation to Cabourg in 1914, he explained to her that there were more guests at the hotel than in previous years as many of them had given up their residences because of the war. Albaret, *Monsieur Proust,* 30.

CHAPTER 14: THE CRY OF THE VALKYRIES

1. Proust, "Dans les Mémoires de Saint-Simon," in *Pastiches et mélanges*, 44–46. The title of Princess Murat's family was imperial and of recent acquisition, just like that of her cousin Louis d'Albufera.

2. On Proust's affection and attraction for Paul Morand, see Citati, *La colomba pugnalata,* 226–28.

3. Tadié, *Marcel Proust,* 141, 164, 202, 411.

4. Duchêne, *L'impossible Marcel Proust,* 191.

5. This is probably an allusion to the forth stanza of Jean Cocteau's *La Visitation*, the first piece of the 1912 collection entitled *La Danse de Sophocle.* See COR XVI, 97 [note 11].

6. Proust is punning here on the French verb *prendre,* which is used to mean both "taking" a direction and "catching" a cold.

7. Proust is alluding here to a three-act comedy by Georges Feydeau and Maurice Desvallières. See COR XVI, 97 [note 14].

8. A previous version of this paragraph appeared in Balsamo, "Proust and the Lessons of War," 215.

9. Proust, *Le temps retrouvé,* 337–38.

10. Ibid., 342, 379, 413.

11. Montaigne, "De la solitude," 271.

12. Archives Nationales du Monde du Travail, Fond Rothschild, cote 132Q T58, Dossier "Dr Adrien Proust, succession (1905–1906)".

CHAPTER 15: THE MISTRUST OF FRIENDSHIP

1. Proust, *Le* côté de Guermantes II.ii, 688–89. As he denounces "the partiality of Proust's knowledge of Nietzsche," Large maintains that the latter would have been "quite prepared to admit, with Proust, that the friend 'superficializes.'" However, "Nietzsche . . . recognise[d] the value of the 'superficiality' of friendship in a more positive way than [did] Proust, with his rather begrudging admission that friends can simply help cheer up the despondent individual when his Muse deserts him. More importantly,

though, Nietzsche [was] just as adamant as Proust that the independence of the creative . . . individual must not be trammeled" (Large, "Proust on Nietzsche," 621–22).

2. Compagnon, "Introduction," *Carnet 3*, 247, in Proust, *Carnets*, 244–48.

3. Forcheville will marry Odette after Swann's death, giving a posthumous confirmation to Swann's suspicions.

CHAPTER 16: ENTER HENRI ROCHAT

1. Proust, *In the Shadow of Young Girls in Flowers II*, 83.

2. Proust, *Le* côté de Guermantes II.ii, 689.

CHAPTER 17: A FAIRY-TALE PRINCESS AND AN AMERICAN TENNIS PLAYER

1. Edel, "Walter Berry and the Novelists: Proust, James, and Edith Wharton," 514–15.

2. See COR XVII, 44, 47, 60, 96, 99, 101, 102, 169, 171, 196, 199, 207, 209, 210, 216, 218, 219, 220; XVIII, 4, 5, 6, 28, 29, 44, 45, 260.

3. Zanden, *Appendices. Figures and Explanations, Collective Bibliography, and Index*, Tables 2.4.1 and 2.4.2.

CHAPTER 18: IN SEARCH OF TIME SQUANDERED

1. Among contemporary psychologists there were also visionaries of the caliber of William James, who would have certainly agreed with the thrust of Proust's experiment with his cup of tea. Alluding probably to the novels of his brother Henry James, William James complained that in order to find interesting insights on the nature of emotions, and especially on the interconnection of bodily sensation and spiritual emotion, one had to read contemporary literature rather than "scientific psychology." See James, *The Principles of Psychology* (1890), vol. 2, chapter 25, particularly p. 448, for the reference to literature. It is equally important to stress that in 1927 Henri Bergson published *Essai sur les données immediate de la conscience*, in which he repeated Proust's experiment with the cup of tea, applying it to a rose's scent (121–22). As regards the recent and very rich scientific debate about Proust's cup of tea, Kirsten Shepherd-Barr and Gordon Shepherd have argued that the introspective self-analysis undertaken by Proust's Narrator while he sits in front of his famous cup of tea circumscribes a neurological field with "multiple pathways" that connect his "neural mechanism of smell perception" to "the highest cognitive perceptual regions of the forebrain as well as the most deeply embedded primal emotional areas of the brain." Simon Chu and John Joseph Downes, in turn, have referred to the same episode to argue that early-life memories are more effectively "cued" (that is, more easily triggered) "by odors rather than [word] labels." Shepherd-Barr and Shepherd, "Madeleines and Neuromodernism," 51; Chu and Downes, "Long Live Proust," B41–B50.

2. See Proust, *Du côté de chez Swann*, 45.

3. See Clarac, "Notice 2," 983.

4. Proust, *Le temps retrouvé*, 450.

5. Ibid., 450–51.

6. Ricoeur, *Time and Narrative*, 143.

7. Proust, *Le temps retrouvé*, 610. I have described Proust's *ars poetica* in Balsamo, "The Fiction of Marcel Proust's Autobiography," 601–2.

8. Roger Duchêne was of the opinion that Proust's theory of involuntary memory was not original since his friend Fernand Gregh, under the influence of Proust's same professors from the Sorbonne, had written of it as early as 1896 in a short piece, "Mystères," which appeared in the *Revue Blanche*—a piece, moreover, whose subject, namely, the intense déjà-vu experience provoked in a young man by the sound of church bells at Easter, was developed a few years later by Proust himself in an episode from his aborted novel *Jean Santeuil*. The only problem in this interpretation is that Gregh's short piece (by all means, not a "novella," as Duchêne defines it) is a concise sketch of the aesthetic agenda which Proust would soon transfer from *Jean Santeuil* to *In Search of Lost Time*. Gregh's first-person narrator reports verbatim the explanation about a déjà-vu experience given him by a friend who just went through it, who has been familiar with that kind of experience for years, and who expresses the rhetorical wish that somebody would write one day a whole book on the way one's earliest memories are affected by sudden episodes of unexpected recollection. Either Proust ran off with Gregh's idea and spent the rest of his life chiseling it—and enriched it, in the process, with a poetic and an erotic agenda—or Gregh's piece, more likely, recorded a real-life conversation between the two friends. Duchêne, *L'impossible Marcel Proust*, 360–61; Gregh, "Mystères," 259–70.

9. Updike, "More Love in the Western World," 231–32.

CHAPTER 19: THE THREE LEVERS OF THE NEW WORLD

1. Proust, *Sodome et Gomorrhe* II, 423. The 2005 edition of John Sturrock's translation of this passage from *Sodom and Gomorrah* is misleading: "It is legitimate, admittedly, for the man who drafts reports, lines up figures, answers business letters, or follows prices on the Bourse to feel, *when you say to him sneeringly*, 'It's all right for you, who have nothing to do,' an agreeable sense of his own superiority" (*Sodom and Gomorrah*, 423; my emphasis). The correct translation of the phrase I emphasized reads, "when he says to you sneeringly" ["quand il vous dit en ricanant"] (Proust, *Sodome et Gomorrhe* II.iii, 423). This passage comes from Proust's *Cahier 6* (Bibliothèque Nationale, Nouvelles Acquisitions Françaises, no. 16713); it was therefore completed before the end of World War I, and was not subsequently corrected or reformulated by Proust when he edited the pages of the typewritten version of *Sodome et Gomorrhe*, prepared by the Éditions de la N. R. F. in 1921. See Antoine Compagnon, "Notes sur le texte [de *Sodome et Gomorrhe* II]," 1291, 1291 no. 1.

2. Proust is alluding here to Virgil's *Aeneid*, Book X, line 284. See COR XVII, 46 [note 2]).

3. La Fontaine, Livre XI, 8. See COR XVII, 81 [note 3].

4. Hauser was alluding to the new piece of heavy artillery adopted by the German army. See COR XVII, 81 [note 4].

5. See Wise, "Une lettre inédite de René Dumesnil à Marcel Proust du 19 janvier 1920," 4; COR XII, 126 [note 8].

6. Proust, "À propos du 'style' de Flaubert," 586–87.

CHAPTER 20: TURNING CARESSES INTO GOLD

1. Rey, "Introduction [À l'*ombre des jeunes filles en fleurs*]," 1291.

2. Proust, À l'*ombre des jeunes filles en fleurs* I, 613.

3. Collomb, *Paul Morand écrivain,* 292.
4. Tadié, *Marcel Proust,* 720.
5. Ibid., 680.
6. Proust, *La prisonnière,* 572.
7. In *Proust, Class, and Nation,* Edward J. Hughes shows in minute detail how the "working-class youth is instrumentalized" in these encounters, which are "moulded to shape and satisfy the sexual needs of the protagonist and others of his social class" (158; also 126).
8. Bibliothèque Nationale, Nouvelles Acquisitions Françaises, no. 16746, pp. 81, 84–101. See Hughes, *Proust, Class, and Nation,* 165 note 13; Robert, "Notes et variantes [de *La prisonnière*], note to p. 687; 1737–38.
9. Proust, *La prisonnière,* 688–89.
10. Hughes, *Proust, Class, and Nation,* 126.
11. Ruskin, *Sesame and Lilies,* 34–35, and *The Political Economy of Art,* 37.
12. Proust, *La prisonnière,* 689.
13. In "La Bourse ou le temps," Stéphane Chaudier and Clément Paradis have remarked the "alchemical metamorphosis" inherent in the language whereby the Narrator describes old Bergotte's creative resourcefulness. However, they detect in this language an accusation, however mild, of artistic sterility, neglecting thereby the Ruskinian overtones that bespeak a degree of shared aims between Bergotte's artistic achievement and Proust's artistic goal with *In Search of Lost Time* (87).
14. Proust, *Jean Santeuil,* 399.
15. Ruskin, *Sesame and Lilies,* 34–35.
16. Ruskin, *The Political Economy of Art,* Addenda, 153–54.
17. Marsh, "Of *Sesame and Lilies,*" 147.
18. Ruskin, *Sesame and Lilies,* 34–35.
19. Proust, *Le côté de Guermantes* II.i, 622.
20. In this passage from *The Guermantes Way,* the term *filles* is concordant in intended meaning with the term *fillettes* in the passage from *The Prisoner* I have just been discussing, and which Carol Clark renders aptly as "girls" (*Guermantes Way,* 322; *Prisoner,* 165–66). It seems evident to me that, in the case of the old Bergotte, the "filles qu'on aime mais dont . . . les bruyants plaisirs vous fatiguent" are those very young women which venality draws into the writer's bedroom, where they trade "fiery pleasures" for gold.
21. Ruskin, *The Political Economy of Art,* 75.

CHAPTER 21: LOVE'S BOOKKEEPER

1. Bergson's reputation as a theorist of memory work went unchallenged in Paris in the days of Proust's composition of *In Search of Lost Time.* Notwithstanding Proust's declaration to *Le Temps* of November 13, 1913, the day before the appearance of *Swann's Way,* that his novel was not a "roman bergsonien," it is generally agreed that Proust's views of memory work feed on and occasionally clash with those of Bergson, indicating that he paid close attention to his older acquired cousin's theories. See Shattuck, *Marcel Proust,* 144; Chassick, "The Search for the Authentic Self in Bergson and Proust," 19; Nalbantian, *Memory in Literature,* 62–65. Proust elaborates his most detailed critiques of Bergson's views on memory and dreams in his *Cahier 59.* See à propos Megay, *Bergson et Proust,* 84–85.

2. This lecture, entitled "Le Rêve," was to appear in 1919 as the fourth chapter of *L'énergie spirituelle*. The pertinent sentence reads: "[J]e crois que notre vie passé est là, conservée jusque dans ses moindres details, et que nous n'oublions rien." Bergson, *L'énergie spirituelle*, 93.

3. Bergson, *L'énergie spirituèlle*, 93–94, 137, 139, 183. Although Bergson does not provide a scientific explication of this motion of reciprocal "harmonization" between past memory and present situation, his description suggests the phenomenon analogous to what contemporary immunology and neuroscience call "binding": the "harmonization" of past and present is permitted, that is, by a matching or recognition whereby a preexistent memory turns out to fit a present sense perception better than all other competing memories. For a definition of *binding*, see Piattelli-Palmarini, "Evolution, Selection, and Cognition," 1–44. Bergson discussed the same theory of the pyramid of remembrance and the same concept of the "attention to life" in *Matière et mémoire*, 103–8, 165–66, 189–90. See also Balsamo, "The Place of the Soul in Augustine and Proust," 458.

4. Proust, *Contre Sainte-Beuve*, 224; *Le temps retrouvé*, 451.

5. Bergson, *L'énergie spirituèlle*, 137.

6. Bergson, *Essai sur les données immédiates de la conscience*, 97.

7. See Balsamo, "The Place of the Soul in Augustine and Proust," 457–58. See also Bergson, *L'énergie spirituelle*, 137, 183.

8. Proust, *À l'ombre des jeunes filles en fleurs* II, 77–79. James Grieve translates Proust's phrase "J'étais triste comme si je venais de . . . mourir à moi-même" with "I was as sad as though I . . . felt something die in myself" (*Young Girls in Flower*, 299). This rendering, which is tolerably correct per se, fails to capture fully the Narrator's quest for his true self, which I discuss on several occasions. It seems to me that the Narrator's sadness is rather caused by his impression that "he died to his own self," as I translate it; or, in other words, that he just betrayed that very self for which he constantly searches.

CHAPTER 22: MISSION ACCOMPLISHED

1. Proust, *Pastiches et mélanges*, 49–51.
2. Mozand, "Ode á Marcel Proust," lines 38–41.
3. Ibid., 46.
4. COR XVIII, 242, 242 [note 19], 24.
5. COR XVIII, 253 [notes 2 and 3]; XIX, 3, 3 [note 6].
6. In a letter of praise for Proust's article, René Dumesnil, future editor of Flaubert's correspondence, tried to persuade him that one could not judge fairly Flaubert's epistolary style on the basis of the available evidence. See Wise, "Une lettre inédite de René Dumesnil à Marcel Proust du 19 janvier 1920," 8, 13.
7. On a memorable occasion, Antoine Bibesco's fiancée, Elizabeth Asquith, was smuggled into Proust's bedroom with a subterfuge. See Carter, *Marcel Proust,* 686.
8. COR XVIII, 10, 29, 48, 49, 84; XIX, 69, 367. Proust paid the bank back by the end of 1920.
9. Albaret, *Monsieur Proust,* 318.
10. Ibid.
11. Duchêne, "Un inédit proustien," 676–78.
12. Balsamo, "Proust and His Banker: Numerical Documentation," Item 2.

13. Monnot, *Principles of Turbulent Fired Heat*, 190.

14. Pharmacie Rullier, "*Datura* et traitement de l'asthme," July 11, 2014; Charpin et al., "Bronchodilator Effects of Antiasthmatic Cigarette Smoke (*Datura stramonium*)," 259–61; Duchêne, *L'impossible Marcel Proust*, 316, 371; Albaret, *Monsieur Proust*, 16, 27, 56, 272.

15. Albaret, *Monsieur Proust*, 323.

16. Proust was alluding to Sainte-Beuve's poem "À Ernest Fouinet."

17. Albaret, *Monsieur Proust*, 79, 234.

18. For the sake of rigorous statistics, this lower price would require that the value attributed to the packet of Royal Dutch shares in 1918 be proportionately decreased. As I explain in Item 6 (Quantitative Methodology) of Balsamo, "Proust and His Banker: Numerical Documentation," the available data made it systematically impossible to adjust the value of various portfolios subsequent to the price changes of some of the securities held in them. Therefore, I abstain in the present case from adjusting the entire value of Proust's packet of Royal Dutch shares, even if it could be calculated with good approximation. In Item 6, I explain the effects of this quantitative procedure on the respective reliability of the time series showing the worth of Proust's portfolios, both in absolute and relative terms.

CHAPTER 23: WORDS LIKE A HAIL OF BLOWS

1. See COR XVIII, 59 [note 2].

2. Rachilde, "Revue de la quinzaine: Les romans," *Mercure de France* 107 (1 Janvier–1 Février 1914): 364; "Revue de la quinzaine: Les romans," *Mercure de France* 137 (1 Janvier–1 Février 1920): 199–203.

3. COR XIX, 14. In June 1920, Rachilde invited Proust to join Les Amis des Lettres Françaises, which she presided over with Rosny Aîné, and specifically the section devoted to poets and novelists. Yet subsequent exchanges between Proust and Aîné reveal that the invitation had come under the demeaning condition that Proust should buy his own membership. Aîné himself was horrified by such a request for money, explaining, with unintentional sarcasm, that only people of leisure and amateur writers were expected to pay a membership fee. A great admirer of Oscar Wilde, Rachilde went out of her way to show disrespect for Proust. See COR XIX 140, 142.

4. White, *Marcel Proust*, 75.

5. This is an obvious retort of Hauser's intimation that Proust could never grasp the psychology of people as different from him and his blasé friends as the Russian Bolsheviks.

6. Bergson, *Matière et mémoire*, 245–46.

7. Bergson, *L'énergie spirituelle*, 104, 142–43.

8. Proust, *Jean Santeuil*, 399.

9. The term *qualia*, used in current neuropsychological discourse, was introduced by William James in *The Principles of Psychology*, vol. 2, 156–57, note *.

10. Proust, À l'ombre des jeunes filles en fleurs I, 450.

CHAPTER 24: FINANCIAL COMEBACK

1. COR XIX, vii, 92; Proust and Gallimard, *Correspondance*, 334 note 2, 311, 624, 632; Kolb, *La correspondance de Marcel Proust*, vol. 6, 196–97.

2. "Index of Stock Prices for France, Federal Research Bank of St. Louis," https://research.stlouisfed.org/fred2/series/M11024FRM324NNBR, accessed September 6, 2015.

3. Zanden, *Appendices. Figures and Explanations, Collective Bibliography, and Index,* Tables 2.4.1 and 2.4.2.

CHAPTER 25: A RELATIVITY THEORY OF SEX

1. Gide, *Journal,* vol. 1, 1126–27 (July 17 or 24, 1921).
2. Gide, *Journal,* vol. 2, 296–97 (July 28, 1931).
3. Ibid., 44 (October 1, 1927).
4. See à propos Duchêne, *L'impossible Marcel Proust,* 96–116.
5. Vieuille, "Préface," 25.
6. Hughes, *Proust, Class, and Nation,* 126–27, 158–59, 158 note 2, 192.
7. Landy, *Philosophy as Fiction,* 21.
8. Proust, *La prisonnière,* 678–79.
9. Proust, *Albertine disparue* I, 126–27, 129.
10. Ibid., 36.
11. As he did later in *In Search of Lost Time,* already in *Jean Santeuil*—the aborted novel destined to remain unpublished in Proust's lifetime—the writer postulated that imagination was a faculty that, unable to apply ("qui ne peut . . . appliquer") the full power of its evocations to present circumstances or to past memories, "floats" ("flotte") around that past reality which is "captured" ("qui se trouve prise") by present experience via the mediation of memory and the exercise of "contemplation" (*Jean Santeuil,* 399). Hence, Proust's Narrator can desire Albertine's sexual intimacy thanks to the intensifying effect of his imagination's being, as he would phrase it, "applied to it" (*Finding Time Again,* 180; *Le temps retrouvé,* 450)—thanks to that "memory of the present" which, as Proust knew well, Aristotle deemed impossible to perform (Aristotle, "On Memory," 714–15).
12. Vettard, "Proust et Einstein," *NRF* no. 107 (August 1922): 246–52, and "Proust et le temps," *NRF* no. 112 (January 1923): 204–11.
13. Proust, *Le temps retrouvé,* 451.
14. See Rivers, *Proust and the Art of Love,* chapter 5: "Monsters of Time."
15. Proust, *Du côté de chez Swann,* 4; *Le Temps retrouvé,* 625; Rivers, *Proust and the Art of Love,* 250.
16. Maeterlinck, *L'intelligence des fleurs,* 57–107.; Compagnon, "Lost Allusions in À la recherché du temps perdu," 142; Hullu-van Doeselaar, "Compte rendu," 222; see also Viers, "Evolution et sexualité des plantes dans *Sodome et Gomorrhe,*" 105–7. The translation of Darwin's *Different Forms of Flowers on Plants of the Same Species* (1878) was by Édouard Heckel. In "Gay Incipit: Botanical Connections, Nosegays, and Bouquets," George Bauer indicates also Darwin's *Various Contrivances by which Orchids Are Fertilized by Insects* among Proust's sources, but I found no confirmation of his view anywhere else (70).
17. Rivers, *Proust and the Art of Love,* 239.
18. Proust, *Sodome et Gomorrhe* I, 6–7, 29–30.
19. Proust and Gallimard, *Correspondance,* 18 (Proust to Gallimard, circa November 8, 1912).
20. Proust, *La prisonnière,* 686.
21. Proust, *Du côté de chez Swann,* 13; *La prisonnière,* 520 ; see also Proust, *Jean Santeuil,* 399. Julia Kristeva offers several penetrating insights into the discordant analogies between the "infantile and maternal pleasure" given to the Narrator, in his infancy,

by the oscular contact with his mother, and the erotic effects of "the greedy *oralité* of the young girls in flower," and especially by Albertine's goodnight kiss, an alternating source of comfort, arousal, and anguish. Kristeva, *Le temps sensible*, 140–41, 144.

22. Proust, *Le temps retrouvé*, 451; Updike, "More Love in the Western World," 231.
23. Proust, *Du côté de chez Swann* II, 375.
24. Proust, *La prisonnière*, 679.
25. Balsamo, "The Fiction of Marcel Proust's Autobiography," 574, 583–84; see also Balsamo, "Figural Literalism," 15–16, 28.
26. Auerbach, *Studi su Dante*, 224–26.
27. Proust, *Le temps retrouvé*, 459.
28. Duchêne, *L'impossible Marcel Proust*, 732–35.

CHAPTER 26: SUICIDAL OBSTINACY

1. Proust is ostensibly alluding to Alphonse de Lamartine's poem "Novissima verba," in *Harmonies poétiques et religieuses*, book IV, poem xi, stanza 15, https://fr.wikisource.org/wiki/Novissima_Verba. Accessed April 20, 2016; see à propos COR X, 56 [note 8].
2. Proust, "À propos de Baudelaire," 622.
3. It seems that Gallimard ended up paying Proust better than any other author. See COR XXI, 258, 258 [note 10].
4. COR XX, 265; Proust and Gallimard, *Correspondance*, 334 note 2, 311, 624, 632. See also Kolb, *La correspondance de Marcel Proust*, vol. 6, 196–97; Tadié, *Marcel Prouust*, 733.
5. Proust is here alluding to *Sodom and Gomorrah* II, which was set to appear in 1922.
6. Albaret, *Monsieur Proust*, 265.
7. Gregh, *L'age d'or*, 148–67.
8. In his "Dans les Mémoires de Saint-Simon," Proust fictionalizes an analogous episode, in which the very Madame Straus says to a Monsieur de Noyon, "Ah! Monsieur, j'allais le dire!" Proust, *Pastiches et mélanges*, 53.
9. Gregh, *L'age d'or*, 168–69.
10. Albaret, *Monsieur Proust*, 300, 325.
11. Letter of Adolphe Ferrière to Elisabeth Rotten, December 16, 1925. Archives Institut J. J. Rousseau (IJJR), Fonds Adolphe Ferrière, Correspondance alphabétique. Cote : AdF.C.I/63, my translation. Cited in Haenggeli-Jenni, "Pour *l'Ère Nouvelle*," 88.
12. Haenggeli-Jenni, "Pour *l'Ère Nouvelle*," 10–19, 92, 104, 188, 191 note 247.
13. See also Gutierrez, "L'Éducation nouvelle et l'enseignement catholique en France (1899–1939)," and *Histoire du movement de l'Education nouvelle en France.*

CHAPTER 27: *ARS LONGA, VITA BREVIS*

1. Proust, "À propos du 'style' de Flaubert," 586.
2. Proust, *Le temps retrouvé*, 625
3. Proust, À l'ombre des jeunes filles en fleurs I, 548. See also Balsamo, "The Fiction of Marcel Proust's Autobiography," 600.
4. Kristeva, *Le temps sensible*, 341.
5. Proust, *Le temps retrouvé*, 625.
6. Proust, *La prisonnière*, 693.
7. Proust, *Le temps retrouvé*, 610.

WORKS CITED

Albaret, Céleste. *Monsieur Proust.* Translated by Barbara Bray. New York: McGraw-Hill, 1976.

Aristotle. "On Memory." In *The Complete Works of Aristotle.* Vol. 1, 714–20. Edited by Jonathan Barnes Bollingen Series LXXI-2. Princeton: Princeton University Press, 1984.

Auerbach, Erich. *Studi su Dante.* Translated by M. L. De Pieri Bonino, Dante Della Terza. Milano: Feltrinelli, 1963.

Balsamo, Gian. "The Fiction of Marcel Proust's Autobiography." *Poetics Today* 28, no. 4 (2007): 573–606.

——. "Figural Literalism: Metaphor, Altruism, and Alterity in Dante and Caterina da Siena." *Exemplaria* 18 (Spring 2006): 1–30.

——. "The Place of the Soul in Augustine and Proust: Amorous Memory versus Neuroscience." *Journal of Religion* no. 88 (October 2008): 439–65.

——. "Proust and His Banker: Numerical Documentation," http://www.academia.edu/24415226/Documentation. Accessed April 15, 20165.

——. "Proust and the Lessons of War." *Salmagundi* nos. 166–167 (Spring–Summer 2010): 204–19.

——. "Son, Knight, and Lover: Perceval's Dilemma at the Castle of Beaurepaire." *Exemplaria* 5 (October 1993): 263–81.

Bauer, George H. "Gay Incipit: Botanical Connections, Nosegays, and Bouquets." In *Articulations of Difference: Gender Studies and Writing in French,* edited by Dominique D. Fisher and Lawrence R. Schehr, 64–82. Stanford: Stanford University Press, 1997.

Benjamin, Walter. "The Image of Proust." In *Illuminations: Essays and Reflections,* by Walter Benjamin, translated by Harry Zohn, 201–16. New York: Schocken Books, 1969.

Bergson, Henri. *L'énergie spirituelle.* Geneva: Skira, 1946.

——. *Essai sur les données immédiates de la conscience.* Paris: Quadrige/PUF, 2007.

——. *Matière et mémoire: Essai sur la relation du corps à l'ésprit.* Paris: Alcan, 1914.

Bergstein, Mary. *In Looking Back One Learns to See: Marcel Proust and Photography.* Amsterdam: Rodopi, 2014.

Bibesco, Antoine. "The Heartlessness of Marcel Proust." *Cornhill Magazine* no. 983 (Summer 1950): 421–28.

Boella, Alessandro, and Antonella Galli. "Presentazione." In *Adamo l'uomo rosso, o gli elementi di una gnosi per il matrimonio perfetto,* by René Adolphe Schwaller de Lubicz, 9–44. Rome: Edizioni Mediterranee, 2006.

Brooke, Jocelyn. "Proust and Joyce: The Case for the Prosecution." *Adam: International Review* nos. 297–298 (1961): 5–66.

Carter, William C. *Marcel Proust: A Life.* New Haven and London: Yale University Press, 2000.

Charpin, D., J. Orehek, and J. M. Velardocchio. "Bronchodilator Effects of Antiasthmatic Cigarette Smoke (*Datura stramonium*)." *Thorax* no. 34 (1979): 259–61.

Chassick, Richard. "The Search for the Authentic Self in Bergson and Proust." In *Psychoanalytic Approaches to Literature and Film,* edited by Maurice Charney and Joseph Reppen, 19–36. London: Associated University Presses, 1987.

Chaudier, Stéphane, and Clément Paradis. "La Bourse ou le temps: L'imaginaire financier de Marcel Proust." In *Les Frontières littéraires de l'économie (XVII*[e]*–XX*[e] *siècles),* edited by Martial Poirson, Yves Citton, and Christian Biet, 79–91. Paris: Desjonquères, 2008.

Chevalier, Anne. "Notice" (sur *Albertine disparue*). In À la recherche du temps perdu, by Marcel Proust. Vol. IV, edited by Jean-Yves Tadié, 993–1038. Paris: Gallimard, 1989.

Chu, Simon, and John Joseph Downes. "Long Live Proust: The Odor-Cued Autobiographical Memory Bump." *Cognition,* no. 75 (2000): B41–B50.

Citati, Pietro. *La colomba pugnalata: Proust e la Recherche.* Milan: Mondadori, 1995.

Clarac, Pierre. "Notice 1." In *Contre Sainte-Beuve (*précédé de *Pastiches et mélanges,* et suivi de *Essais et articles),* by Marcel Proust, edited by Pierre Clarac, 819–29. Paris: Gallimard, 1971.

——. "Notice 2." In *Jean Santeuil (*précédé de *Les plaisirs et les jours),* by Marcel Proust, edited by Pierre Clarac, 980–86. Paris: Gallimard, 1971.

Clark, Carol, trans. *The Prisoner,* by Marcel Proust. In *The Prisoner* and *The Fugitive,* by Marcel Proust. New York: Penguin, 2003.

Collier, Peter, trans. *The Fugitive,* by Marcel Proust. In *The Prisoner* and *The Fugitive,* by Marcel Proust. New York: Penguin, 2003.

Collomb, Michel, ed. *Paul Morand écrivain.* Montpellier: Université Paul-Valéry, 1993.

Compagnon, Antoine. "Lost Allusions in À la recherché du temps perdu," translated by Jane Kuntz. In *Proust in Perspective: Visions and Revisions,* edited by Armine Kotin Mortimer and Catherine Kolb, 133–46. Chicago: University of Illinois Press, 2002.

——. "Notes sur le texte [de *Sodome et Gomorrhe,* II]." In *À la recherche du temps perdu,* by Marcel Proust. Vol. III, edited by Jean-Yves Tadié, 1291–99. Paris: Gallimard, 1988.

Davis, Lydia, trans. *Swann's Way,* by Marcel Proust. New York: Penguin, 2004.

Duchêne, Roger. *L'impossible Marcel Proust.* Paris: Laffont, 1994.

——. "Un inédit proustien: le testament de 'L'Oncle Adolphe.'" *Revue d'Histoire Littéraire de la France* 104, no. 3 (2004): 673–85.

Duplay, Maurice. "Proust avant Proust." *Les Nouvelles Littéraires, Artistiques et Scientifiques* no. 1570 (October 3, 1957): 4.

Edel, Leon. "Walter Berry and the Novelists: Proust, James, and Edith Wharton." *Nineteenth-Century Fiction* 38 (March 1984): 514–28.

Ellmann, Richard. *Oscar Wilde.* New York: Vintage, 1988.

Fontaine, Jean de la. *Les Fables de la Fontaine.* http://www.lesfables.fr. Accessed April 20, 2016.

Frank, Joseph. *The Widening Gyre: Mastery in Modern Literature.* New Brunswick: Rutgers University Press, 1963.

Gamble, Cynthia J. *Proust as Interpreter of Ruskin: The Seven Lamps of Translation.* Birmingham, Ala.: Summa Publications, 2002.

Gide, André. *Journal.* Vol. 1, 1887–1925. Edited by Éric Marty. Paris: Gallimard, 1996.

——. *Journal.* Vol. 2, 1926–1950. Edited by Martine Sagaert. Paris Gallimard, 1997.
Goethe, Johann Wolfgang. "Simple Imitation of Nature, Manner, Style." In *Goethe on Art,* edited and translated by John Cage, 21–24. Berkeley and Los Angeles: University of California Press, 1980.
Goux, Jean-Joseph. "Cash, Check, or Charge?" In *The New Economic Criticism,* edited by Martha Woodmansee and Mark Osteen, 114–28. New York: Routledge, 1999.
Gregh, Fernand. *L'age d'or: Souvenirs d'enfance et de jeunesse.* Paris: Grasset, 1947.
——. "Mystères." In *La fenêtre ouverte,* by Fernand Gregh, 259–70. Paris: Bibliothèque-Charpentier, 1901.
Grieve, James, trans. *In the Shadow of Young Girls in Flower,* by Marcel Proust. New York: Penguin, 2005.
Gutierrez, Laurent. "L'Éducation nouvelle et l'enseignement catholique en France (1899–1939)." Doctoral thesis, Université Paris VIII-Saint-Denis, 2008.
——. *Histoire du movement de l'Éducation nouvelle en France,* http://hmenf.free.fr. Accessed February 27, 2015.
Haenggeli-Jenni, Béatrice. "Pour *l'Ère Nouvelle*: une revue-carrefour entre science et militance (1922–1940)." Doctoral thesis, Université de Genève, 2011, no. FPSE 491, August 2011, http://archive-ouverte.unige.ch/unige:18162. Accessed February 27, 2015.
Hopkins, Gerard, trans. *Jean Santeuil,* by Marcel Proust. New York: Simon & Schuster, 1956.
Hughes, Edward J. *Proust, Class, and Nation.* Oxford University Press, 2011.
Hullu-van Doeselaar, Nell. "Compte rendu." In *Marcel Proust Aujourd'hui: 9,* edited by Sjef Houppermans et al., 215–26. Amsterdam and New York: Rodopi, 2004.
Kilmartin, Joanna, trans. *Selected Letters,* by Marcel Proust. Vol. 4, 1918–1922. Edited by Philip Kolb. London: HarperCollins, 2000.
Kilmartin, Philip, trans. *Selected Letters,* by Marcel Proust. Vols. 2 and 3, 1904–1909 and 1910–1917. Edited by Philip Kolb. New York: Oxford University Press, 1989, 1992.
Kolb, Philip, ed. [Marcel Proust's] *Correspondance* 1892–1922, 21 vols. Paris: Plon, 1970–1993.
——, ed. *La correspondance de Marcel Proust: Chronologie et Commentaire Critique.* Urbana: University of Illinois Press, 1949, Vol. VI.
——. "Marcel Proust speculateur." In *Cahier Marcel Proust, nouvelle série 6,* 177–81. Études Proustiennes I. Paris: Gallimard, 1973.
Kristeva, Julia. *Intimate Revolt: The Powers and Limits of Psychoanalysis.* Translated by Jeanine Herman. New York: Columbia University Press, 2003.
——. "Le temps, la femme, la jalousie, selon Albertine." Journée d'études "À la recherche d'*Albertine disparue.*" Université Paris 7, January 27, 2007, *Acta Fabula.* http://www.fabula.org/colloques/document470.php. Accessed February 27, 2015.
——. *Le temps sensible: Proust et l'expérience littéraire.* Paris: Gallimard, 1994.
James, William. *The Principles of Psychology.* 2 vols. London: Macmillan, 1890.
Landy, Joshua. "'*Les moi en moi*': The Proustian Self in Philosophical Perspective." *New Literary History* 32 (Winter 2001): 91–132.
——. *Philosophy as Fiction: Self, Deception, and Knowledge in Proust.* Oxford: Oxford University Press, 2004.
——. "Proust, His Narrator, and the Importance of the Distinction." *Poetics Today* 25, no. 1 (2004): 91–135.
Large, Duncan. "Proust on Nietzsche: The Question of Friendship." *Modern Language Review* 88 (July 1993): 612–24.

Lauris, Georges de. "Préface." In À un ami: Correspondance inédite, 1903–1922, by Marcel Proust, 7–43. Paris: Amiot-Dumont, 1948.
Maeterlink, Maurice. *L'intelligence des fleurs.* Paris: Bibliothèque-Charpentier, 1907.
Mallarmé, Stéphane. *Collected Poems and Other Verse.* Translated by E. H. Blackmore and A. M. Blackmore. Oxford: Oxford's World Classics, 2008.
Man, Paul de. *Allegories of Reading: Figural Language in Rousseau, Nietzsche, Rilke, and Proust.* New Haven: Yale University Press, 1979.
Manheim, Ralph, trans. *Selected Letters,* by Marcel Proust. Vol. 1, 1880–1903. Edited by Philip Kolb. New York: Doubleday, 1983.
Marsh, Jan. "Of *Sesame and Lilies:* Education in a Humane Society." In John Ruskin. *Sesame and Lilies,* by John Ruskin, edited by Deborah Epstein Nord, 142–64. New Haven: Yale University Press, 2002.
Martin-Chauffier, Louis. "Proust et le double 'je' de quatre personnes." *Confluences* 21 (July–August 1943): 55–69.
Megay, Joyce N. *Bergson et Proust: Essai de mise au point de la question de l'influence de Bergson sur Proust.* Paris: Vrin, 1976.
Monnot, Georges. *Principles of Turbulent Fired Heat.* Paris: Technip Editions, 1985.
Montaigne, Michel de. "De la solitude." In *Essais,* by Michel de Montaigne, edited by Maurice Rat, chapter XXXIX, 267–79. Paris: Garnier Frères, 1952.
Morand, Paul. "Ode á Marcel Proust." http://lesdiagonalesdutemps.over-blog.com/article-ode-a-marcel-proust-par-paul-morand-1888-1976-83497725.html. Accessed April 22, 2016.
Nalbantian, Suzanne. *Memory in Literature: From Rousseau to Neuroscience.* New York: Palgrave, 2003.
Painter, George D. *Marcel Proust: A Biography.* 2 vols. London: Chatto & Windus, 1989.
Pareyson, Luigi. "La prima estetica classica di Goethe." *Rivista di estetica,* no. 1(1971): 5–67.
Patterson, Ian, trans. *Finding Time Again,* by Marcel Proust. New York: Penguin, 2003.
Pharmacie Rullier, "*Datura* et traitement de l'asthme," July 11, 2014, http://www.pharmacie-rullier.fr/spip.php?page=imprimir_articulo&id_article=495. Accessed February 27, 2015.
Piattelli-Palmarini, Massimo. "Evolution, Selection, and Cognition: From 'Learning' to Parameter Setting in Biology and in the Study of Language." *Cognition,* no. 31 (1989): 1–44.
Prestwich, P. F. *The Translation of Memories: Recollections of the Young Proust.* London: Peter Owen, 1999.
Proust, Marcel. *Albertine disparue.* Original edition of the last version reviewed by the author. Edited by Nathalie Mauriac and Étienne Wolff. Paris: Grasset, 1987.
——. *Albertine disparue.* In À la recherche du temps perdu, by Marcel Proust. Vol. IV. Edited by Jean-Yves Tadié. Paris: Gallimard, 1989.
——. *À l'ombre des jeunes filles en fleurs* I. In *À la recherche du temps perdu,* by Marcel Proust. Vol. I. Edited by Jean-Yves Tadié. Paris: Gallimard, 1987.
——. *À l'ombre des jeunes filles en fleurs* II. In *À la recherche du temps perdu,* by Marcel Proust. Vol. II. Edited by Jean-Yves Tadié. Paris: Gallimard, 1988.
——. "À mon ami Willie Heath" (dedication of *Les plaisirs et les jours*). In *Jean Santeuil* précédé de *Les plaisirs et les jours,* by Marcel Proust. Edited by Pierre Clarac with Yves Sandre, 5–8. Paris: Gallimard, 1971.

——. "À propos de Baudelaire." In *Contre Sainte-Beuve* précédé de *Pastiches et mélanges* et suivi de *Essais et articles,* by Marcel Proust. Edited by Pierre Clarac with Yves Sandre, 618–39. Paris: Gallimard, 1971.

——. "À propos du 'style' de Flaubert." In *Contre Sainte-Beuve* précédé de *Pastiches et mélanges* et suivi de *Essais et articles,* by Marcel Proust. Edited by Pierre Clarac with Yves Sandre, 586–89. Paris: Gallimard, 1971.

——. *À un ami: Correspondance inédite, 1903–1922.* Paris: Amiot-Dumont, 1948.

——. "Beg-Meil." In *Jean Santeuil* précédé de *Les plaisirs et les jours,* by Marcel Proust, edited by Pierre Clarac with Yves Sandre, 354–402. Paris: Gallimard, 1971.

——. *Le Carnet de 1908.* Edited by Philip Kolb. Paris: Gallimard, 1976.

——. *Carnets.* Edited by Florence Callu and Antoine Compagnon. Paris: Gallimard, 2002.

——. *Contre Sainte-Beuve* précédé de *Pastiches et mélanges* et suivi de *Essais et articles.* Edited by Pierre Clarac with Yves Sandre. Paris Gallimard, 1971.

——. *Correspondance* (1892–1922). Edited by Philip Kolb. 21 vols. Paris: Plon, 1970–1993.

——. *Du côté de chez Swann.* In *À la recherche du temps perdu,* by Marcel Proust. Vol. I. Edited by Jean-Yves Tadié. Paris: Gallimard, 1987.

——. *Le côté de Guermantes* I and II. In À la recherche du temps perdu, by Marcel Proust. Vol. II. Edited by Jean-Yves Tadié. Paris: Gallimard, 1988.

——. "Esquisse 13." In *À la recherche du temps perdu,* by Marcel Proust. Vol. III, edited by Jean-Yves Tadié, 1032–48. Paris: Gallimard, 1988.

——. *Finding Time Again.* Translated by Ian Patterson. New York: Penguin, 2003.

——. *The Fugitive.* Translated by Peter Collier. In *The Prisoner* and *The Fugitive,* by Marcel Proust. New York: Penguin, 2003.

——. *The Guermantes Way.* Translated by Mark Treharne. New York: Penguin, 2005.

——. *In the Shadow of Young Girls in Flower.* Translated by James Grieve. New York: Penguin, 2005.

——. *Jean Santeuil* (précédé de *Les plaisirs et les jours).* Edited by Pierre Clarac. Paris: Gallimard, 1971.

——. *Pastiches et mélanges.* In *Contre Sainte-Beuve* précédé de *Pastiches et mélanges* et suivi de *Essais et articles,* by Marcel Proust. Edited by Pierre Clarac with Yves Sandre. Paris: Gallimard, 1971.

——. *Les plaisirs et le jours.* In *Jean Santeuil* précédé de *Les plaisirs et les* jours, by Marcel Proust. Edited by Pierre Clarac with Yves Sandres. Paris: Gallimard, 1971.

——. *The Prisoner.* Translated by Carol Clark. In *The Prisoner* and *The Fugitive,* by Marcel Proust. New York: Penguin, 2003.

——. *La prisonnière.* In À la recherche du temps perdu, by Marcel Proust. Vol. III. Edited by Jean-Yves Tadié. Paris: Gallimard, 1988.

——. *Sodom and Gomorrah.* Translated by John Sturrock. New York: Penguin, 2005.

——. *Sodome et Gomorrhe* I and II. In *À la recherche du temps perdu,* by Marcel Proust. Vol. III. Edited by Jean-Yves Tadié. Paris: Gallimard, 1988.

——. *Le temps retrouvé.* In À la recherche du temps perdu, by Marcel Proust. Vol. IV. Edited by Jean-Yves Tadié. Paris: Gallimard, 1989.

——, and Gaston Gallimard. *Correspondance.* Edited by Pascal Fouché. Paris: Gallimard, 1989.

Quennouëlle-Corre, Laure. "The Paris Bourse and the International Capital Flows Before 1914." MPRA paper no. 6264, September 12, 2007, http//mpra.ub.uni-muenchen.de/6264/1/MPRA_paper_6264.pdf. Accessed February 27, 2015

Rey, Pierre-Louis. "La guerre dans *Le temps retrouvé*," January 15, 2009, http://centreproust.univ-paris3.fr. Accessed June 23, 2011.

——. "Introduction [À l'ombre des jeunes filles en fleurs]." In *À la recherche du temps perdu,* by Marcel Proust, Vol. I, 1282–1302. Paris: Gallimard, 1987.

Revah, Louis-Albert. *Un maranne d'aujourd'hui: Juif, mais pas simplement.* Paris: L'Harmattan, 2007.

Ricoeur, Paul. *Time and Narrative.* Vol. 2. Translated by Kathleen Blamey and David Pellauer. Chicago: University of Chicago Press, 1990.

——. "Time Traversed: *Remembrance of Things Past.*" In *A Ricoeur Reader: Reflection and Imagination,* edited by Mario J. Valdes, 355–89. Toronto: University of Toronto Press, 1991.

Rivers, J. E. *Proust and the Art of Love: The Aesthetics of Sexuality in the Life, Times, and Art of Marcel Proust.* New York: Columbia University Press, 1980.

Robert, Pierre-Edmond. "Notes et variantes [de *La prisonnière*]. In À la recherche du temps perdu, by Marcel Proust. Vol. III, edited by Jean-Yves Tadié, 1699–1795. Paris: Gallimard, 1988.

Robichez, Jacques. *Précis de litterature Française du XXᵉ siècle.* Paris: PUF, 1985.

Rousset, Jean. *Forme et signification: Essai sur les structures littèraires de Corneille à Claudel.* Paris: José Corti, 1995.

Ruskin, John. *The Political Economy of Art.* London: Cassell, 1907.

——. *Sesame and Lilies.* Edited by Deborah Epstein Nord. New Haven: Yale University Press, 2002.

Shattuck, Roger. *Marcel Proust.* Princeton: Princeton University Press, 1982.

Shell, Marc. *The Economy of Literature.* Baltimore: Johns Hopkins University Press, 1993.

——. "The Issue of Representation." In *The New Economic Criticism,* edited by Martha Woodmansee and Mark Osteen, 53–74. New York: Routledge, 1999.

——. "Ruskin and the Economy of Literature." *Journal of the History of Ideas* 38 (January–March 1977): 65–84.

Shepherd-Barr, Kirsten, and Gordon M. Shepherd. "Madeleines and Neuromodernism: Reassessing Mechanisms of Autobiographical Memory in Proust." *a/b: Auto/Biography Studies* 13 (Spring 1998): 39–60

Sturrock, John, trans. *Sodom and Gomorrah,* by Marcel Proust. New York: Penguin, 2005.

Tadié, Jean-Yves. *Marcel Proust.* Translated by Euan Cameron. New York: Viking, 2000.

Terdiman, Richard. *The Dialectics of Isolation: Self and Society in the French Novel from the Realists to Proust.* New Haven: Yale University Press, 1976.

Updike, John. "More Love in the Western World." In *Assorted Prose,* by John Updike, 283–300. New York: Random House Trade Paperbacks, 2012.

Vellucci, Giuseppe. "L'interpretazione 'unitaria' e l'interpretazione 'dualistica' della *Commedia* nella critica dantesca dal Romanticismo al Novecento." In *Unità o dualità della Commedia: Il dibattito su Dante da Schelling ad Auerbach,* by Gianfranco Frigo and Giuseppe Vellucci, 65–106. Florence: Leo O. Olschki, 1994.

Vettard, Camille. "Proust et Einstein," *NRF* no. 107, (August 1922): 246–52.

——. "Prouse et let Temps." *NRF* no. 112 (January 1923): 204–11.

Vidal, Emmanuel. *The History and Methods of the Paris Bourse.* Washington, D.C.: Government Printing Office, 61st Congress, 2nd Session, Doc. no 573, 1910.

Viers, Rina. "Evolution et sexualité des plantes dans *Sodome et Gomorrhe*." *Europe* nos. 502–503 (1971): 100–113.

Vieuille, Marie-Françoise. "Préface." In *Jalousie,* by Marcel Proust, 7–31. Paris: Le Castor Astral, 2007.

Virgil. *Eneide.* Translated by Rosa Calzecchi Onesti. Turin: Einaudi, 1995.

White, Edmund. *Marcel Proust.* New York: Viking Penguin, 1999.

Wise, Pyra. "Une lettre inédite de René Dumesnil à Marcel Proust du 19 janvier 1920." *Flaubert: Revue critique et génétique,* http://flaubert.revues.org/815. Accessed February 27, 2015.

——. "Marcel Proust et Albert Nahmias: quelques lettres inédites," *Bulletin d'informations proustiennes,* no. 37. Paris: Éditions Rue d'Ulm, Presses de l'École normale supérierre, 2007.

——. "Trois lettres et une dédicace inédites de Marcel Proust conservées à la Pierpont Morgan Library." *Bulletin d'informations proustiennes,* no. 35. Paris: Éditions d'Ulm, Presses de l'École normale supérieure, 2005, http:www.item.ens.fr/index.php?id=76053. Accessed February 27, 2015.

Zanden, Jan Luiten van. *Appendices. Figures and Explanations, Collective Bibliography, and Index.* Volume 4 of *A History of Royal Dutch Shell,* by Stephen Howarth et al. Oxford: Oxford University Press, 2007.

INDEX

ABOUT THE AUTHOR

GIAN BALSAMO, a financial data scientist with a Ph.D. in comparative literature from Vanderbilt University, has taught literature at Northwestern University and Stanford University. He is the author of *Joyce's Messianism*, *Rituals of Literature*, and the novel *The Book of Breathing* (attributed to Luigi Ferdinando Dagnese). Balsamo is a member of Statistics without Borders and is currently affiliated with the Department of Mathematics at the University of York in the United Kingdom.